I0760113

The Ancient Germans and Rome 120 BC to AD 68

Also by Raoul McLaughlin

Germania: The Ancient Germans in Greek and Roman Sources: Geography, Society, Warfare, Religion and Customs

Rome and the Distant East: Trade Routes to the Ancient Lands of Arabia, India and China

The Roman Empire and the Indian Ocean: the Ancient World Economy & the Kingdoms of Africa, Arabia & India

The Roman Empire and the Silk Routes: The Ancient World Economy and the Empires of Parthia, Central Asia and Han China

Rome and China: Points of Contact (co-authored with Professors Hyun Jin Kim and Samuel N.C. Lieu)

The Ancient Germans and Rome 120 BC to AD 68

Records of Contact and Conflict

Raoul McLaughlin

Pen & Sword
MILITARY

First published in Great Britain in 2025 by
Pen & Sword Military
An imprint of Pen & Sword Books Limited
Yorkshire – Philadelphia

ISBN 978 1 03613 291 0

A CIP catalogue record for this book is
available from the British Library.

Typeset by Mac Style
Printed in the UK by CPI Group (UK) Ltd, Croydon, CR0 4YY.

The Publisher's authorised representative in the EU for product safety is Authorised Rep Compliance Ltd., Ground Floor, 71 Lower Baggot Street, Dublin D02 P593, Ireland.
www.arccompliance.com

For a complete list of Pen & Sword titles please contact:

PEN & SWORD BOOKS LIMITED
47 Church Street, Barnsley, South Yorkshire, S70 2AS, England
E-mail: enquiries@pen-and-sword.co.uk
Website: www.pen-and-sword.co.uk
or
PEN AND SWORD BOOKS
1950 Lawrence Road, Havertown, PA 19083, USA
E-mail: uspen-and-sword@casematepublishers.com
Website: www.penandswordbooks.com

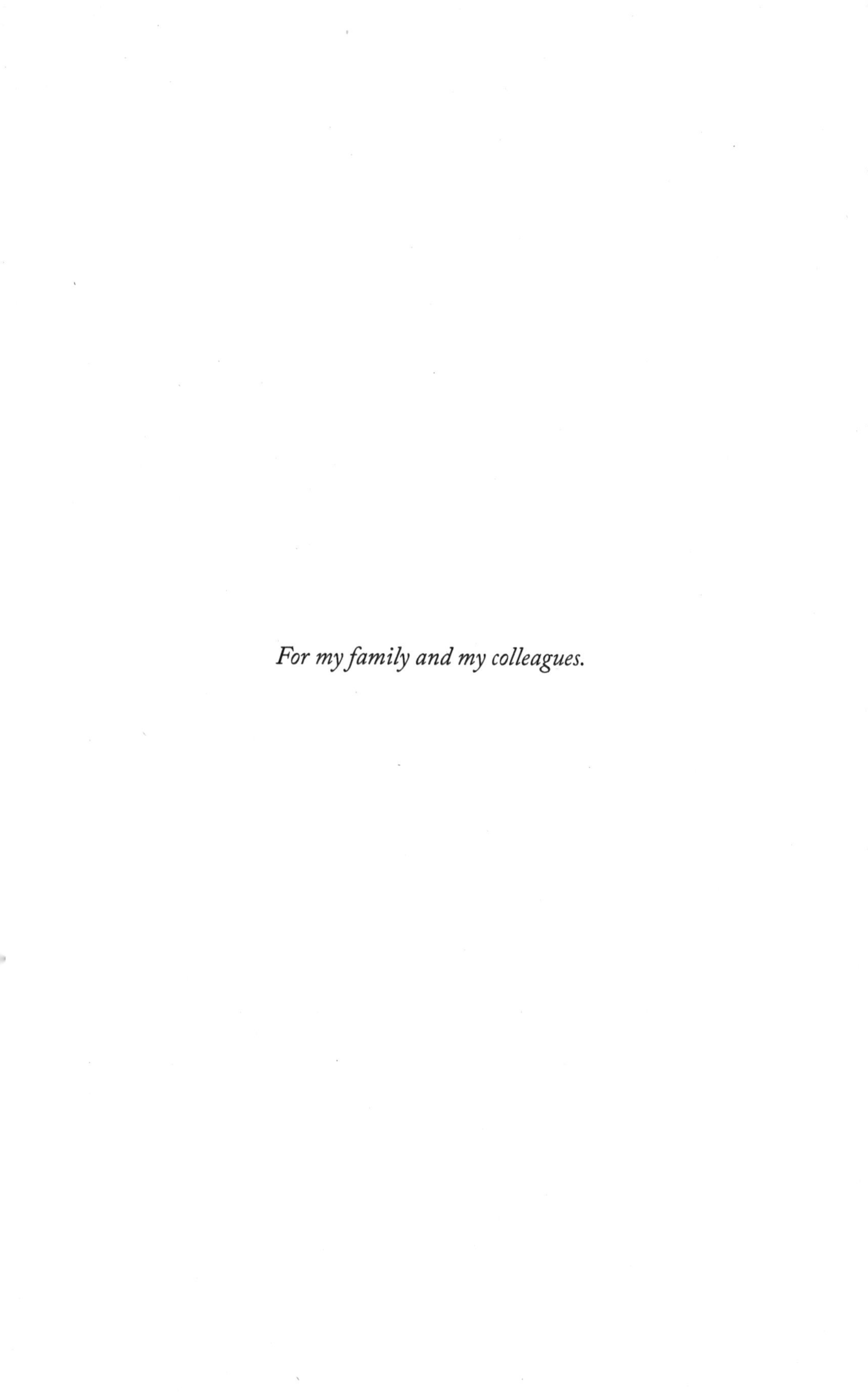

For my family and my colleagues.

Contents

Maps and Illustrations

Maps

Illustrations

Reverse: victory image formed from war trophies. Two Germanic shields, two pairs of spears, two war trumpets, and a *vexillum* (Roman military banner). Text: *DE GERMANIS.*

10. Lower part of the Gemma Augustea, a Roman cameo cut from onyx. The scene depicts the raising of a *tropaion* (victory monument fashioned from war trophies). Bound male and female figures are captured Celts or Germans.
11. Gilded silver roundel from a Roman military standard. The victorious general is Germanicus, or the future Emperor Tiberius, standing triumphant on a mound of Germanic captives, weapons and war trumpets.
12. Silver Roman skyphos (two-handled wine cup) possibly depicting the imperial prince, Tiberius, during his triumph of 8 BC. He carries an eagle-headed ivory sceptre and a laurel branch.
13. Roman silver drinking cup depicting Augustus and Drusus. The enthroned Augustus receives defeated barbarian chieftains offering their children as political hostages.
14. Roman silver drinking cup depicting King Priam of Troy appealing to Achilles for the return of his son Hector's body. Found in a Germanic chieftain's grave at Hoby, Denmark (first century BC). The Greek champion Achilles is depicted as Augustus and the cup was possibly a diplomatic gift.
15. Life-size Roman bronze statue of Germanicus discovered at Amelia, Italy. Germanicus died in AD 19, but the statue dates to about AD 40 (the reign of the Emperor Caligula). The breastplate depicts the Greek hero Achilles attacking Troilus, the youngest son of King Priam, outside the walls of Troy.
16. Marble Roman bust of a young German ('Arminius', in the Capitoline Museum in Rome).
17. Marble Roman statue depicting a Germanic woman, perhaps a personification of the country (Rome, second century AD) ('Thusnelda', currently installed at the Loggia dei Lanzi, Florence).
18. Cenotaph of Centurion Marcus Caelius. Killed by Germanic warriors during the Teutoburg massacre (AD 9). Monument from Xanten.
19. Silver Roman faceplate found at the Teutoburg Forest battle site.
20. Roman cavalry mask discovered at Hellvi, Gotland, Sweden. The eyes have been infilled, but one was damaged, perhaps to represent the Germanic god Oden.

Acknowledgements

I was educated at Lagan College in Belfast, the first integrated cross-community school to be established in Northern Ireland, founded for young people of all cultural and economic backgrounds. I am grateful for an education free from the divisions of race, religion, or social class.

My undergraduate degree was in Archaeology and Ancient History at Queen's University Belfast and I am indebted to the Northern Ireland Department of Education and Learning for financing the early stage of my doctoral research.

In the absence of further funding, I used my spare time and limited earnings to continue my research. In 2010 I completed my monograph, *Rome and the Distant East*. This was followed by the publication of *The Roman Empire and the Indian Ocean* in 2014 and *The Roman Empire and the Silk Routes* in 2016, presenting a new model for the ancient world economy.

For eight years I taught tutorial groups in Ancient History at Queen's University Belfast. From 2016, I worked in a clinical care home that provides nursing care for patients with complex medical needs, including palliative care for elderly people with dementia. During the Covid-19 pandemic, a specialised Covid care unit for the elderly and infirm was opened at the facility. I left health care in April 2024 to resume my research.

I would like to thank Dr John Curran for his steadfast support throughout my academic career, and all my colleagues at the Classical Association in Northern Ireland who strive to preserve the relevance of Classics and ancient history. I especially mention Dr Peter Crawford and Dr Helen McVeigh. I am grateful for their friendship.

Publishing this work in a series of books without an academic position has created personal hardship. This book is therefore dedicated to my immediate family: my parents, my brother Leon and my sister Thayna. Thank you for all your support.

Dr Raoul McLaughlin
Bangor, Northern Ireland
September 2025

Map 1. Roman world view: Claudius Ptolemy's map (AD 150).

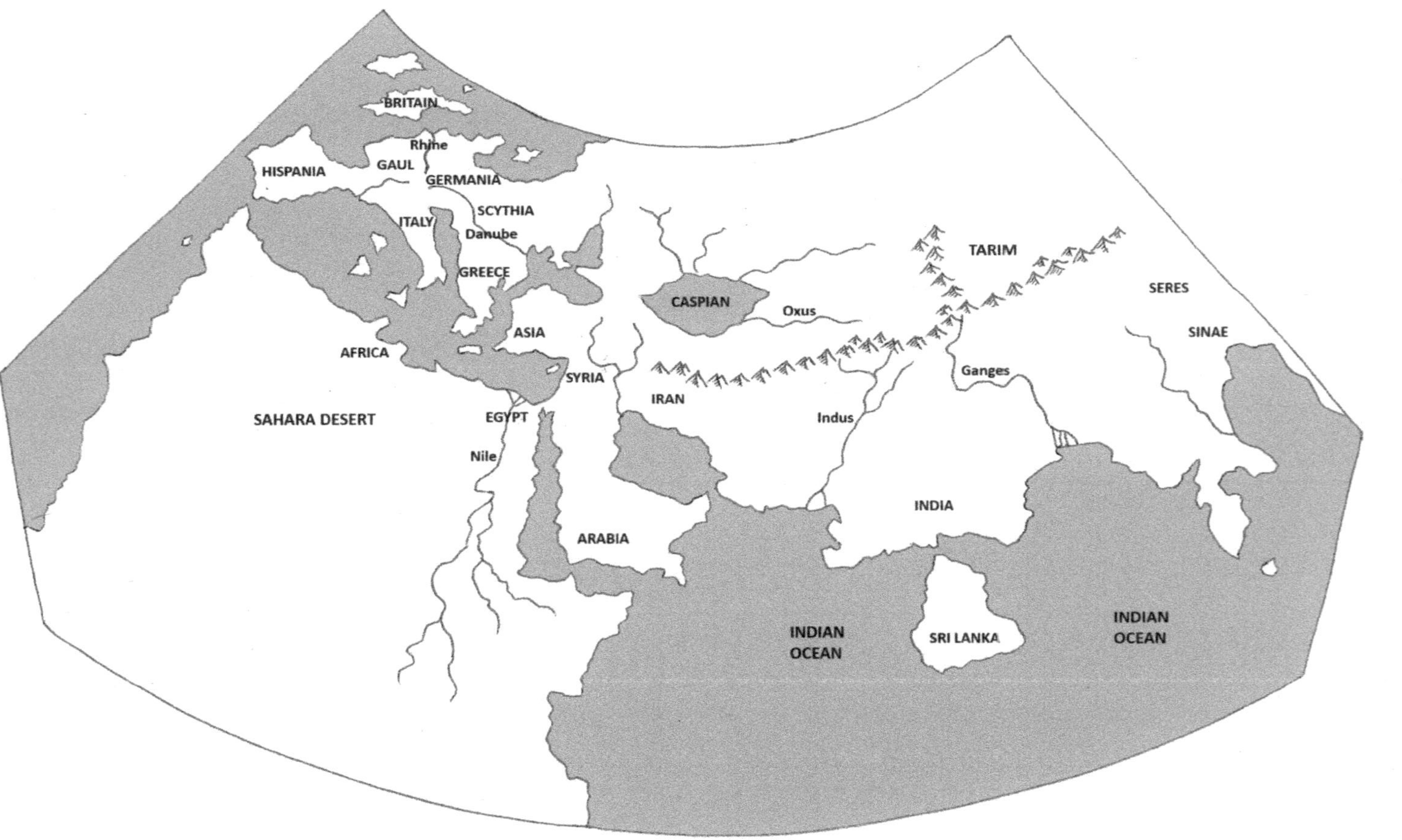

Map 2. Claudius Ptolemy's map of Germania (based on map drawings).

Map 3. The Roman Empire and Northern Europe.

Map 4. Peoples of Ancient Germania.

Introduction

The Germans and Rome*

This book is an account of the ancient Germans as provided by Greek and Roman sources. Ancient Germania extended from the Rhine to the Vistula rivers and included southern Scandinavia. According to Claudius Ptolemy, a second-century Roman geographer, there were about fifty-five tribal groups in this territory. Roman accounts suggest that each tribe could muster at least 10,000 fighting men, indicating that Germania had a population of more than half a million warriors (550,000). This is confirmed by Julius Caesar, who suggests that the Germans were a nation with 430,000 people able to engage in warfare (adult men). In contrast, the early Roman Empire maintained an army of about 300,000 professional soldiers guarding the conquered territories extending from Spain and Britain to Syria and Egypt.

Ancient Germania was about the same size as Greater Gaul, a territory conquered by the Roman general Julius Caesar between 58 and 50 BC. However, Germany was less intensely farmed, and its southern territories were dominated by a vast woodland zone known as the Teutoburg Forest. The total population of Germania was probably smaller and more widely dispersed than Gaul and the country lacked large-scale settlements (*oppida* – proto-towns). Nevertheless, Germania may have had a total population approaching 5 million people. This was less than a tenth of the population of the Roman Empire, which was estimated between 50 and 60 million during the early imperial era.

Despite their smaller numbers, the Germans represented a unique threat to the Romans. Their populations were highly mobile and German tribes could easily migrate great distances. Families would board wagons and travel to new territories, bringing their livestock with them. In antiquity, sections of the Rhine and Danube frontiers often froze, permitting easy crossings of river systems using temporary 'ice roads'. On these occasions vast numbers of Germans could cross the frontiers accompanied by formidable warrior warbands. They sought settlement in Roman territories, and displaced established tax-paying populations to acquire the best farmlands. In conquered territories they also

* See appendices for data and references.

established themselves as overlords, redirecting regional taxes and tribute into their communities.

The first major Germanic migration occurred in about 120 BC when the population of Jutland (Denmark) was displaced by tidal floods. The territory was occupied by the Cimbri and Teutones, who began a mass migration southwards into Gaul. By 113 BC, they had reached Roman-controlled territory north of the Alps, where they inflicted a severe defeat on imperial forces. Up to 80,000 Roman soldiers were massacred at the Battle of Arausio, near the Rhone River (105 BC). To provide context, the Carthaginian general Hannibal killed 50,000 Roman troops during the Battle of Cannae, usually recognised as one of the Republic's greatest defeats (216 BC). During the era of the Cimbric invasion, almost 400,000 citizens were registered in the Roman census.

After Arausio, a force of several hundred thousand Germans and Gauls attempted to cross the Alps and overrun Roman Italy. The Roman legions defeated and massacred the incomers, but the state was forced to institutionalise new measures to improve its military response. This included the recruitment of citizens who did not own property as professional soldiers in long-term service. Half a century later, Julius Caesar intervened in Celtic Gaul to prevent a major Germanic expansion across the Rhine. He used the military power he amassed from this campaign to override the Republican system and appoint himself perpetual dictator.

Figures from the Republican era suggest the manpower potential of migratory Germanic tribes. Julius Caesar records that the Harudes crossed the Rhine with a population that included 24,000 men. Other Germanic invasions were composed of military warbands with a force of 15,000 Sequani. By 58 BC, Julius Caesar estimated that up to 120,000 Germans had crossed the Rhine to settle in Gaul (mainly Suebi).

With the conquest of Gaul, the threat of German expansion became a long-term concern of Rome. Roman accounts suggest that the Suebic tribes in central Germania might have possessed up to 100,000 fighting men, while the emerging Marcomannic kingdom in southern Germany could mobilise up to 70,000 well-trained warriors. In Late Antiquity, a Germanic confederation called the Alemanni could assemble 35,000 fighters for attacks across the Rhine frontiers. In comparison, the Goths who invaded across the Danube frontier could mobilise more than 26,000 fighters (Thervingi and Greuthungi).

The early Roman Empire contained the German threat by stationing about half its military forces along the Rhine and Danube frontiers. The armies were based in military camps and fortresses that developed into significant urban centres. The river systems also functioned as significant routes for the movement of goods and supplies, as riverine travel incurred about one-sixth the cost of land haulage. During the early imperial era, a legion consisted of about 5,000 Roman soldiers supported by an equivalent force of auxiliaries. In total, 8 legions, or about 80,000 troops, guarded the Rhine frontier extending from the North Sea to the Swiss Alps (700 miles). A further 6 legions, or 60,000 soldiers, protected the Danube River extending east from the Black Forest to the Black Sea (a longer frontier stretching more than 1,100 miles).

The Romans maintained at least 3 legions in Britain (30,000 troops) with a fleet of perhaps 40 military vessels guarding the North Sea crossings to Germania (the *Classis Brittanica*). A similar sized fleet operated in the Black Sea safeguarding the coasts of the Caucasus and Crimea (the *Classis Pontica*). These fleets could transfer troops, supplies and materials into the Rhine or Danube networks in the event of military emergencies. The Rhine River fleet included perhaps fifty war galleys, troop transport ships and military supply vessels (the *Classis Germanica*). In contrast, the longer Danube River was patrolled and guarded by two fleets and perhaps a hundred ships (the *Classis Pannonica* and the *Classis Germanica*). A large trireme war galley required about 200 crew to operate and a light *liburna* bireme had sixty personnel on board. The Roman frontiers therefore represented a massive and costly investment of wealth, manpower and materials.

The Failed Conquests

During the reign of the first Emperor Augustus, the Romans campaigned across the Rhine and managed to conquer about half of Germania (12–9 BC), halting at the Elbe River. These campaign routes crossed more than 400 miles and involved several armies including more than 30,000 soldiers. The Romans held this territory for about two decades, until a revolt led by several dominant Germanic tribes ended the conquest. These tribes ambushed the occupying Roman army and annihilated three entire legions in the Teutoburg Forest (AD 9). In response, the Empire withdrew from the country and fortified the Rhine frontier.

In the second century, the Emperor Marcus Aurelius campaigned across the Danube frontier to suppress and conquer southern Germany, including the territories of the Quadi and Marcomanni. By the close of the final campaign, the Romans had occupied and garrisoned the region with about 20,000 troops (AD 177–180). However, when Marcus Aurelius died, his son and successor Commodus withdrew Roman forces from the newly conquered territory.

These campaigns suggest that the Roman Empire would have required about 5 legions or 50,000 troops to fully conquer the greater part of Germania (Rhine to Elbe and the Marcomannic realm). If this conquest had been attempted, then the frontier legions could have been advanced from the Rhine or Danube lines to new positions in west Germania and the expanded Elbe boundary. A conquered west Germania might have added about 20 million sesterces to Roman revenues, based on what Julius Caesar was able to obtain from newly occupied Gaul.

Roman Revenues

During the early imperial era, the Roman Empire received revenues of about 900 million sesterces per annum. About 380 million sesterces came from the conquered provinces in the form of tribute payments that were delivered directly to the imperial government. Greater Gaul contributed about 40 million sesterces a year, while a typical wealthy province or kingdom might contribute about 5 million sesterces per annum. Egypt was the exception, as the territory incorporated the highly productive Nile Valley and the country had been subject to well-developed tax systems for many centuries. Egypt therefore produced monetary revenues that were close to 300 million sesterces per annum, equivalent to almost a third of imperial finances. Egypt also produced an enormous tax-generated grain surplus that was shipped to Rome to feed an enlarged population in the imperial capital (29,000 tons supplied to 200,000 citizens).

Other major sources of revenue to the Roman state were only productive during the early imperial era. The Roman regime received about 120 million sesterces per annum from the output of gold and silver mines located mainly in the Iberian Peninsula (Spain and Portugal). The government also imposed a quarter-rate import tax on all goods crossing the imperial frontiers. This is significant because the Roman Empire maintained large-scale trade connections with the Indian Ocean via Egypt and the Red Sea. According to the geographer Strabo, at least 120 Roman ships sailed to India every year and a legal contract known as the Muziris papyrus puts the value of a single return cargo at over 9 million sesterces. This suggests that eastern trade was worth over a billion sesterces per annum and the Roman state received over 270 million sesterces a year from taxing this commerce.

The vast revenues generated from mineworks and customs taxes were relatively easy to collect and did not require a large-scale state bureaucracy. In the case of frontier commerce, Roman garrisons located at key sites on restricted desert frontiers could safeguard and extract enormous revenues. A Roman conquest of Germania would never have been a safe or secure financial asset.

The cost of a Roman legion and its auxiliary support can be calculated using ancient figures for unit size and military pay. This data suggests that a legion supported by an equivalent force of auxiliaries must have cost the early Roman

Empire about 11 million sesterces per annum. The Rhine frontier, with its eight legions, must have been defended at a cost of about 90 million sesterces per annum, excluding the cost of the riverine fleet. A further 70 million must have been spent on the six legions defending the Danube frontier. Three legions at a cost of 33 million sesterces were required to conquer and retain northern Germany between the Rhine and the Elbe. By contrast, two legions at a cost of 22 million sesterces would have been needed to conquer Marcomannic territory in southern Germany. These conquests would have cost the Roman state over 60 million sesterces per annum to gain tribute revenues of just 20 million sesterces. This is a policy that the Emperor Augustus dismissed as 'fishing with a golden hook' – for if the line snaps, then the loss of the investment is greater than all the fish that might have been caught (Suetonius, *Augustus*, 25). Perhaps Augustus was thinking about the three Roman legions massacred in the Teutoburg Forest. In total, the Romans might have required five legions to combat and overcome threats from Germany. This would have meant large-scale redeployments, or the raising of new units.

Roman military costs increased when army pay was enhanced, as additional troops were raised and deployed to preserve imperial interests. Bureaucratic costs were minimal in the early Empire, since governors were selected from the Roman ruling elite who had private wealth. The army managed most of the state services, bureaucracy and infrastructure required in the provinces. It has been estimated that the early Roman 'civil service' consisted of about 160 personnel. The Roman regime therefore existed mainly as a permanent military force guarding a tax-paying population and guaranteeing the continuation of lucrative commercial networks.

Military Manpower

The conquest of Germania was more than a financial calculation. The Roman capture of this territory would have removed a serious threat and provided the Empire with an important reserve of military recruits to enhance essential armies. This potential is revealed by Roman relations with the subject German peoples on the Rhine frontiers.

By the Augustan era there were significant German populations occupying the eastern territories of Gaul next to the Rhine frontier. Some of these populations had crossed the Rhine decades earlier during the era of Julius Caesar, but the Emperor Augustus permitted others to cross into Roman Gaul. The Romans accepted these Germanic populations into their Empire and created two border provinces in Gaul known as Germania Superior (in the south) and Germania Inferior (in the north). These 'flanking' frontier provinces encompassed distinct

German communities living among Gallic populations. The Romans granted them special privileges, but also placed obligations on their communities and leaders.

The northern frontier also included a territory called Batavia, located on the North Sea coast between several major branches of the Rhine (modern Netherlands). The Romans considered this low-lying territory to be almost an island due to the encroachment of the sea and the extent of the wide waterways flowing through the vast Rhine delta. Batavia incorporated a territory that was about 8,500 square miles in area and formed a 100-mile-long stretch of the lower Rhine frontier. This was a strategic location since Roman ships operating on the North Sea and the Gallic coast delivered cargoes into the Rhine River systems. The Romans also sent cargoes downstream along the Rhine to supply the frontier military and deliver goods to seaports on the north coast of Gaul.

The Germanic population of Batavia was not subject to ordinary taxes. Instead, the Batavians regularly provided high-quality recruits for the Roman army, maintaining at least 16 cohorts (8,000 troops). Roman arrangements with other Germanic tribes, on or beyond the frontiers, also provided a significant supply of essential military recruits for the armies of Rome. Soon after the Emperor Commodus came to power in AD 180, he imposed new terms on the defeated Marcomannic kingdom. The territory delivered a force of nearly 13,000 fighters to the Roman army as new military recruits. This represented about one-fifth of the former Marcomannic military potential.

Germanic leaders with experience in the Roman army were dangerous opponents when they rebelled against the Empire. These experienced soldiers could manipulate, anticipate and counter Roman strategies. The Germanic leader Arminius proved this in the Battle of the Teutoburg Forest, leading a revolt that annihilated about 20,000 Roman troops (AD 9). In AD 47, a Germanic deserter from the Roman army, named Gannascus, used his knowledge and training to conduct seaborne raids into Gaul. In AD 69, the war leader Civilis led a large-scale mutiny of Germanic auxiliaries and a full revolt of the Batavian nation. In the aftermath of this conflict, two Roman legions had to be disbanded due to severe losses and three legions were renamed or reconstituted to evade the shame of defeat. Warfare in the late Roman Empire was characterised by conflicts against similar Germanic peoples who were experienced in Roman tactics. These included the Goths, Vandals, Franks, Angles and Saxons.

Late Empire

The first major shock to the Roman system was a smallpox pandemic that struck the Empire in the AD 160s. The Roman population had no natural resistance to this strain of the disease, which reached the Empire through silk routes crossing Central Asia. The disease inflicted great losses in areas where people lived in close proximity to each other, such as urban sites or military garrisons. The frontier armies therefore suffered severe losses during sustained outbreaks. As many as a third of people in affected communities may have died or been debilitated by this disease, including sight loss and other chronic conditions. The Germanic tribes, who lived in small, scattered family units, were not so severely affected. As Roman garrisons were depleted, the Germans launched savage attacks on the imperial frontiers. In response and retaliation, the Emperor Marcus Aurelius spent over a decade campaigning against the Germanic tribes located north of the Danube (the Marcomannic Wars, AD 166–180). During this conflict, the Roman army suffered losses as severe as the Varus massacre (Teutoburg Forest, AD 9), with 20,000 soldiers killed in a single battle north of the Danube (AD 170).

Roman trade with the Indian Ocean declined rapidly during this era and the mining of precious metals drastically decreased (confirmed by particle pollution in arctic ice cores). This greatly reduced the revenues received by the Roman state and forced the regime to increase taxes, along with other direct extractions from the provinces (food and materials to sustain the armies). This new system required the development of an extensive and costly civilian state bureaucracy, charged with arranging and administering the wider tax burdens. It also led to increased intra-state competition for regional revenues, which was a cause of military mutiny and civil war. To administer this new state apparatus and defend the threatened frontiers, the Emperor Diocletian separated the Empire into eastern and western divisions (AD 286).

Civil wars were rare in the early Empire, but by the third century these events were common occurrences. Tacitus records that during the civil war of AD 69, about 40,000 Roman soldiers were killed at the First Battle of Cremona. About 70,000 soldiers took part in this engagement, meaning that total Roman losses were over 50 per cent. Cassius Dio records that during the Roman civil war of AD 194, about 20,000 soldiers were killed on one side during the Battle of Issus, which was the third major engagement in this conflict. Roman losses during the civil wars of the Tetrarchy (306–324 AD) produced casualties equivalent to almost a third of the Roman military. Combined Roman losses from the battles of Augusta Taurinorum, Tzirallum, Cibalae, Chrysopolis and Mursa probably included more than 164,000 soldiers. Figures from the Battle of Mursa suggest that a victorious Roman force might lose more than a quarter of its soldiers in an engagement with other imperial troops. The defeated side might suffer casualty rates eliminating two-thirds of their army. Roman civil wars inflicted greater damage on the Empire then the Germans or Persians could ever achieve.

Roman losses also led some imperial factions to employ large groups of Germanic fighters to restore and bolster their armies. These practices ultimately had a fatal impact on the Western Roman Empire.

State Resources and Military Capacity

During the civil wars of the third century AD, the Romans lost control over several crucial territories. These territories were depleted of troops and overrun by foreign peoples. The Romans maintained a naval base on the Farasan Islands near the entrance of the Red Sea, 600 miles from the southern frontiers of Egypt. This outpost was to protect shipping and was probably abandoned in the third century AD as troops were transferred to other conflict zones.

The Romans also abandoned Dacia, a province north of the Danube conquered by the Emperor Trajan in AD 106 (modern Romania). This had been a valuable source of new gold bullion at a time when other mine works in the Empire were becoming exhausted. A further loss to the Empire involved a Germanic people called the Goths who had migrated from southern Sweden down the Dnieper River towards the Black Sea. During the mid-third century, they seized and settled the Roman protectorate of the Crimean Peninsula, one of the major grain producers in the ancient world. Well-established seaborne trade routes delivered Crimean grain through the Black Sea to cities in the eastern Mediterranean, including Athens (700 miles distant). Ancient accounts suggest that Crimea provided revenues of about 6 million sesterces to the Roman state and exported over 29,000 tons of grain annually (enough to feed 70,000 people). The region also delivered grain to the Roman Danube armies via the adjacent coastline. After the Gothic takeover, all this potential for wealth and population increase was diverted into the new Germanic settler population. During the third century the Romans exploited this growing Gothic population as their military allies and recruits for new wars against the Sassanid Empire of ancient Persia.

Later Roman armies remained highly effective, and accounts of conflict suggest that a well-led force could expect to defeat a barbarian army about three times its size. This is comparable to military success rates in the early imperial era. At the Battle of Mons Graupius in AD 83, a Roman force, including 11,000 auxiliaries, defeated 30,000 Caladonians. Close to 10,000 enemy were slain and 360 Romans killed. At the Battle of Argentoratum in AD 357, a Roman force of 13,000 soldiers defeated 35,000 Alemanni, killing 6,000 and suffering only 360 deaths.

The Roman situation was radically altered by the arrival of a Hunnic nation in territories north of the Black Sea. The Hunnic nations originated in the orient and migrated through Central Asia. They were highly mobile with a politically sophisticated regime. The eastern Huns had maintained a powerful tribal coalition on the northern frontiers of ancient China, where they posed a serious political and military threat to the Han Empire (202 BC–AD 220). During the fourth century, various Hunnic factions had migrated westwards across the vast Eurasian Steppe. By AD 370, the western Huns had reached the Black Sea. They expelled the existing Pontic Steppe populations and caused up to 200,000 Goths to seek refuge behind the Danube frontiers maintained by Rome.

In this era, the main function of the Roman state was to maintain the cost of its armies and preserve the tax-collecting bureaucratic system that the military required in order to function. However, provincial populations preferred to pay tax in cash, rather than submit to military conscriptions. The import of barbarian populations gave the bureaucrats a way to increase the number of tax-paying subjects in a region. It also gave the state a reserve of new recruits available for immediate military service, an obligation that the migrant settlers accepted. The government could therefore meet its military needs and still charge the provincials its usual defence costs to defer conscription. The surplus income amassed by the state enriched the new bureaucratic elites.

In AD 376, the Eastern Emperor Valens permitted an entire migrant population of Goths to cross the Danube frontier and settle in Roman territory. According to Roman accounts, this migrant force might have included more than 200,000 foreign people. The Visigoths revolted in AD 378, destroying the Eastern Roman Field Army and killing the emperor. Recognising the existence of a foreign rival regime in their territories, the Romans were forced to negotiate terms. Faced with further civil wars and foreign invasions, various Roman factions competed for this Gothic military support. The Visigoths became a mobile well-armed ethnic state within imperial territories, eventually becoming a prominent political challenger and rival to both imperial courts. The Western Roman Empire would only last one more century before its collapse.

The Hunnic expansion into central Europe created further large-scale population movements. In AD 406, an east Germanic people called the Vandals broke through the Rhine frontiers to plunder and occupy Gaul. Their population, which included more than 50,000 warriors, migrated southwards, seizing lands in Spain before crossing to North Africa in AD 435. They exploited the reduction of Roman garrisons to conquer the imperial province that incorporated Tunisia. This was another major grain-producing region and during the height of the Roman Empire it had yielded more than 88,000 tons of tax-generated grain for delivery to Rome. This great wealth and productivity was incorporated in the newly established Vandal kingdom of North Africa. Their population increased, and within a century this Vandal regime could mobilise up to 80,000 fighting men.

In AD 361, the Emperor Julian completed a major restoration of supply lines and trade routes designed to deliver large quantities of British grain to Roman forces on the Rhine frontiers. But in the following era, Roman garrisons in Britain were depleted by military mutinies and costly civil wars. The coastal tribes of northern Germany began to cross the sea to settle on the east flank of the island. The Roman British recruited these North Germans to serve as mercenaries to defend wealthy villas from Irish and Pictish raiders. But as their numbers increased, they rebelled and Angles, Jutes and Saxons overran eastern Britain (AD 449).

By AD 450, the Hunnic King Attila ruled an empire extending around the Black Sea from the Pontic Steppe to the Danube frontier. His political dominance stretched across southern Germany, and he claimed fealty over several large Germanic tribes who bolstered his steppe armies. In AD 451, Attila invaded Roman Gaul with a vast army capable of inflicting unprecedented damage on the Western Empire. The Huns had an ethnic force of about 60,000 steppe cavalry, supported by tens of thousands of Germanic warriors assembled from tribes who had submitted to the Hunnic king. In response, the Romans united with the Visigoths to resist and expel the invaders. But their triumph at the Battle of the Catalaunian Plains massively depleted the remaining Roman armies of the Western Empire. In AD 453, Attila died, and the Hunnic Empire disintegrated into civil war. However, by this stage, the Rhine frontiers had been annihilated. In AD 478, the last emperor of Roman Italy was deposed and the Western Empire fragmented under the pressure of incoming Germanic tribes. Five centuries after Julius Caesar had opposed the Germans and set the Rhine limits, the barriers had been breached and the Germans had overthrown Roman civilisation. This process can only be explained by the surviving ancient sources. This book contains the ancient accounts of the Germanic threat and reveals Roman efforts to contain the severe challenge and perpetual danger.

Chapter One

Invasion of the Cimbri and Tuetones (113–101 BC)

The first conflict between Rome and the Germans occurred in 113 BC. In this era the Romans controlled all of Italy, large parts of southern Spain (Hispania) and the Mediterranean coast of southern Gaul (Gallia Narbonensis). The Celtic territory of Noricum (Austria) on the eastern flank of the Alps was also under Roman protection.

The Cimbri and Tuetones were Germanic peoples from the Jutland Peninsula who migrated towards the Alps with the hope of seizing and settling Roman territory.

Main events of the Cimbrian War:

- **113 BC:** Gnaeus Papirius Carbo is defeated at the Battle of Noreia in Noricum (north-east of the Alps). An army of 30,000 Roman troops is annihilated.
- **109 BC:** Marcus Junius Silanus is defeated in Gallia Narbonensis (the Roman province in southern Gaul).
- **105 BC:** The consul Gnaeus Mallius Maximus and the proconsul Quintus Servilius Caepio are defeated at the Battle of Arausio (southern Gaul). Perhaps 70,000–80,000 Roman and Italian soldiers are killed. The Roman legate Marcus Aurelius Scaurus is taken prisoner.
- **102 BC:** The consul Gaius Marius defeats the Cimbri at the Battle of Aquae Sextiae (southern Gaul). Quintus Lutatius Catulus cannot prevent the Tuetones crossing the Alps.
- **101 BC:** The consul Gaius Marius and the proconsul Quintus Lutatius Catulus defeat the Cimbri at the Battle of the Raudian Plain in northern Italy.

Origin of the Cimbri and Tuetones

001 Plutarch, *Marius*, 11

The Teutones and Cimbri remained a coherent population, even though they had traversed a vast stretch of territory to reach their current location. The distance was so great that the Romans were not familiar with the origin of their populations and could not clearly ascertain where their homelands might have been.

The most prevalent conjecture is that the Teutones and Cimbri belonged to the German peoples who occupy lands extending to the great northern ocean (Scandinavia). This conjecture was based on their large stature, their light-blue eyes, and the fact that the Germans call raiders 'Cimbri'.

Some authorities give an alternative origin for the Teutones and Cimbri. They suggest that Gaul was once large and wide enough to reach to the outer sea and the subarctic regions (of Scandinavia). From there, the territory extended eastwards to the Maeotic Sea in Pontic Scythia (the Azov expanse north of the Black Sea). Celtic territories therefore adjoined Scythia and in these regions, Celts and Scythians mingled. These mixed populations left their home and moved westwards. But they did not travel the distance in a single continuous journey. Instead, they pushed forwards each spring and fought to occupy new lands. Eventually they crossed the entire continent. These people had many different names for their population groups, but they called their whole force by the common name of Gallo-Scythians.

Other authorities connect the Cimbri with the people known to the ancient Greeks as the Cimmerians. They say that Cimmerians were not an entire nation, but a group or faction expelled from lands near the Maeotic Sea (northern Black Sea). The Cimmerians were expelled by the Scythians and fled into Asia under the leadership of Lygdamis. But the largest and most warlike part of their people remained in their homelands near the outer ocean at the very edge of the earth. They occupy a land that is shaded and sunless due to the height and thickness of their forests, which stretch as far as Hercynia (the Black Forest in Germany).

These people look up at a sky where the Pole Star has a greater elevation due to the reduction in parallels (converging latitudes on a globe). Here, the viewer sees the star in a position closer to its zenith. In this region a single day and night divide the year into two equal parts. This is why Homer in his story of Odysseus, has his hero consult the shades of the dead (in the land of the Cimmerians).

So, these barbarians were first called 'Cimmerians' and then known as 'Cimbri'. From these most distant regions they emerged and came forth against Italy. But all this background is based on conjecture, rather than clear historical evidence.

Cimbri among Celtic Invaders of Greece (279 BC)

In 279 BC, Celtic invaders sacked Delphi, one of the main cultural and religious centres in ancient Greece. Appian was writing in the second century AD.

002 Appian, *Illyrian Wars*, 1.4
The Autarienses (an Illyrian tribe) joined Molostimus and the Celtic people called the Cimbri in their military expedition against the Temple of Delphi. But the greater part of their force was destroyed by storm, hurricane, and lightning just before the sacrilege was committed.

Greek Deities enter Battle at Delphi (279 BC)

003 Pausanias, *Description of Greece*, 1.4
When the Greek defenders engaged the Celts, thunderbolts struck from the sky and rocks from the cliffs broke loose and fell upon the invaders. Terrifying phantom shapes of armed warriors harassed the foreigners. It is said that two of these ghostly figures were from Hyperborea (the Artic North). These spectres were named Hyperochus and Amadocus. The third figure was Pyrrhus, son of Achilles (a red-haired Greek warrior also known as Neoptolemus – the 'New Warrior').

Cursed Greek Temple Treasures

004 Justin, *Histories*, 32.3
The Gauls returned to their own country after their disastrous attack upon Delphi. (…) There they were advised by their soothsayers to cast all the gold and silver which they had won in war and sacrilege, into the waters of Toulouse (a sacred lake). This treasure included 110,000 pounds of silver and 1,500 pounds of gold. Later the Roman consul Caepio managed to seize this wealth (during his military command in the region). But this was a sacrilegious act that cursed Caepio and his army. The Cimbrian War seemed to pursue the Romans as vengeance for the removal of those sacred treasures.

Cimbri Displaced by an Ocean Flood (120 BC)

005 Strabo, *Geography*, 7.2.1

Concerning the Cimbri, some things that are written about them are incorrect and others are improbable. For example, it is said that the Cimbri lived on a large peninsula (Jutland) and they began their hostile migration when their settlements were overwhelmed by a great flood tide (a North Sea inundation). But they still live in that country and in fact they have recently presented the Emperor Augustus with a sacred cauldron (diplomatic gift). This object was given with a plea for friendship and a request that their earlier offences against the Roman state be forgiven. Their petition was granted and the Cimbri returned by ship to their homeland (a sailing from the Rhine to Jutland).

It is ridiculous to suppose that the original Cimbri left their homelands because of tidal effects. This is because the ocean tides are a natural and persistent phenomenon which predictably occurs twice a day (Strabo was from the Black Sea region, which experiences minimal tidal flow). The claim that an excessive flood tide once occurred therefore seems to be a fabrication. The ocean is subject to increases and diminutions (tidal effects), but these are always limited and periodical.

Anyone who claims that the Cimbri began their hostile migrations due to flood tides must be mistaken. Ephorus writes that the coastal-dwelling Celts meekly tolerate the destruction of their homes by the ocean tides and then resolutely rebuild them (the effects of Atlantic storms). They see this enterprise as training in the virtue of fearlessness and endurance. In fact, it is said that they suffer greater losses from the tides than from warfare (therefore, why would the Cimbri migrate?).

(As stated) the excuse of flood tides is absurd. This part|of the world is subject to continual inundations and the tidal phenomenon occurs twice every day (regular tides on the Atlantic coasts). It is impossible to believe that the original Cimbri saw this phenomenon as anything other than natural and harmless. In fact, it occurs in every country that faces this ocean (to include Britain and northern Gaul).

Cleitarchus says that some of the Cimbri horsemen saw the sea suddenly rushing in (possibly occurring at tidal estuaries in shallow coastal areas) and although they rode away at speed, they were almost caught and cut off by the rising water. This must be a false narrative and the tide cannot invade the land in this manner. We know that the incoming tide is an imperceptibly slow advance by the sea. Furthermore, it occurs daily, and its presence is audible to anyone near the shore, even if they cannot see the water (the sound of the lapping waves). The incoming sea could never have caused men to flee in terror as if it was a sudden and unexpected event.

Errors and Assumptions

The Cimmerians were an East Iranic people occupying lands near the Black Sea in the 600s BC. Their name sounded like 'Cimbri', so certain Greeks wrongly assumed a connection.

006 Strabo, *Geography*, 7.2.1
Poseidonius is right to criticise historians who make these assertions (claiming that the Cimbri migration was caused by flood tides). His own ideas are also reasonable. He suggests that the Cimbri began as a migratory people engaged in raiding. They may even have made an expedition as far as Lake Maeotis (the Azov expanse located north of the Black Sea). Poseidonius suggests that the Greek word for Cimbri was 'Cimmeri' and this would explain the 'Cimmerian' Bosphorus (the ancient name for the Crimean Peninsula).

Migration of the Cimbri

007 Strabo, *Geography*, 7.2.2
Poseidonius records that in earlier times the Hercynian Forest was occupied by the Boii (a Celtic tribe). When the Cimbri tried to enter this territory, they were forced back, and they therefore followed a route along the Ister (Danube) to the country of the Scordiscan Galatae (Celtic territories on a western stretch of the Danube). Then they crossed the territories of the Teuristae and Taurisci who were also Galatae (Celts) to the lands of the Helvetii (Swiss Plateau). The Helvetii were rich in gold, but peaceable (not at war with neighbouring Celtic nations). They observed the wealth which the Cimbri had acquired from plundering other territories and were excited to see that it surpassed their own riches. Two of the Helvetii tribes therefore joined the Cimbri in their further migrations. These were the Tigurini and Toygeni.

But the Romans subdued all these people (the hostile migrants), both the Cimbri and those who had joined their expedition. Some of them were defeated as they tried to cross the Alps (the Tuetones) and the rest were overcome in Italy, on the far side of the mountains (the Cimbri).

Gallic Allies

Celtic warriors from the populus Helvetii tribe in the Swiss Plateau joined the Germanic forces.

008 Strabo, *Geography*, 4.3.3
The Helvetii were said to be rich in gold, but they still decided to engage in plundering raids when they observed the great wealth of the Cimbri. Two of their three tribes joined the Germans on their campaigns, but they were obliterated in the wars that followed.

First Roman Contact with the Cimbri and Teutones

009 Florus, *Roman History*, 1.38
The Cimbri, Teutones and Tigurini were fugitives from the extreme parts of Gaul (Germany, northern Europe). The ocean flooded their territories, so they sought new places to live. But their settlement in Gaul was opposed and their progress into Spain was halted. They therefore descended upon Roman Italy. They sent representatives to the headquarters of the Roman commander Silanus and offered a message to the Senate. They requested that:

> O, Romans, followers of the War God Mars, grant us land as payment and use our manpower and weapons for any purpose you wish.

But what land could the Roman people give them? They were involved in their own disputes about land shortages and agrarian legislation.

When their requests were denied, the Germans prepared to take by military force that which they could not obtain by negotiation.

Invasion

010 Plutarch, *Marius*, 11
The Romans received news that Jugurtha (the Numidian king of North Africa) had been captured (ending one conflict). But soon afterwards reports reached them concerning the Teutones and Cimbri. Information regarding the numbers and strength of the invading hosts were at first disbelieved, but afterwards these details were found to be accurate. The reports said that 300,000 fighting men carrying weapons were advancing on Italy and far

larger hordes of women and children accompanied these warriors. These people were searching for lands to support a vast multitude and for cities in which to settle and live. The circumstances resembled the earlier Gallic invasion of Italy. These new invaders had learnt how the Gauls had seized and occupied the best part of Italy from the Tyrrhenians and they planned to do likewise. Both tribes (the Teutones and Cimbri) therefore descended upon Gaul and Italy like a vast cloud. (…)

Many writers report that the force approaching Italy was larger than the figure mentioned above. Furthermore, nothing could withstand their courage and daring. When they engaged in battle, they rushed forth with the swiftness and violence of fire. No one could withstand their assault and all who opposed them became their prey and plunder. Several large Roman armies had been stationed in Transalpine Gaul to protect the region. But they too were destroyed, along with their commanders, in an inglorious way. In fact, these armies offered such feeble resistance that their defeat encouraged the onrushing barbarians to head south and challenge Rome. The invaders conquered all who opposed them and acquired an abundance of plunder in their victories. Now they were determined not to settle anywhere until they had utterly destroyed Rome and ravaged all of Italy.

011 Livy, *Periochae*, 63
A total of 394,336 citizens were registered in the Roman census.

Bad Omens (113 BC)

012 Julius Obsequens, *Prodigies*, 38
Mount Alban (near Rome) seemed to be on fire that night when a small temple and a statue were struck by lightning. The altar of Salus (the goddess of wellbeing) was smashed by a lightning strike and the land in Lucania and Privernum gaped open (seismic activity). In Gaul the sky seemed to be on fire (perhaps a spectacular sunset). After reaching the Alps, the Cimbri and Teutones cruelly slaughtered the Romans and their allies.

First Engagement with the Cimbri and Tuetones (113 BC)

013 Livy, *Periochae*, 63 (Latin summary of lost books in Livy's *History of Rome*)
A nomadic tribe known as the Cimbrians came to Illyricum (north of the Alps) in pursuit of plunder. They defeated the consul Papirius Carbo and his army.

014 Appian, *Gallic Wars*, 3, fragment 17 (Constantine Porphyrogenitus, *The Embassies*)
A large horde of Teutones invaded the territory of Noricum determined to plunder the region. The Roman consul, Papirius Carbo, was afraid that they would cross into Italy, so he occupied the Alps at a place where the pass is at its narrowest. When the enemy made no movement in this direction, he attacked them. They had invaded Noricum and the people of this region were foreign 'friends' of the Romans. It was the practice of the Romans in this era to acknowledge foreign nations as 'friends'. They did this when they wanted to intervene in the territory of foreign peoples, without being obligated to defend them as allies.

As Carbo was approaching, the Teutones sent envoys explaining that they had not known anything about the 'friendship' between Rome and Noricum. They pledged that in the future they would not intrude into this territory. Carbo praised the ambassadors and gave them guides for their return journey. But he secretly instructed the guides to take the envoys by a longer route (delaying their return). Then he marched his army by a shorter route to reach the Teutones while they were ceasing hostilities and were still unprepared for conflict. But Carbo suffered severely for this treachery and a large part of his army was destroyed. The entire Roman force might have perished, if the gloom of a tremendous thunderstorm had not overtaken the armies when the fighting was in progress. The storm forced the combatants to separate, and the terror of heaven ended the battle (severe winds, torrential rain and lightning strikes). The Romans fled in small bands through the woods and only reformed (into a fighting force) three days later after enduring many difficulties.

Confused Account of Battle Site

015 Strabo, *Geography*, 5.4.8
Aquileia is outside the territory of the Veneti. The boundary between the two peoples is formed by a river flowing from the Alps. This waterway can be travelled 1,200 *stadia* inland (about 100 miles) by river craft to reach the town of Noreia. Nearby is where Gnaeus Carbo fought the Cimbri without obtaining a victory. This region has places that are naturally well-suited to gold-panning (prospecting) and has also ironworks (tools and weaponry).

Suicide of Carbo

016 Cicero, *Letters to his Friends*, 9.21 'To Papirius Paetus (at Naples) from Cicero at Rome' (43 BC)
Not one person from that family has been a good or useful citizen. (…) Even his father, when accused by Marcus Antonius, is thought to have escaped condemnation by ingesting a dose of shoemaker's vitriol (sulfuric acid used as a mordant for leather dyes).

Bad Omens (105 BC)

017 Julius Obsequens, *Prodigies*, 43
The moon and a star were visible for a long time between the third and the seventh hour of the day. Fugitives and deserters ransacked territories near Thurii (a Greek colony in southern Italy). After devastating Spain, the Cimbri crossed the mountains and joined with the Teutones. A wolf entered the city of Rome. Vultures on a tower were killed by a lightning bolt. At the third hour of the day the sun disappeared and all light was obscured (probably an eclipse).

Battle of Arausio (105 BC)

A Roman force prepared to engage the invaders near the Rhone River in southern Gaul (Gallia Narbonensis). The Ambrones were probably a Celtic population who joined the German migrants. Orosius mentions Gauls among the invaders and some of the Celtic settlers in northern Italy shared this tribal name.

018 Cassius Dio, *Roman History*, 27.91
Quintus Servilius caused great harm to the Roman army due to the jealousy he felt towards his colleague Gnaeus Mallius (the other commander). Both men had equal authority, but Servilius felt inferior because Mallius was a consul. Mallius had sent for Servilius, after the death of Scaurus (defeated, captured and executed by the Cimbri in 105 BC).

Servilius suggested that each commander should guard his own province. But then he became concerned that Mallius might gain some great glory on his own. He therefore moved his army nearby but refused to join the other Roman encampment or formulate a common plan of action. Instead, he took position between Mallius and the Cimbri, clearly intending to join battle before his rival general and thus winning the greater glory of the war.

Their enemies were filled with dread since they did not know that the Roman commanders were in dispute. The Cimbri desired peace and made overtures to Mallius as consul (the more senior commander), but Servilius was indignant and refused any reconciliation. He also contemplated killing the envoys. Finally, the soldiers forced Servilius to go to Mallius and consult with him about the situation. But the meeting caused greater hostilities between the commanders, and they parted in a disgraceful state of strife.

019 Granius Licinianus, *Roman History*, 33.11

The consul Mallius was alarmed by the success of the Cimbri. He therefore sent a letter to Servilius Caepio urging him to join forces and confront the enemy with a large, combined army. But Servilius refused and crossed the Rhone in command of his own forces. He boasted to his soldiers that he would bring help to the frightened consul, but he did not meet with him to discuss the conduct of the war. He also ignored envoys sent by the Senate asking the generals to co-operate and jointly protect the Roman state.

The Cimbri sent envoys to arrange peace terms and to ask for land to settle and grain to sow. But Servilius dismissed them with such harshness that the following day they attacked the Romans. His military camp was situated close to the camp of Mallius, but he could not be persuaded to combine their armies into a single force.

Most of the Roman army was destroyed (…) (the battle took place) the day before October. Rutilius Rufus claims that at least 70,000 regular and light-armed soldiers were killed on this one day.

020 Orosius, *History*, 5.16

The following events occurred 642 years after the founding of Rome (105 BC). The consul Gaius Marius and the proconsul Quintus Caepio were dispatched against the Cimbri, Teutones, Tigurini and Ambrones. These Gallic and Germanic tribes had formed a conspiracy to destroy the Roman state. The Roman leaders divided the command between themselves and established the Rhone River as the boundary for their military operations. But they began disputing and contending their command roles and responsibilities. This produced ill will between the commanders, and they failed to co-ordinate their military actions. The result was a major defeat with both commanders bringing great disgrace and peril to the Roman nation.

In this battle, Marcus Aemilius, who was of consular rank, was captured and killed and the two sons of the serving consul were slain. According to Antias, 80,000 of the Romans and their allies were slaughtered in the disaster and 40,000 servants and camp followers were killed. It is said that only ten men survived from the entire Roman army. These men reported the desperate events in a manner that greatly increased the distress of the Roman populace. (…)

Having gained possession of both military camps and a vast amount of booty, the enemy acted in a strange and unusual manner. As though performing a curse or a sacrifice they utterly destroyed everything they had captured. They tore the Roman clothing into pieces and had it strewn about the landscape. The captured gold and silver were cast into the river. The Roman breastplates were hacked to pieces and horse trappings were deliberately destroyed. The horses they seized were drowned in whirlpools and the captured soldiers had nooses fastened around their neck before being strung up to die on trees. Thus, the conqueror received no booty while the conquered obtained no mercy. At Rome there was great sorrow, but also intense fear that the Cimbri would immediately cross the Alps and destroy Italy.

021 Livy, *Periochae*, 65

The consul Marcus Junius Silanus unsuccessfully fought against the Cimbrians. The Senate ignored the envoys of the Cimbrians who demanded land and a place to settle.

Effect of the Roman Defeat

022 Livy, *Periochae*, 67

The consuls Gnaeus Mallius and the proconsul Quintus Servilius Caepio were both defeated by these same enemies (the Cimbrians). Their military camps were plundered and the Romans suffered great losses. Valerius Antias records that 80,000 soldiers, and 40,000 servants and camp followers were killed near Arausio.

Caepio, who had caused this defeat by his earlier rashness, was convicted by the Roman state. His powers of office were revoked, and all his possessions were confiscated. This was the first time this had occurred since the era of King Tarquinius (the last monarch of Rome).

023 Florus, *Roman History*, 1.38

Silanus could not withstand the first attack of the barbarians. The Roman commander Mallius was overwhelmed in the second engagement and

Caepio defeated in the third encounter. The Romans were routed, and their military camps captured by the enemy.

This would have been an end to Rome except that they appointed Marius as their commander.

Fate of Scaurus (105 BC)

024 Granius Licinianus, *Roman History*, 33.11
The ex-consul Marcus Aurelius Scaurus was thrown from his horse and captured (by the Cimbri). He was brought before their governing council, but he did not do or say anything that was unworthy of a Roman who had held high honours. He could have escaped death, but he refused to act as a collaborator or guide. He was ashamed to have survived the loss of his army and therefore submitted to execution.

025 Livy, *Periochae*, 67
After the defeat of his army, Marcus Aurelius Scaurus, a deputy of the consul, was captured by the Cimbrians and brought before their council. He managed to deter them from crossing the Alps and entering Italy, by claiming that the Romans were unconquerable. But he was killed by a savage young man named Boiorix.

Heroic Action by Sertorius

026 Plutarch, *Sertorius*, 3
Quintus Sertorius served under Caepio when the Cimbri and Teutones invaded Gaul (105 BC). When the Romans were defeated and forced to flee, Sertorius lost his horse and suffered a wound to his body. But he still managed to cross the Rhone, swimming in his breastplate (perhaps a leather cuirass) and holding his shield (for buoyancy). He could withstand the adverse river currents due to his great physical strength and endurance to hardship enabled by his training.

Later, these same enemies continued their advance (into Italy) approaching with dreadful threats and a vast multitude of fighting men (102 BC). At this time it was challenging for any Roman soldier to remain in his post and obey his senior officers. But while Marius was in command, Sertorius undertook a mission to spy upon the enemy. He disguised himself in a Celtic outfit and learnt some of the commonest expressions in this language. This was enough to conduct a basic conversation if required (presenting himself as a Celtic ally to Germanic warriors). Then he mingled with the barbarians, seeing and hearing what might be important before reporting back to Marius (troop movements, the size and composition of enemy forces). For this action he received an award for valour. During the rest of this campaign, he performed many deeds which demonstrated daring and good judgement. Sertorius was therefore advanced by his commanders to further positions of greater honour and trust. When the war against the Cimbri and Teutones was concluded, he was sent out to Spain as a military tribune to serve in the territory of the Celtiberians.

Unrest among the Celts (104 BC)

027 Frontinus, *Stratagems*, 1.2.6 'On Discovering Enemy Plans'
During the war with the Cimbrians and Teutones, the consul Gaius Marius wanted to test the loyalty of the Gauls and Ligurians (Alpine Celts). He therefore sent them a letter commanding them, in the first part of the dispatch, to only open the specially sealed inner document on a certain date. Then, before the appointed day had arrived, he demanded that the letter was returned. When he found that all the seals were broken, he knew that trust was breached and hostilities were being planned.

Gaius Marius takes Command

A senior politician named Gaius Marius was selected to lead the Roman forces with the support of the Roman populace.

028 Velleius Paterculus, *History of Rome*, 2.12
An immense horde of the German peoples called the Cimbri and the Teutones defeated and routed the consuls Caepio and Mallius in Gaul (105 BC). The armies of Carbo (113 BC) and Silanus (109 BC) had also been defeated and scattered. The ex-consul Scaurus Aurelius had been killed in the fighting along with other renowned men. The Roman people therefore believed that Marius was the most qualified person to take command and repel these mighty enemies.

Therefore, Marius achieved a succession of consulships. His third year of office was spent in preparation for this war against the Cimbri and Tuetones (104 BC).

029 Plutarch, *Marius*, 11

Soon all the envy, hatred and slander directed at Marius dissipated due to the great peril that threatened Italy from the north. It seems the Romans required a mighty general, and they looked for a helmsman who could save the state from a great flood tide of war. But the Roman populace did not support anyone of high birth, or private wealth, who sought office at the consular elections. Instead, they proclaimed Marius a consul, even though he was absent from the city.

030 Livy, *Periochae*, 67 (104 BC)

Gaius Marius entered the Senate in full military triumphal attire, something no one had ever done before. It was permitted because his consulship had been prolonged due to the fear and apprehension caused by the Cimbrian War. (…)

Meanwhile, the Cimbri devastated all the territories between the Rhone River and Pyrenees Mountains. Then they crossed through a mountain pass into Hispania and destroyed many districts until they were routed by the Celtiberians. So, the Cimbri returned to Gaul and rejoined the Teutones in the land of the Veliocassians (northern Alps).

Improvements in the Military

031 Plutarch, *Marius*, 13

Marius set out on the campaign, but he worked to drill and improve his army on the march. He made his men practise all types of running and he conducted very long marches (extreme fitness to counter the Germanic physique). He also forced them to carry their own baggage and to prepare their own meals (tasks previously conducted by surplus slaves, attendants and other camp followers). These soldiers would obediently perform great labours without complaint, so they became known as 'Marian Mules' (men with the strength and endurance of pack animals).

Germanic Invasion is Delayed

032 Plutarch, *Marius*, 14

Fortune favoured Marius, for the barbarians deviated from their course (north Italy) and surged into Spain. This gave the commander time to further exercise his soldiers for improved physical strength. He raised their spirits and gave them a sturdier courage (increased morale and mental fortitude). Most important of all, this training gave the soldiers time to discover what sort of man Marius was (a stern disciplinarian who won the long-term loyalty and respect of his soldiers).

(...) the Romans were unwilling to risk battle under any other general. The barbarians were expected to return in the following spring, but they did not reappear. Once again, the period of Marius' consulship expired (requiring his reappointment as commander).

Improvements to Rhone River Infrastructure (Gallia Narbonensis)

033 Plutarch, *Marius*, 15

Marius learned that the enemy were near (approaching northern Italy). He therefore crossed the Alps with his army and established a fortified camp next to the Rhone River (southern Gaul). He brought an abundance of stores into this encampment. This guaranteed that his army would not be compelled to give battle due to a lack of provisions (the need to preserve and protect vulnerable supply lines). It had been a long and costly process to supply his army with essentials (including thousands of tons of food). But he rendered this process rapid and easy via the maritime route (supply sailings from Italy to southern Gaul). The river channels which led from the Rhone into the sea were obstructed by great quantities of mud and sand. Due to the action of the tides, this material formed densely packed clay-like banks (semi-submerged barriers). This made it difficult, laborious, and slow for vessels carrying supplies to enter the river (a process required for upstream travel).

Marius therefore brought his army to the place and since his soldiers would otherwise have been idle, he began to divert the river (a massive labour project). He redirected a large part of the river to a more suitable position on the coast. This was a deep bay where ships could anchor, and the water could flow through a calm and uninterrupted channel directly into the sea. This canal still bears his name (an important economic feature during the imperial era).

034 Polyaenus, *Stratagems*, 8.10.1

The Cimbri and Teutones were a savage people with an immense stature. They had a horrible appearance and a language that was scarcely human (a Greek perspective). When they began to enter Italy, Marius avoided any close engagement (a decisive battle). Instead, he ordered his soldiers to advance no further than the outer ditches of their defences (large fortified Roman encampments). Furthermore, if skirmishing occurred at a distance, then his soldiers were instructed to remain at least a javelin's throw away from the enemy. By this means the Romans became familiar with the appearance of their foe (to diminish fear). They learned to despise their opponents as savages and urged Marius to lead them forth to defeat these barbarous invaders. When Marius finally engaged 100,000 of the enemy in battle, few escaped and most of the foe were taken prisoner or slain.

Confrontation with the Tuetones

035 Plutarch, *Marius*, 15

The barbarians divided themselves into two groups with the Cimbri passing through Noricum in the direction of Catulus (the second Roman commander located in north-east Italy). Meanwhile, the Teutones and Ambrones planned a march along the Ligurian sea coast to engage Marius (the north-west approach into Italy)

The Cimbri delayed, but the Teutones and Ambrones marched immediately through the intervening lands to reach Marius. Their numbers seemed limitless, their appearance was terrifying (physical size) and their speech and cries did not resemble the sound of any other people (a Germanic language). Their horde covered a large part of the plain and after pitching their camp, they challenged Marius to battle.

Marius ignored these challenges and kept his soldiers securely within their fortifications. He severely rebuked any over-eager officers who tried to display their courage by urging a rush into combat. He denounced these men as traitors to their country. He said that their ambition should not be for immediate triumphs or trophies (battle honours). Their objective was to negate the storm of war and secure the long-term safety of Italy.

This was his message to his officers and equals (men in the senior military and political classes). But he had a different approach to his soldiers (ordinary fighting men). He would station them in detachments on the fortifications closest to the enemy. He urged these soldiers to observe the foe and become accustomed to them. They must not fear their physical size or dread their strange and ferocious calls (perhaps bellowing challenges to combat). They must become acquainted with their war gear and military movements (observing their manoeuvres or bouts of practice fighting). Over the course of time, these observations allowed the soldiers to perceive a formidable enemy as something familiar (no longer inducing fear).

Marius thought that the unknown will provoke terror through many imagined attributes that simply do not exist (false fears). But familiarity with a genuinely dreadful phenomenon can remove the power of fear. So, he applied this principle to his soldiers. They were daily exposed to the sight of the enemy, which lessened their fear and astonishment. Eventually, when they heard the threats and the intolerable boasting of the barbarians, they were only filled with anger and the impulse to act.

The enemy had begun ravaging and plundering all the surrounding countryside. They often attacked the Roman fortifications with great audacity and confidence. The disgruntled soldiers began to talk, and news of their anger reached Marius. They said:

> Why does Marius treat us like cowards? He keeps us from battle like women locked in the household. Let us act like free men and demand an answer. Is he waiting for other soldiers to fight in defence of Italy? Are we to be used only as workmen, digging ditches, clearing out mud and diverting rivers? Have we trained and toiled for this purpose? Are these the achievements of his consulships? Are these the only acts he will reveal to his fellow citizens in Rome?
>
> Or does Marius fear defeat from the enemy like the generals Carbo and Caepio? But those men never had the reputation or ability of our commander and their armies were far inferior to our current force. Surely it is better to act, even if we perish, than to remain here idly watching as our allies are overrun and plundered.

Marius was glad to hear these sentiments from the soldiers (expressing confidence and enthusiasm for battle). Nevertheless, he tried to restrain them, saying that he trusted their abilities, but certain oracles would decide the exact time and place of his victory. He had in his entourage a Syrian woman (a mystic), named Martha, who had the gift of prophesy and would make the required sacrifices (to determine when battle might be favourable to Rome). (…)

Many strange omens were observed. In the Italian cities of Ameria and Tuder flaming spears and shields were seen streaking across the night sky (meteors). These objects seemed to clash together then move in different directions (splitting apart). Their movements resembled men in battle formations, with some groups fleeing and others following in pursuit (meteor showers). They all streamed away towards the west.

036 Plutarch, *Marius*, 18

Finally, since Marius did not act, the Teutones attempted to storm the Roman camp (a provocation). But the Romans hurled many missiles against them from the fortifications, and the Tuetones began to suffer casualties. They therefore halted their attack and prepared a march onwards (into Italy). They expected to cross the Alps without opposition (since the Roman army would not fight an open battle).

The Tuetones packed up their baggage and began to march past the Roman camp. Their immense numbers were revealed by the length of their marching lines. It is said that it took six days for them to file past the fortifications of Marius, although they moved in a near continuous progression. As they marched close to the Roman camp, the warriors called out to the soldiers, asking them if they had any special messages for their wives at home, saying, 'we shall soon be with them.'

Marius waited, but then acted when the barbarians had passed and were on their way (towards Italy). He ordered his army to leave their camp and follow close behind the enemy. On this march they always halted near to the enemy, but in strongly fortified camps that were secure throughout the night. Thus, the two armies moved forwards to a site called Aquae Sextiae that was only a short march from the Alps. Marius prepared to give battle in this location. The place chosen for his military camp offered strong protection, but it was poorly supplied with water. It is said that this was a deliberate ploy by Marius to induce his soldiers to fight.

Much of the army was dissatisfied by the location of their military camp. But when they complained that they might suffer from thirst, Marius pointed to a river that flowed close to the fortified barbarian camp. He told them they could get water from that place, but it would cost them in blood. They replied, 'then you must lead us against the enemy, while our blood is still moist.' Marius calmly responded: 'First we must fortify our military camp.'

Rome fights the Tuetones
The Battle of Aquae Sextiae (102 BC)

037 Florus, *Roman History*, 1.38

Marius did not immediately engage the enemy in battle. Instead, he kept his soldiers in their fortified camps until the barbarians had exhausted themselves with irresistible fury and rage. This behaviour takes the place of courage in their forces.

Finally, the overconfident barbarians departed, jeering at our troops by saying that they would soon capture Rome. They mocked them, asking if they could deliver any messages to the soldiers' wives in Italy. Then with threatening speed the barbarians in three large detachments advanced towards the Alps and the northern barriers of Italy.

Marius immediately acted with great swiftness. He led his soldiers by a shorter route to overtake the Teutonic enemy force. With the power of the gods, he engaged them in battle at the very foot of the Alps at a place called Aquae Sextiae. The enemy were in a valley with a river flowing through it, while our troops had no water supply. It is not known whether the general acted according to a plan or whether he converted a mistake into an advantage.

Other Accounts of the Pre-Battle Engagement

038 Orosius, *History*, 5.16

After Marius was made consul for the fourth time, he acted against the enemy (102 BC). He established his fortified military camp near the confluence of the Isara and Rhone rivers. The Cimbri, Teutones, Tigurini and Ambrones fought continuously for three days, trying to force the Romans from their ramparts and make them fight in open battle. When this was not possible, they decided to invade Italy by dividing their forces into three armies.

When the enemy had departed, Marius also moved his army. He occupied a hill overlooking a river and plain where part of the enemy had spread their camp. But his army lacked drinking water and Marius was subject to numerous complaints issued from every quarter. He answered his soldiers that there was water in direct view, but they would need to use their swords to claim it. The servants in the camp cheered loudly and they were the first to rush downhill into combat. The main army immediately followed. Lines of battle quickly formed for regular engagement and so the Romans were victorious in this first encounter.

039 Florus, *Roman History*, 1.38

The Roman bravery was one of necessity and this made them victorious. When his soldiers demanded water, Marius replied, 'your water is in front of you – if you are man enough to take it.' The Romans fought with great determination and inflicted a great slaughter on the enemy. So, when the victors reached the river and drank, there was as much barbarian blood as water in that gory stream.

040 Frontinus, *Stratagems*, 2.7.12 'On Concealing Reverses'

When Marius was fighting against the Cimbrians and Teutones, his surveyors carelessly selected an unsuitable site for the Roman military camp. This gave the barbarians control over the main water supply in the area. When the soldiers demanded water, Marius pointed towards the enemy and said, 'you can get it from there.' This inspired the Romans to immediately drive the barbarians from the strategic place they held.

041 Plutarch, *Marius*, 19

When Marius ordered that the river should be seized, the soldiers reluctantly obeyed. Only a few of the enemy engaged them at first. Warm streams emerge from the ground near this site and the main enemy host were some distance away taking their meals after bathing in these warming pools. The Romans were surprised by the number of barbarians who were engaged in this activity and enjoying the pleasant environment of the plain. But there was a mass of Roman camp attendants who lacked water for themselves and their pack animals. They were the first to rush down to seize the objective. These servants carried hatchets and axes, and some even brought swords and lances along with their water jars. They were determined to get water even if they had to fight for it.

The shouts of the first barbarians who engaged the camp attendants brought more of the enemy running to the encounter. Marius had difficulty restraining his soldiers since they saw that their servants were in danger. The most warlike division of the enemy, the Ambrones, had already leapt up from their meals and were running to grab their weapons. These were the elite warriors who had defeated the Roman armies led by the commanders Mallius and Caepio. They numbered more than 30,000 fighting men.

However, the Ambrones were still lethargic from their heavy meals and disordered by the effects of drinking strong wines. So, they did not attack as expected. They did not rush straight at the Romans in a frantic charge, yelling their inarticulate battle cry. Instead, they stood in a crowd rhythmically clashing their shields and weapons. The warriors performed bouncing jumps where they stood. When the excitement of the rhythm had built up, they would all shout in unison their tribal name – 'AMBRONES!' They did this to encourage one another and to terrify their enemies by their declaration.

The first Italians to engage the Ambrones were the Ligurians (descendants of Celtic settlers who had crossed the Alps generations earlier). They claimed the name 'Ambrones' as their own ancestral title and claimed to be 'Ambrones' by common descent. The Ligurians heard and understood what the enemy were shouting, so they yelled the same name back at them. The same shout therefore echoed and re-echoed across the field of conflict. Both battle hosts tried to outdo the other in the magnitude and rousing ferocity of their shouts. Thus, each side roused the spirits of their combatants before the two forces engaged.

Not all the enemy Ambrones managed to cross the stream in time to form a full battle array. Their foremost fighters crossed, but the Ligurians immediately rushed at them and engaged them in fierce hand-to-hand fighting. The other Roman units came to the aid of the Ligurians, charging downhill to overwhelm the enemy and turn them back. Most of the Ambrones crowded together to make a stand and were killed in the river. The entire river was filled with their corpses and blood.

042 Plutarch, *Marius*, 20–21

Night was approaching, so the Romans withdrew back to their military camp after destroying a vast number of the Ambrones. The army had achieved a great success, but after the battle they did not celebrate with triumphal *paeans* (victory songs). There was no opportunity to safely drink together in their tents, converse over suppers, or gain a peaceful and restorative night's sleep. That night was full of extreme fears and commotions. The Roman encampment had no wall or palisade (bank and ditch perimeter topped with stout wooden barriers) and there was still a vast multitude of barbarians in the vicinity who had suffered no defeat.

The Ambrones who had survived the battle had joined the main host (the Tuetones) and their cries of grief could be heard all night. Their lamentations did not resemble the mournful groans of ordinary men (Romans in grief). The Ambrones howled and bellowed like wild beasts, while uttering threats and cries of sorrow. The sound came from such a vast multitude that it echoed among the surrounding hills and reverberated down the river valley. The whole plain was filled with this terrible sound which provoked great fear among the Romans. Marius also spent the night in dismay, awaiting some chaotic and confused night battle. However, the barbarians did not attack that night, or the following day. Instead, they spent the time in assembling their forces and making further preparations for battle.

The barbarians occupied a position overlooked by sloping glens and tree-covered steep ravines. Marius sent Claudius Marcellus into these woodlands with a force of 3,000 men. These soldiers were instructed to lie concealed in ambush until the main battle had begun. Then they were to charge into the rear of the enemy. The rest of the Roman army ate well and with restored confidence, they received a full night's sleep (the defences had been completed).

At daybreak Marius led his army out and assembled them in front of his military camp (overlooking the proposed battle site). Meanwhile, the Roman cavalry prepared to ride down onto the plain (on the flanks). When the Teutones saw this, they could not wait for the Romans to descend and fight them on level ground. They quickly armed themselves and, full of vengeance, they immediately charged up the hill.

Marius sent officers to all parts of the Roman line to ensure that the soldiers stood firmly in their ranks. As the enemy rushed forwards the Romans launched their javelins. They drew their swords and began to crowd forwards and batter the barbarians back with their shields. The enemy were on treacherous ground (a downward slope) so their blows lacked force and their shield walls could not lock together with sufficient strength. The uneven ground disrupted the enemy battle line as shields were flipped and turned. This action by the Romans fulfilled the orders hurridly issued by Marius (a rapid response by intensely trained troops). In fact, Marius was the first to engage the enemy with these attack methods, since he was better trained than any of his soldiers and more daring.

As instructed, the Romans had awaited the enemy's charge. They closed the distance, withstood their upward rush, and by crowding them back, pushed them down, little by little back onto the plain. Here the foremost barbarians could at last form battle lines on level ground (gaining an advantage). But suddenly there was shouting and commotion at their rear.

Marcellus had been waiting for this opportunity (the Roman ambush force located on the upper slopes). When the noise of battle had reached the hills, he had sent his soldiers running (a flanking action). Now they charged into the rear of the enemy uttering loud shouts and killing the warriors at the back. The rear fighters pushed into the men in front and the whole enemy army was soon in confusion. The Tuetones could not retain their composure while exposed to this double attack. The enemy broke formation and fled. The Romans pursued them and either slew, or took captive, over 100,000 people. They also seized all the possessions of their enemies including their tents and wagons.

The soldiers agreed that all the captured gear that had not yet been claimed was to be presented to Marius (spoils of war). This was a splendid gift, but it was still thought to be inadequate considering the great services the commander had performed on such a dangerous campaign.

Some writers give a different account of how the plunder was divided and offer different figures for the number of enemies who were slain. But it is said that the people of Massalia made boundary walls around their vineyards with the bones of the fallen (clearing the land for farm plots). After the battle, when the rains fell, the decomposing corpses imparted a great store of nutrients into the earth. This rich soil therefore produced an exceedingly great harvest in later years (ideal soil for grapevines).

043 Polyaenus, *Stratagems*, 8.10.2

Before battle with the Teutones and Cimbri, Marius ordered Marcellus to take command of 3,000 heavily armed troops. He was to leave in the night and make a circuit around the mountains. His force marched through remote and difficult terrain to reach the enemy's rear. When this was achieved, Marius ordered his troops to retreat from the high ground into the plain. The enemy felt superior (with greater numbers) and were thus decoyed onto level ground (the base of the valley). Then the manoeuvre was successfully launched. Marius attacked the enemy from the front and Marcellus charged them from the rear (a surprise assault with downhill momentum). He thus obtained a brilliant victory.

044 Frontinus, *Stratagems*, 2.4.6

Marius planned to fight a decisive battle against the Teutones at Aquae Sextiae. The night before the battle, he sent a small detachment of cavalry and infantry to the rear of the enemy (unnoticed by his opponents). To complete the illusion that this was a larger military force, he ordered all the servants and camp followers to accompany them. These men were issued with weapons and they led many of the pack animals (mules) draped in saddlecloths, so they had the appearance of cavalry.

Marius commanded these men that, as soon as battle had begun, they were to assail the enemy from the rear. The enemy were so terrified by this sudden attack (from an unexpected quarter) that despite their great ferocity, they turned and fled.

045 Orosius, *History*, 5.16

On the fourth day, both sides assembled in full formation upon the exposed plane. The combat raged until midday with neither side having the advantage. But under the burning rays of the sun, the swollen bodies of the enemy weakened like melting snow (heat exhaustion). The conflict became more like a massacre than a battle and the fighting continued into the night. It is reported that 200,000 enemy combatants were slain in the battle. By contrast 80,000 enemy were captured and 3,000 fled.

046 Velleius Paterculus, *History of Rome*, 2.12
In the year of his fourth consulship (102 BC), Marius engaged the Teutones beyond the Alps at the Battle of Aquae Sextiae. More than 150,000 of the enemy were slain by the Romans on a single day. The following day his army exterminated this entire population of Teutones.

047 Livy, *Periochae*, 68 (102 BC)
The consul Gaius Marius defended his military camp against a ferocious attack by the Teutones and Ambronians. Afterwards, he defeated these enemies in two battles near Aquae Sextiae. It is claimed that 200,000 enemies were killed in this conflict and 90,000 captured.

Fate of the Tuetonic Women

048 Plutarch, *Marius*, 19
The Romans fought their way across the stream and from this moment onwards, the fleeing enemy did not dare turn round to face them. The Romans slew everyone in their path until they advanced as far as the wagons surrounding the enemy encampment. The women in the encampments stood ready with swords and axes in their hands. They screamed at their fleeing warriors with furious shrieks, calling them deserters. Then they tried to drive back their foes with fearsome cries. Women who became mixed up with the combatants, used their bare hands to tear away the shields of the Romans. Some grabbed the blades of the Roman swords with their unprotected hands, thereby suffering horrific wounds and mutilations. But their fierce spirits remained unvanquished to the end.

This battle had begun at the river and occurred in the manner described. The engagement was an accident of circumstances, rather than a planned intention by the commander.

049 Orosius, *History*, 5.16
The wives of the enemy showed great determination in their defeat. They informed the consul (Marius) that he should meet their requirements for surrender, or they would take their own lives. They insisted that their chastity should remain inviolate, and when taken to Rome they must be assigned duties serving the gods and the Vestal Virgins (the sacred priestesses). When their requests were refused, they bludgeoned their infants to death on the rocks. Then they committed suicide using swords, or by hanging. This was also the fate of the Tigurini and Ambrones (the Celtic allies).

050 Jerome, *Letter*, 123.8

The Teutones came from the remote shores of the Germanic Ocean. They overran Gaul, and slaughtered several Roman armies before Marius finally defeated them at Aquae Sextiae. As a condition of their surrender, 300 of their married women were to be handed over to the Romans. When the Teuton matrons heard of this arrangement they begged the consul (Marius) that they might serve in the Temples of Ceres and Venus (Roman goddesses associated with harvests and fertility). When they failed to obtain their request, they were silenced by the lictors (official agents of the consul). So they slew their little children. Next morning they were all found dead in each other's arms, having strangled each other in the night.

Aftermath of Battle

051 Plutarch, *Marius*, 22

After the battle, Marius ordered all the intact weapons and fine plunder collected from the fallen barbarians to be retained for his triumphal procession in Rome (an impressive victory show and exhibition of enemy war gear). All the remaining spoils were heaped up onto a huge pyre and burned as a magnificent sacrifice (including tents, wagons and fabrics). The soldiers stood around the pyre in armed ranks with wreaths on their heads (victory honours). Marius appeared in his purple-bordered toga and, as custom required, he held the lighted torch up to the heavens. He was about to set fire to the pyre when some dispatch messengers were seen riding swiftly towards him (news from Rome). The assembled soldiers waited in deep silence and expectation. When the horsemen drew near, they leaped onto the ground and saluted Marius. They brought good news, with letters confirming that Marius had been elected consul for the fifth time (his command would continue). The delighted army rejoiced for their general and their great victory. In unison they shouted their acclamation and clattered their weapons together in a loud clashing din. After this, the Roman officers crowned Marius with new wreaths made from bay leaves and he set fire to the pyre, to complete this sacrificial offering.

Fate of the Tuetonic King

052 Florus, *Roman History*, 1.38

Now, Teutobodus, the king of the Tuetones, had previously demonstrated his physical prowess by vaulting over four or six horses at a time. But when his need for strength came, he could scarcely find a single mount able to carry him in his escape. He was captured in a nearby forest and displayed in the triumphal procession held in Rome. Teutobodus had great stature with extraordinary height and bearing and even in defeat he towered over the other trophies of battle. Thus, the Teutones were destroyed, and the Romans could direct their attention to the Cimbri.

Cimbri advance through the Alps

053 Plutarch, *Marius*, 23

Catulus, who was opposing the Cimbri, was concerned that his army would be weakened and rendered inactive if they kept dividing into smaller forces to guard the mountain passes. He therefore gave up trying to guard all the routes through the Alps. Instead, he decided to march his army down into the plains of Italy and place himself beyond the Adige River (a defensive feature). He would then construct strong fortifications on both banks of the river to prevent any enemy crossing. He would also have a bridge constructed across the stream so that reinforcements could be sent into the passes, to assist any forts attacked by the enemy.

Meanwhile, the enemy were approaching the main Roman encampment in the passes held by Catulus (advancing before his plan could be enacted). They were so bold and contemptful of the Romans that they endured snowstorms without protective clothing. This was a display of their daring and strength (supreme resistance to hardship). They endured routes through ice and deep snow up to the mountain summits. Then, placing their shields under them, they slid down the smooth mountainsides between deeply fissured cliffs.

The enemy observed the stream flowing through the mountain pass (the Roman camp was next to the river, a timber bridge connecting the Romans to their main route of retreat). They therefore began to dam the river upstream, causing landslides to block the watercourse. Like primordial giants (using the power of nature against their foe), they dislodged cliff faces and raised mounds of earth to redirect and concentrate the course of the river. Then they placed entire trees, complete with roots, in the accumulating water. (Releasing the barrier) these objects hurtled downstream (with the surging water) to smash into the struts that held the bridge upright. The Roman bridge shook with these heavy impacts. Most of the Roman soldiers were overcome with fear, and abandoning their main camp, they began to retreat.

In this crisis Catulus acted as a skilful commander. He demonstrated that he cared more for the honour of his soldiers than for his own military reputation. He could not persuade the troops to remain in camp, or halt their terrified retreat. So, he ordered his battle standard to be carried forward and he ran to a position ahead of the soldiers leaving the camp. From there he led their retreat, so it seemed that the men were following their general, rather than fleeing an enemy (an ordered retreat that would allow him to pursue his earlier battle plan – to fortify the Adige River).

The barbarians attacked and captured the Roman strongholds located north of the Adige River (securing the mountain passes). The Roman garrisons demonstrated extreme bravery in defence of their country. The enemy so admired these soldiers that they allowed them to depart the forts without further harm (a truce while the Romans evacuated their positions). But first they made the soldiers take an oath on their bronze bull (a tribal idol). This object was subsequently captured by the Romans (when the Cimbri were defeated). It is said that it was taken to the house of Catulus as the main prize of his victory. The countryside (north of the Adige) was now destitute of defenders and the barbarians surged into the region to ravage the territory.

054 Valerius Maximus, *Memorable Deeds and Sayings*, 5.8

Marcus Aemilius Scaurus held the highest office and respect in his country (the Roman consul in 115 BC). But his son was with the Roman army that was defeated by the Cimbri at the river Athesis (Adige). He was among the cavalry that fled in terror, deserting the proconsul Catulus to escape back to the city. Scaurus sent someone to tell his son that he would rather find his carcass slain in the battlefield, than see him alive and guilty of such shameful cowardice. So, if he had any integrity left, he would shun the sight of his enraged father. For Scaurus recalled his own youth and questioned how he could have produced such a son. So he fully condemned him. When his son received this message, he was compelled to make a more lethal use of his sword against himself, than he had against his former enemies (suicide by self-inflicted wounds).

055 Frontinus, *Stratagems*, 4.1.13 'On Discipline'

Marcus Scaurus forbade his son to enter his presence, since he had retreated before the enemy in the Tridentine Pass (102 BC). Overwhelmed by the shame of this disgrace, the young man committed suicide.

056 Frontinus, *Stratagems*, 2.5.8 'On Ambushes'

Fulvius, a commander in the Cimbrian War, pitched his camp near the enemy. Then he ordered his cavalry to approach the barbarian defences. They were to perform a limited attack, and then retreat in the pretense of flight. He repeated these actions over the course of several days, with the Cimbrians fiercely pursuing on each occasion. Fulvius noticed that when this occurred, the enemy camp was regularly left exposed and vulnerable. So, on the next occasion, he secretly took position near the rear of the enemy camp with a force of light-armed troops. Then, when the enemy rushed out as expected, he suddenly attacked. He demolished the unguarded rampart and captured their camp.

057 Frontinus, *Stratagems*, 1.5.3 'On Escaping Difficult Situations'

Quintus Lutatius Catulus had been driven back by the Cimbrians. His only safe route for retreat was across a stream which was securely held by the enemy. He therefore displayed his troops on the nearest mountain, as though intending to camp there. But he commanded his men not to loosen their packs, or set down their loads. They must not leave their ranks and standards (unit formations). Then, to increase the impression that he intended to remain, he ordered a few tents to be erected in full view of the enemy. Campfires were constructed, and while some soldiers began to build a rampart, others went to gather firewood. The Cimbrians thought these performances were genuine, so they began to choose a place for their own camp and scattered across the nearest fields to gather the necessary supplies for their stay. This gave Catulus an opportunity to suddenly cross the stream and attack the enemy camp.

058 Pliny, *Natural History*, 22.4; 6

Crowns (military awards and laurels) acknowledge sovereignty over people, rulership over a territory, or the valour of citizens. Some crowns are made from gold and adorned with gems, such as the Vallar, Mural, Rostrate, Civic, and triumphal crowns (awards for different military accomplishments such as successful sieges, naval victories and territorial conquests). But they are all inferior, for a single commander can confer these crowns on his colleagues, or his soldiers. These crowns can also be awarded by the Senate who are far from the war zone, or the idle populace in Rome who can approve triumphal honours. None of these have greater glory than the 'Crown of Grass'.

The 'Grass Crown' is only conferred in times of crisis and extreme desperation. It is only approved by the acclamation of the entire active army and granted to a single man who has saved or preserved them. Other crowns were awarded by the generals to their soldiers, but this award alone is granted by the soldiers to the person they honour.

The Grass Crown is sometimes known as the 'Obsidional Crown' ('under siege crown'). This is because a beleaguered army will have been delivered from danger and preserved from some fearful disaster. Consider how glorious and hallowed the Civic Crown is (an award given for saving the life of a fellow citizen). This honour is given for saving even the humblest soldier, so a far greater award is therefore granted to the courageous soldier who saves or preserves an entire army. By tradition this greatest of crowns is woven from green grass pulled up from the very site where the oppressed or besieged men were rescued. (…)

Up to the present time, only a single centurion has received the Grass Crown. His name was Cneius Petreius Atinas and he fought in the war against the Cimbri. While serving as *Primus Pilus* (First Centurian) under Catulus, he discovered that every route of retreat for his legion was cut off by the enemy. He berated the reluctant troops, and killed his dithering tribune. He led his legion through the enemy encampment, fighting a path to safety. Some authors also state that in addition to the Grass Crown, Petreius appeared clad in a purple toga. While the sacred flute played, he conducted offerings at the sacrificial altar in the presence of the consuls Marius and Catulus (supreme military honours).

059 Livy, *Periochae*, 68 (101 BC)

Although he was absent from Rome, Marius was elected consul for the fifth time. He postponed the triumph offered to him (for defeating the Tuetones) until he had also defeated the Cimbrians.

The proconsul Quintus Catulus wanted to block the passes leading through the Alps. But the Cimbrians drove the Romans back and forced Catulus to flee. A cohort had been left to guard a mountain stronghold near the river Athesis (Adige). They resorted to their own valour and managed to break through the enemy force to follow the fleeing proconsul and his army.

060 Orosius, *History*, 5.16

Meanwhile, the Cimbri crossed through the snows covering the Alps and with their forces intact they swept across the plains of Italy. But these hardy peoples quickly became softened by the milder climate of this region. They enjoyed its abundance of fine wines, luxury foods and hot baths.

Battle of the Raudian Plain (101 BC)

061 Plutarch, *Marius*, 24

Marius was summoned to Rome where he was expected to celebrate his triumph which the Senate had already approved (his victory over the Teutones). But he declined the offer (...) and sending messages of encouragement to Catulus, he set out to join him. Meanwhile, he summoned his own soldiers from Gaul (his recently victorious army, recalled to Italy).

When his army arrived, Marius led them across the Po River planning to keep the barbarians from crossing into the greater part of Italy. But the barbarians refused to engage the Roman army in battle. They claimed to be waiting for their brethren, the Teutones, and wondered why they had been delayed (in the invasion). Perhaps they were truly ignorant of their destruction, or maybe this was a ploy against the Romans. Anyone who brought news of the defeat was subject to severe mistreatment (suggesting angry disbelief).

The Cimbri sent envoys to Marius demanding territory for themselves and their brethren, with enough settlements for them all to dwell in (Italian possessions). When Marius asked, 'who are your brethren?', the envoys replied, 'the Teutones'. At this, the Romans in attendance roared with laughter, and Marius said in contempt: 'Don't worry about your brethren, we have given them land to settle in, and they will be keeping it forever' (a mass grave).

The envoys understood the meaning of this scorn and launched a sudden tirade of abuse against the Romans. They told Marius that he would be punished for his comments, first by the Cimbri, and then by the Teutones when they reached this place. Marius replied, 'In truth, you can greet your brethren before you leave here.' Then he ordered that the captured kings of the Teutones were to be brought forward in chains. For the Sequani (Gallic allies of the Romans) had captured these men when they had been fleeing in defeat through the Alps.

062 Florus, *Roman History*, 1.38

It seems incredible, but the Cimbri had already crossed the Alps during the winter when the mountain heights are more inaccessible. They therefore descended from the Tridentine ranges into Italy like an avalanche. Their first obstacle was the Athesis River (Adige) which they did not attempt to cross using a bridge or boats. Instead, with the stupidity of barbarians, they tried to swim the river against the strong current. Finally, they reduced the river current by casting trees into the stream and using their shields to block the water flow. This allowed their force (including wagons) to ford the river.

The danger to Rome would have been very great if the hostile Cimbri had immediately marched upon the city of Rome. But they delayed in Venetia, a district in which the Italian climate is very gentle and pleasant. This mild country depleted their vigour and dulled their urgency. They were gradually demoralised by soft breads, cooked meats, and delightful wines.

When Marius approached the enemy with his army, the barbarians displayed no trace of fear. They came forth of their own accord and asked our general to set a date for the battle. He nominated the following day and the two armies met on a very wide and level expanse known as the Raudian Plain. The battle commenced and continued all day.

During the battle, Marius added craft to his courage and followed the strategy that Hannibal had used at Cannae. Firstly, he had chosen a misty day to charge into the enemy while they were still unaware. It was also windy, and the dust of the plain was blown into the eyes and faces of the enemy. Finally, he was able to draw up his main battle line facing west so that, according to the prisoners, the morning sky seemed to be on fire behind them with the glint reflected from the bronze Roman helmets. Almost 65,000 of the enemy were killed while our army suffered less than 300 deaths. (…)

Their king, Boiorix, died fighting with great fury in the forefront of the battle, after he had inflicted many vengeful injuries upon his foes.

Battle against the Cimbri

063 Plutarch, *Marius*, 25–27

When the Cimbri were informed of these events they advanced against Marius. But the Romans remained subdued in their carefully guarded military camps. It is said that Marius had introduced an innovation in javelin design for this campaign. Previously, the iron head of the Roman javelin was fastened to the wooden shaft by two iron nails. One of these nails was now replaced by a wooden pin that would break on impact. After striking an enemy shield, the long iron head would therefore bend and trail along the ground while still connected to the shaft (impeding removal and preventing any further use of the shield).

Boiorix, the king of the Cimbri, rode up towards the Roman camp with a small retinue. He challenged the Romans to come forth and for Marius to set a day and a place for the battle that would decide ownership of this country (northern Italy). Marius replied that the Romans never allowed their enemies to give them advice about fighting, but he would gratify the Cimbri in this matter. They agreed that the battle would take place three days later on the plain of Vercellae (Raudian Plain). This battlefield would give the Roman cavalry space to manoeuvre and allow the Cimbri an area large enough to accommodate their vast numbers.

When the appointed time had come, the two Roman armies formed up for battle. The army led by Catulus included 20,300 soldiers, while Marius deployed 32,000 troops from his forces. Catulus took the centre of the Roman battle line, while the forces of Marius formed the two wings. Sulla fought in this battle, and he claims that Marius hoped that the two battle lines would engage at their outer extremes. The fiercest fighting would therefore occur on the wings and his own soldiers would have the greater credit for claiming victory. Marius expected that the centre of the Roman army, formed by the soldiers of Catulus, would be enveloped by the flank engagements, as often occurs when battle lines are extended across a very wide area. It is said that Catulus also expected this outcome and accused Marius of malice in assigning him the centre position in the Roman formation (depriving him of battle glory).

The Cimbri infantry advanced slowly from their defences. The depth of their ranks was almost equal to the length of their battle line, which extended over more than 3 miles. Meanwhile, a force of Cimbri horsemen, including 15,000 cavalry, rode forth in a splendid display. Their helmets were crafted to resemble the jaws of terrifying wild beasts or the outline of strange animals. Towering crests of feathers (large plumes) made the fighters appear taller than they already were. These warriors were equipped with iron breastplates and carried gleaming white shields. Each man was equipped with two lances and a large heavy sword for close-quarter combat.

The Cimbri horsemen did not charge directly towards the Romans. They swerved to the right and tried to draw the left part of the Roman battle line out of position, to where they would be caught between themselves and advancing infantry. The Roman commanders perceived the strategy, but they could not restrain their units on the left flank. One of the soldiers yelled that the enemy was fleeing, and they all rushed forwards in pursuit. Meanwhile, the barbarian infantry surged forwards to attack, like a vast sea set in motion.

It is said that Marius had conducted a (pre-battle) offering to the gods and when he inspected the innards of the animal (divination), he cried out in a loud voice, 'The victory is mine!' He had washed his hands (concluding the ceremony), but (when he saw his battle plan failing) he appealed directly to the gods, lifting his hands upwards and vowing a hecatomb (elaborate mass sacrifices). Catulus performed the same customs, offering entire fortunes for divine assistance.

Sulla records that other events on the battlefield signalled divine displeasure for Marius. The two armies raised an immense cloud of dust as they advanced which obscured their vision. So, when Marius (still on the outer wing) led his forces forwards to attack, he bypassed the enemy host (which had swerved right to converge on the Roman centre). His forces moved aimlessly up and down the plain for some time (with the actual battle obscured). Meanwhile, the barbarians fought fiercely against Catulus. Sulla was posted in this quarter (the Roman centre) which bore the brunt of the combat.

The Romans had the advantage in this contest. Sulla says that the sun was shining in the faces of the Cimbri, exposing them to greater glare and heat. They sweated profusely, breathed with difficulty, and were forced to hold their shields before their faces (to provide shade and avoid sunstroke and heat exhaustion). By Roman reckoning, the battle was fought just after the summer solstice, three days before the new moon in August in the month previously known as 'Sextilis'. The dust also assisted the Romans and gave them encouragement, since they could not see the vast numbers of the enemy. Instead, each man avoided this terrifying sight and concentrated only on the enemy he engaged in immediate hand-to-hand combat.

According to Catulus, his soldiers were so supremely fit and well trained that they barely sweated or panted with effort as they fought in the great heat. They had even run into combat and scarcely felt the effects of this added effort. Anyhow, this is what Catulus wrote in praise of his soldiers.

> Most of the Cimbri army was soon cut to pieces by the Romans, including their best fighters. Their leading warriors had bound themselves together with long chains passed through their belts. This ensured that their ranks would never break. But the other fighters were forced back from the battlefield towards their own entrenchments (the outer defences of their camp). And there the Romans witnessed a tragic sight. The Cimbri women were dressed in black garments, and they stood at the wagons killing any of their menfolk who fled the battlefield. They slew their husbands, brothers, or fathers (flinging themselves at exhausted and panic-stricken men fleeing the enemy). Then they strangled their little children and placed babies to be crushed beneath the wheels of wagons, or the hooves of cattle. Finally, they cut their own throats.

> It is said that one woman was found dangling from the tip of an upturned wagon pole (noose around her neck). She had hung herself with the dead bodies of her two small children tied to each ankle (also hung). The men would have hung themselves from branches, but there were no suitable trees at the site. So, they fastened their nooses to the necks, horns, or hind legs of cattle. Then they goaded the beasts forwards and were dragged or trampled to death as the cattle dashed away. Despite this self-destruction, more than 60,000 Cimbri were taken prisoner. It is thought that more than double this number died in the fighting (120,000).

The soldiers of Marius claimed the enemy property as their booty (Cimbri camp belongings). But Catulus had the spoils of battle (salvaged weapons, armour and ornaments) taken to his own camp, along with the Cimbri battle standards and war trumpets (trophies). Catulus used these items to claim that the greater share of the victory had been won by his soldiers (who had looted the actual battleground).

A dispute arose among the soldiers concerning who could claim the greater honour for the victory. An embassy from Parma was present (a north Italian city) so their envoys were chosen to act as independent arbitrators. The soldiers of Catulus showed the envoys the dead bodies of the enemy who had been pierced by their javelins. This was confirmed by the shaft of these weapons which had been incised with the name 'Catulus' (marked before battle). But despite this evidence the entire victory was attributed to Marius, due to his former military glories and superior rank.

The Roman population now hailed Marius as the third founder of Rome (a saviour of the state). They said that he had saved them from a danger that was as great as the Gallic invasion (the Gauls who sacked Rome in 390 BC). They all celebrated with their wives and children, presenting ceremonial offerings and libations of wine to Marius and the gods. The Roman people demanded that Marius alone should celebrate both triumphs (victory over the Tuetones and Cimbri). But Marius insisted that Catulus jointly participate in his second triumphal victory.

Another Account of the Battle

064 Orosius, *History*, 5.16

Marius was made consul for the fifth time (in 102 BC). He was sent with Catulus against this enemy. He followed Hannibal's clever scheme of selecting both the day for battle and also the field of combat. The consuls arranged their battle line under the cover of a morning mist, but later they had to fight the main engagement under the scorching sun. When the enemy realised that the Roman battle lines were assembled and ready for action they demonstrated their first sign of disorder and uncertainty, before they had even reached the field of combat. The enemy formed up and advanced, but their wounded cavalrymen were driven back towards their own men. This threw the entire advancing force into such confusion that they met the Romans in an uncertain and irregular formation. By this stage, the bright sun was shining directly into their faces and a wind was rising against them. The wind cast dust into their eyes and the glaring sun restricted their vision. They suffered immense casualties under these conditions. Consequently only a few survived this disaster, while Roman losses were minimal. According to reports, 140,000 enemy were slain in that battle, while 60,000 were captured. (...)

The enemy suffered many wretched forms of death. It was reported that two chieftains attacked each other with drawn swords, each inflicting killing blows on his comrade. The kings Lugius and Boiorix were both killed on the battlefield, while the royal commanders Claodicus and Caesorix were captured.

065 Polyaenus, *Stratagems*, 8.10.3

Marius knew the Cimbri came from a cold country and could endure frost and snow much better than heat and sun. Therefore, in his war against them, he selected August as the best time for battle and approached with the sun behind him. So, when the barbarians turned about to engage the Romans, they also faced the beaming hot sun. They tried to shade their faces with their shields and protect themselves against the heat and glare. But this left their bodies exposed to Roman attack. The Romans slew 120,000 of them, and 60,000 were taken prisoner.

Fate of the Cimbri Womenfolk

066 Florus, *Roman History*, 1.38

After the battle there was a severe struggle with the barbarian womenfolk. They had used their wagons and carts to form a barricade and clambering on top of this defence, they prepared to fight with axes and pikes. But first they sent a delegation to Marius requesting that, if their lives were spared, they would willingly become servants of the priestesses (slaves of the

Vestal Virgins in Rome). Since this request could not lawfully be granted Marius refused (he held a military command and not a religious office). In response the women strangled all the infants in their camp or bludgeoned them to death. They fought as fiercely as their men and their death was as honourable as their resistance. They died fighting the enemy, or from wounds inflicted on one another. Some made ropes of their own hair and hanged themselves on trees, or the upward-tilting yokes of their wagons.

067 Orosius, *History*, 5.16

The women fought a conflict that was perhaps more severe than the main battle. The enemy wagons had been drawn up in the form of a fortified camp, so the women defended themselves from an elevated position. They managed to keep the Romans from entering this compound for a long time. But they finally became terrified by the method that the soldiers employed to kill the defenders. When they dragged women down from the barricades, the Romans scalped them in full view. The soldiers then left the exposed and mutilated corpses on sight for the defenders to witness their shameful and horrific wounds. After this, the women began to commit suicide using the very weapons they had employed against the soldiers. They slaughtered their own children and helped to kill each other. Some women cut each other's throats. Some tied cords to the legs of horses and put the end of the nooses round their own necks. When the horses were driven forwards, the women were dragged along and choked to death. Others hanged themselves with nooses suspended from wagon poles raised high in the air. One woman had slipped nooses over the necks of her two sons, and then bound the ropes to her own ankles. She died by hanging with her two sons suspended from her lower limbs.

068 Pliny, *Natural History*, 8.61

When the Cimbri men were killed, their dogs still defended the wagons on which they had their homes.

069 Appian, *Gallic Wars*, 3, fragment 19 (from the *Suda*)

Marius ordered his soldiers to leave the bodies of the Cimbri intact until daylight because he believed they were adorned with gold (items might be missed if the search was conducted in poor visibility).

Fate of the Tigurini

070 Florus, *Roman History*, 1.38
The third group of northern invaders, consisting of the Tigurini, acted as a reserve force and occupied the Norican ranges of the Alps (Austrian Alps). But they resorted to ignoble flight and ran away to disperse in numerous different directions. These refugees suffered many depredations until they finally vanished from attention.

The joyful news that Italy had been delivered and the Empire saved did not reach the Roman populace through any human agency. If accounts are believed, a favourable report came directly from the gods themselves. On the same day as the Alpine battle against the enemy was fought, two young men emerged from the temple of Pollux and Castor in Rome. Standing in front of the sacred building, they presented to the praetor a despatch letter adorned with victory laurels. The rumour that Rome was victor over the Cimbri spread far and wide throughout the city, reaching the crowded venues. (…) At the very moment that the Cimbri were being slaughtered on a distant battlefield, the Roman populace therefore raised a triumphal applause like an excited crowd witnessing a successful gladiatorial show.

Further Omens

071 Julius Obsequens, *Prodigies*, 44
The Temple of Jupiter was struck by lightning when it was closed (empty of adherents). (…)

The Teutones were slaughtered by Marius.

The Sacred Shields moved of their own accord with a rattle (earth tremors). (…) The Cimbri were destroyed.

Conclusion of the War

072 Appian, *Gallic Wars*, 3, fragment 18
Shortly before the consulships of Marius, a numerous and warlike horde of 'Celtic' peoples (Germanic, North Europeans) made incursions into both Gaul and Italy. These people possessed formidable physical strength and managed to defeat several Roman consuls by butchering their armies. But Marius was sent against them, and he destroyed them all.

073 Velleius Paterculus, *History of Rome*, 2.12

During his fifth consulship (101 BC), Marius and the proconsul Quintus Lutatius Catulus engaged the Cimbri. They fought a successful battle on this side of the Alps at a site called the Raudian Plain. More than 100,000 of the enemy were taken captive or slain.

By this victory Marius could claim that his life had not been to the detriment of his country. Any harmful actions he had caused to the state were counterbalanced by this well-performed service.

074 Orosius, *History*, 5.16

These two battles concluded the war. An estimated 340,000 enemy were slain and 140,000 were captured. This does not include the countless number of women who exhibited a manly resolve. They killed themselves and all their infant children in a fit of fearful frenzy.

075 Livy, *Periochae*, 68 (101 BC)

The Cimbri invaded Italy but were defeated in battle by the united forces of Catulus and Gaius Marius. It is said that 160,000 enemies were killed and 60,000 captured.

Marius thus received the acclaim of the entire Roman state. He was offered two triumphs (for defeating both the Tuetones and Cimbri), but he was content with just one victory celebration. The leading men of the state (people with prestigious ancestors) had envied this 'New Man' for the numerous important offices he had obtained ('New Man' – first person in his family to serve in the Senate). Now they acknowledged that he had saved the Roman state. (…)

It is said that the Sacred Shields moved and rattled before the Cimbrian War had ended (twelve sacred shields displayed in the temple of the martial god Mars).

Recognising the Germanic Threat

King Mithridates VI of Pontus sought out enemies of Rome before beginning his own hostilities against the Republic.

076 Justin, *Histories*, 38.3

Mithridates formed an alliance with King Tigranes (of Armenia) in preparation for a war against Rome. (…) He also sent ambassadors to the Cimbri, the Gallo-Graeci (Galatians), the Sarmatians, and the Bastarnians (tribes north of the Danube), to request their aid. He tried to gain the goodwill of these nations with gifts and assurances while he plotted war.

North European Captives and Slaves

Gauls and Germans were involved in the Spartacus Slave Revolt, which occurred in Roman Italy (73 BC).

077 Orosius, *History*, 5.24

During the consulships of Lucullus and Cassius, seventy-four gladiators escaped from the training school of Gnaeus Lentulus at Capua. Under the leadership of Crixus and Oenomaus who were Gauls, and Spartacus who was a Thracian, the fugitives occupied Mount Vesuvius. The praetor, Clodius Glaber, was sent to supress them, but they captured his military camp and he was forced to flee. Afterwards the fugitives increased their plundering activities. They marched through Consentia and Metapontum gathering a vast number of fugitive followers in only a short period (runaway slaves). Soon, according to one report, Crixus had an army of 10,000 and Spartacus had three times that number (30,000). (...)

The consuls Gellius and Lentulus each led an army against these fugitives (72 BC). Crixus fought with great bravery against Gellus, but he was defeated by the Romans. However, the Roman army led by Lentulus was defeated by Spartacus and forced to flee. (...)

The Senate placed Crassus in command of the legions, the consuls, and the new reinforcements (71 BC). He quickly engaged the fugitives in battle, killing 6,000 of them and taking only 900 captives. Then he advanced against Spartacus who was encamped near the head of the Silarus River. Crassus defeated the Gallic and Germanic forces who were supporting Spartacus and slaughtered 30,000 of them along with their leaders. Then he formed up in full battle array to meet the main fugitive army led by Spartacus himself. According to reports Crassus killed 60,000 of the enemy and captured 6,000 prisoners. About 3,000 captive Roman citizens were also recovered and released. The remaining gladiators, who had escaped the battle, wandered around the countryside until they were finally killed off by the Roman troops who relentlessly pursued them.

Another Account of the Slave Revolt confirming German Participation

078 Plutarch, *Crassus*, 9
Spartacus was soon in command of a vast and formidable force. But he took a correct view of the situation and realised that he could not hope to overcome Roman power. He therefore began to lead his army towards the Alps. He thought that if they could cross the mountains, his followers could reach their former homelands, some in Thrace and others in Gaul.

But his followers were now strong in numbers and full of confidence. They would not listen to his appeals and divided themselves into separate forces to ravage Italy. The Senate had previously regarded the revolt as an indignity and disgrace, but now they acted through fear and peril. They prepared for a war of utmost difficulty and magnitude and gave both consuls immediate military commands.

The Germans, who were bold and defiant, separated from the main fugitive force led by Spartacus. The consul Gellius advanced quickly against them and slaughtered the entire company.

Outcome of the 'Slave War' (71 BC)

079 Frontinus, *Stratagems*, 2.5.34 'On Ambushes'
During the 'Slave War', Crassus fortified two military camps close to the enemy encampment near Mount Cantenna. (…) Dividing the Roman cavalry into two detachments, he ordered Lucius Quintius to oppose Spartacus with one force as a diversion. The other Roman force would lure the Germans and Gauls, led by Castus and Cannicus, into combat. Quintius was to feign flight and draw the enemy towards the place where Crassus himself had formed up his troops in full battle array.

When the barbarians followed Quintius as expected, the Roman cavalry withdrew to the flanks of the waiting battle formation. Then the full Roman force was suddenly revealed and rushed forwards with a shout. Livy records that 35,000 armed men along with their leaders were slain in this battle. The victorious Romans recovered five legionary eagles and twenty-six company standards (military trophies lost in earlier defeats).

Descendants in Northern Gaul

A Belgic tribe called the Nervii were said to be descendants of the Cimbri and Teutones. Julius Caesar conquered them in 57 BC.

080 Appian, *Gallic War*, 4.23

Although the Nervii had a force of 60,000 fighters, they were destroyed. These Nervii were descendants of the Cimbri and Teutones (Germanic peoples).

Chapter Two

Julius Caesar and the Conflict with King Ariovistus (58 BC)

The Roman general Julius Caesar began the conquest of Greater Gaul in 58 BC. During these campaigns he came into conflict with a German king named Ariovistus who had crossed the Rhine to settle with his people in eastern Gaul. Initially, Caesar commanded four legions including perhaps 20,000 Roman soldiers with allied support.

081 Florus, *Roman History*, 1.45
Fortuna gave Julius Caesar the opportunity to conquer Europe. The north still contained the most formidable nations, including the Gauls, the Germans, and the Britons. Caesar therefore decided to subdue these people, even though they occupied the edges of the world.

Caesar halts Gallic Migrations but fears German Hostility (58 BC)

082 Plutarch, *Julius Caesar*, 18
Caesar fought the first of his Gallic Wars against the Helvetii and Tigurini. (…) He spared more than 100,000 of the barbarians (migrants) who had survived the battle. But he forced them to resettle their former territory and rebuild the settlements that they had demolished in these abandoned lands (the Swiss Plateau). He did this because he feared that if the territory became vacant, the Germans would cross the Rhine and occupy it.

Conflict between Gallic Tribes

Strabo explains the rivalry between the Celtic Aedui and Sequani tribes. By 60 BC, the Sequani were receiving large-scale military assistance from Germanic peoples.

083 Strabo, *Geography*, 4.3.2
The Aedui tribe inhabit the territories between the Dubis and the Arar rivers (Burgundy). Their city Cabyllinum is on the Arar and there is a

garrison in their territory at Bibracte. The Aedui are considered kinsmen of the Romans. They were one of the first tribes in Gallia to apply for the friendship of the Roman people and enter an alliance.

For a long time the Sequani occupying the adjoining territory were hostile to the Romans and the Aedui. As a result, they often joined forces with the Germans in their attacks upon Italy and increased their military strength in these conflicts. They made the Germans more powerful when they assisted their invasions and greatly weakened them when they refused support. The Aedui disagreed with the Sequani over the Germans and quarrelled with them over the river boundary that separated their territories. Both tribes claimed that the Arar was their sole property and the transportation tolls collected on the river (Rhone) belonged to them alone. However, in the current era, all these territories and tolls are subject to the Romans.

German Presence West of the Rhine

084 Appian, *Gallic War*, 4.21 (preserved in Constantine Porphyrogenitus, *The Embassies*)

Ariovistus, a king of the Germans beyond the Rhine, crossed into Gaul before the arrival of Caesar. But he made war against the Aedui (Celts) who were allied to the Romans (59 BC). When the Romans commanded Ariovistus to cease this conflict, he obeyed and moved his forces away from the Aedui (territories) because he wanted to ally himself with the Roman people. This request was approved and granted by Caesar when he was consul. When Ariovistus had been established as an ally he met with Caesar, but he wished to have another conference. Caesar refused his request and instead sent some of the leading men of Gaul to meet with him. Ariovistus put these representatives in chains and Caesar responded by threatening war. However, due to the military reputation of the Germans, the Roman army was afraid of conflict against this enemy.

085 Plutarch, *Julius Caesar*, 19

(When Caesar was consul in 59 BC) he made the German King Ariovistus a formal ally of Rome. Nevertheless, his second war was to defend Gaul against the Germans. This is because the German presence next to Caesar's Gallic subjects was thought to be intolerable. It was believed that when an opportunity arose, the Germans would not remain quietly in their current territories, but would overrun and occupy further lands in Gaul.

Caesar Plans Action against the Germans after Defeating the Celtic Helvetii

086 Julius Caesar, *Gallic War*, 1.31–35

When the meeting had ended, the same leaders of the Gallic states returned to speak to Caesar. They asked permission to discuss secret matters concerning their own welfare and the common good of the Gallic people. When he agreed, they all wept and threw themselves at Caesar's feet.

They explained that they were anxious to obtain their request, but they did not want the discussions made public. For, if this occurred, they might be subject to terrible punishment (retaliation by more powerful tribes). Their spokesman was the Aeduan (leader) Diviciacus. He explained that there were two main factions within Gaul. One led by the Aedui and the other commanded by the Arverni. For many years the two had been fighting fiercely for supremacy. But then the Arverni and Sequani had hired some German mercenaries. Initially about 15,000 of these warriors had crossed the Rhine. But they were a wild and savage population who had developed a desire to claim further land in Gaul. They wanted the lifestyle and prosperity of Gaul, so more of them had crossed the river (the Rhine). Consequently, there were now about 120,000 Germans in Gaul.

Diviciacus explained that the Aedui and their followers had frequently fought against the Germans, but they had been defeated. They had suffered severe disasters in this conflict and had lost all their aristocracy (warrior noblemen) including their senate (ruling council), and their entire cavalry. Their tribe had once been pre-eminent in Gaul, due to their own excellence and the recognition that the Romans were their allies. But now they had been devastated by catastrophic battles. They had been forced to surrender their most aristocratic citizens as political hostages to the Sequani (Celtic allies of the Germans). They were also made to swear an oath that they would never request hostages (from the Sequani), beg assistance from the Romans, or do anything to resist their perpetual subjection to the power and dominion of the Sequani (and their German allies). Diviciacus revealed that he was the only nobleman in the Aeduan state who had not been compelled to swear this oath, or surrender his own children as political hostages. But due to his refusal he had been forced to flee his homeland. He now sought permission to approach the Roman Senate to plead for help.

Diviciacus explained that a worse fate had now befallen the victorious Sequani than the defeated Aedui had suffered. For a king of the Germans named Ariovistus had settled in their territory and seized one-third of their land. This land was known to be the most prosperous region in Gaul and when 24,000 men from the Harudes tribe (other Germans) had joined Ariovistus, he ordered the Sequani to vacate another third of their territory. These events had occurred only a few months earlier and Ariovistus was already preparing the newly acquired territory for the settlement of the Harudes. If this continued, then far more Germans would soon cross the Rhine and the existing inhabitants would be driven out of the country. This was occurring because these Gallic lands were superior to the Germanic territories and offered a much better way of life.

Meanwhile, Ariovistus engaged the Gallic forces and defeated them in battle at a place called Admagetobriga. Afterwards he began to issue arrogant and cruel commands. He demanded delivery of all the children of the highest-ranking citizens as political hostages, then inflicted many forms of torture on them. This was a warning that nothing should be done contrary to his will and pleasure. Ariovistus was savage, reckless, and impulsive and the Gauls could no longer endure his dictates. Unless Caesar and the Roman people gave their support, the whole of Gaul would be forced to do the same as the Helvetii and leave their homelands in search of new places to settle. They would move far away from the Germans and risk whatever other dangers might befall them.

Diviciacus said that if Ariovistus learnt about this warning, then he was certain that the Gallic hostages would be severely punished (tortured or executed). But he believed that Caesar could discourage Ariovistus from bringing even greater numbers of Germans across the Rhine. This could be achieved through Caesar's political influence, his army, his reputation from the recent victory (against the Helvetii), or even the powerful reputation of the Roman people. Caesar could therefore defend all of Gaul from the outrages planned by Ariovistus.

At the end of this speech by Diviciacus, all (the Gallic representatives) who were present began weeping and pleading for Caesar to help them. But Caesar noticed that the Sequani were not acting in the same manner as the other Gauls. They stood still and serious with their heads bowed, staring at the ground. Wondering why this was so, Caesar asked them, but the Sequani did not reply and maintained the same severe silence. He repeatedly questioned them, but could gain no other response. Finally, Diviciacus the Aeduan answered him and explained that the Sequani had suffered far greater punishments than the other Gallic tribes. Therefore, they did not dare to complain or beg for help, even in secret. They were terrified of the cruelty that Ariovistus could inflict and feared him even in his absence. All the other Gallic tribes had at least some chance of escape, but the Sequani had received Ariovistus within their own homelands. All their towns were under his power, and they would have to endure all the punishments he inflicted.

When Caesar received this information, he spoke words of encouragement to the Gauls and promised them that he would take care of this matter. He assured them that he would use his own powers and influence to force Ariovistus to cease his outrageous actions. Then he dismissed the meeting.

There were many reasons for Caesar to consider it his duty to act on this matter and intervene. The Aedui had more than once been named 'Brothers' and 'Kinsmen' by the Roman Senate. But they were now enslaved under the dominion of the Germans with political hostages detained by Ariovistus and the Sequani. Considering the great power of the Roman people, this was an insult to himself and to the Roman state. Caesar was also aware that if the Germans became accustomed to continually crossing the Rhine and entering Gaul in large numbers, then they would become a serious threat to the Romans. He reckoned that once these fierce barbarians had seized greater Gaul, they would not hesitate to overrun the province (Roman-controlled territory on the Mediterranean coast) just as the Cimbri and Teutoni had done. Then the Germans could cross into Italy, since only the Rhone separated the Sequani from the province (Gallia Narbonensis). Caesar believed that these dangers had to be countered as quickly as possible. Ariovistus had clearly assumed an attitude of supreme arrogance and pride that could not be tolerated.

For these reasons Caesar decided to send envoys to Ariovistus. He asked him to select some location midway between the two powers for a meeting. Caesar announced that he wanted to discuss state affairs and political interests of urgent importance to both leaders. Ariovistus replied to the embassy by saying that if he needed anything from Caesar, he would ask him. But if Caesar wanted something from him, then he should come to him instead. He informed Caesar that he did not dare enter those parts of Gaul under Caesar's control without his army. But he was unable to muster all his warriors in a single place, due to the great effort required to gather sufficient supplies. He ended by saying that he found it remarkable that Caesar, or the Roman people, were concerned by events in Gaul. For the lands he held in Gaul he had made his own by right of conquest in war.

When these words by Ariovistus were reported, Caesar responded by sending envoys back to him with the following message:

> Ariovistus has been treated with great kindness by Caesar and the Roman people. During Caesar's consulship, he was pronounced 'King' and 'Friend' by the Roman Senate. But since then, he has shown his ingratitude to

Caesar and the Roman people by being reluctant to attend a meeting when invited. He has refused to discuss or listen to matters of concern to both powers. Caesar is therefore making the following demands of him. First, he should no longer bring large numbers of men over the Rhine into Gaul. Secondly, he must return the political hostages he has taken from the Aedui and give the Sequani full permission to return all the Aedui hostages they were holding. Furthermore, Ariovistus is to do no harm to the Aedui, or attack them or their allies. If Ariovistus complies with these instructions he will have the lasting favour and friendship of Caesar and the Roman people. The Senate decided, in the consulship of Marcus Messalla and Marcus Piso, that whoever holds command in the Province of Gaul (Gallia Narbonensis) is empowered to act in the state's interest. This includes the defence of the Aedui and the other allies of the Roman people. If Caesar does not receive what he requests, then he will take action over the wrongs inflicted upon the Aedui.

Caesar Confronts Ariovistus

087 Cassius Dio, *Roman History*, 38.34

Caesar did not remain passive for long after this campaign (against the Helvetii). Instead, he acted to fulfil his own ambitions and to advance the objectives sought by the allies of Rome. The Sequani and Aedui (leading Celtic tribes) had noticed that Caesar's ambitions were fulfilled by successful actions. They therefore hoped that he might act to benefit them and take vengeance on the Germans who occupied neighbouring lands. At some time in the remote past these Germans had crossed the Rhine and seized the outlying parts of Gaul. They extracted tribute from surrounding regions and took political hostages from neighbouring Celtic tribes. These Celtic tribes now requested assistance from Caesar and since this is what the general wanted (further campaigns), they easily gained his support.

Ariovistus was the ruler of these Germans (settled west of the Rhine) and his authority had been fully confirmed by the Roman state. During his consulship, Julius Caesar had even formally acknowledged Ariovistus among the political 'friends' and allies of Rome. But this status had to be compared with the glory and power that could be derived from war. The general therefore dismissed previous considerations and used existing arrangements to provoke a quarrel with the barbarian (chief). Caesar did not want to be seen as the aggressor, so he required an excuse for the conflict.

Caesar summoned Ariovistus, pretending that he wished to have a conference with him. But instead of obeying, Ariovistus replied:

> If Caesar wants to say something to me, let him come to me in person. I am not inferior to him in any way. The man who needs the help of another, should go himself to that person.

Caesar displayed anger at this response and declared that Ariovistus had insulted all the Roman people (by arrogantly refusing a political summons). Caesar demanded that Ariovistus immediately surrender all his political hostages to him (the Celtic nobles detained by the Germans would be transferred to Roman authority). Furthermore, he instructed the Germans not to enter any territories claimed by Roman allies (the surrounding Gallic districts) and Caesar forbade them from receiving any reinforcements from their homelands (territories east of the Rhine).

Caesar did not expect to frighten Ariovistus (into compliance) with these demands. Instead, he hoped to enrage and provoke the German leader into actions that could be a plausible pretext for war. This occurred and the outraged Ariovistus sent a long and harsh reply to Caesar. As a result, Caesar no longer engaged in written responses. He immediately marched to occupy Vesontio, a major settlement of the Sequani. This occurred before his opponents were even aware of the general's intentions (the war had already begun).

088 Florus, *Roman History*, 1.45

Caesar cited the complaints of the Aedui (a Celtic tribe allied to Rome) as his just pretext for his first battle against the Germans. The Aedui had suffered armed incursions from Germany, so Caesar sent ambassadors to King Ariovistus (the German chieftain) requesting that he come and meet with him. But the German demonstrated great arrogance and replied:

> Who is this Caesar? Let him come to me if he likes. Why does it matter to him what we Germans do? Do I interfere with Roman affairs?'

The Romans Fear the Germans

089 Julius Caesar, *Gallic War*, 1.38–40

Caesar remained in Vesontio for a few days to gather grain and other supplies. But a terrible panic suddenly seized the whole army and the courage and morale of everyone was affected. The soldiers started asking questions (about their opponents) and the Gauls and traders replied by describing the tallness and physical strength of the Germans. They said that the Germans were exceptionally brave and skilful with weapons. They claimed that those who had encountered the Germans in battle could not withstand their formidable appearance, or even the fierceness of their gaze.

The panic began among the military tribunes and the prefects. But it spread amongst other office holders who had no great military experience and had only followed Caesar from Rome to gain his political friendship. Some of them started giving various excuses for urgent departure and asked his permission to go. But others remained out of shame, since they wanted to avoid an accusation of cowardice. These men could not conceal their fearful expressions and at times they broke down into tears. They hid themselves away in their tents and bemoaned their fate, or gathered with their friends to lament the common danger. Throughout the camp all the soldiers were composing their wills and sealing these documents (with personalised wax seals).

Due to the continual fear and complaining, even men of great military experience began to be affected by this mood (of despondency) including legionaries, centurions, and cavalry officers. Some were eager to appear less cowardly and announced that it was not the enemy they feared. It was dread of the restricted, narrow route of the march through the depths of a forest to reach Ariovistus. Others voiced concern over the arrangements for the supply and transport of sufficient grain for the army. Some even went so far as to tell Caesar that the soldiers would not obey him when he gave the order to leave the military camp and move out. They said the army would simply refuse to lift the standards because of their great fear.

When Caesar became aware of this situation, he called a council and ordered all ranks of centurions to attend. He severely reprimanded them, firstly for thinking that it was their business to inquire about the direction, or the strategy, of the march. He reminded them that during his consulship, Ariovistus had eagerly sought friendly relations with the Roman people. So why would anyone now conclude that he was going to abandon his obligations so impulsively?

He said that he was convinced that, once Ariovistus understood the terms being offered, he would acknowledge the fairness of the conditions and immediately come to an agreement with Caesar and the Roman people.

However, if Ariovistus did start a war, due to some mad fury, then what did the Roman army have to fear? Why did they doubt their own courage and Caesar's concern for their well-being? The danger posed by this enemy had already been experienced by the Romans in the time of their fathers. For the Cimbri and Teutoni had been overcome by Gaius Marius. On that occasion it was clear that the Roman army had deserved as much credit as their commander. This danger (Germanic warrior prowess) had also been experienced more recently during the slave revolt in Italy (led by Spartacus). However, in this instance the slaves had a greater advantage, due to the experience and training which they had received from the Romans (in gladiator schools).

Caesar said that from all these circumstances they should see how crucial it was to maintain a determined purpose. For a long time, the Romans had feared the (Spartacus) slaves when they had few weapons. But later, the Romans defeated these same slaves after they had acquired many weapons and won significant battles. They should also consider how the Germans had often clashed with the Helvetii and the Helvetii had frequently defeated them, not only in their own territory, but also in Germany itself. And yet the Helvetii had proved no match for the Roman army (commanded by Caesar).

Caesar continued by asking why some of the Romans present were disturbed by the defeat the Gauls had recently suffered from the Germans. And were they really troubled that the Gauls had fled from further engagements? He explained that, if they took the trouble to inquire, they would discover that the Gauls had been worn down by the long duration of this conflict. Ariovistus had been skulking in his camp in the marshes, for many months during the fighting, giving the Gauls no opportunity to attack him. Then finally, when the Gauls had abandoned any prospect of battle and dispersed their army, Ariovistus suddenly launched his assault upon them. He had therefore won more by tactical planning than by conspicuous bravery. Perhaps these tactics were successful when dealing with barbarians who had no military skill, but not even Ariovistus could expect such tactics to overcome the Roman army.

Caesar also spoke to those who disguised their fear with a pretend anxiety about grain supplies or the narrowness of the route. He said that they were doing so out of impudence. Clearly, they doubted the commitment of their commander, or else they thought Caesar was simply incapable. Yet his attention was fully focused on all these aspects of conflict. The Sequani, the Leuci, and the Lingones were all providing grain (supplies from Celtic allies). Furthermore, the crops were already ripe in the fields they were marching through and in a short while they would see this for themselves.

Now regarding their declared intention not to follow orders and raise the standards, this did not trouble Caesar at all. For he understood that whenever an army had disobeyed its commander in the past, it was due to other concerns. It was because fortune had deserted this man, or he had failed on the battlefield, or had committed some crime involving profits and these indiscretions had been discovered (payoffs, bribes or the misappropriation of plunder). But Caesar was clearly not guilty of any such crime and this was apparent from the entire conduct of his life. He was a man who enjoyed good fortune and that was evident from his campaign (victory) against the Helvetii.

Caesar concluded that he would begin the conflict (against the Germans) immediately, rather than at a later date. That very next night, during the fourth watch, the Roman army would break camp (in preparation for the march). He would soon know if their sense of shame and duty was stronger than their fear. And even if no one followed him, he would still set out in command of the Tenth Legion, for Caesar had no doubts about their loyalty. This legion would serve and protect him. Caesar gave this legion special favour, for he had the greatest confidence in its courage.

Alternative Account by Cassius Dio

The alternative account by Dio may incorporate some of the political arguments presented by the supporters of Caesar in Rome.

090 Cassius Dio, *Roman History*, 38.35

Meanwhile, reports reached the Roman soldiers that Ariovistus was making vigorous preparations for war. It was reported that many other Germans had either already crossed the Rhine to assist him, or had gathered on the banks of the river to suddenly attack the Romans. The Roman soldiers therefore became deeply dejected. They were alarmed by the large stature of their enemies, their vast numbers, and their boldness. The soldiers felt that they were not being threatened by ordinary men. They were going to engage uncanny and ferocious creatures resembling wild beasts. The talk amongst the army was that this conflict was none of their business. The campaign had not been decreed by the Roman government, so they were deployed merely because of Caesar's personal ambition. Consequently, the soldiers threatened to desert their general if he did not change his course of action.

When Caesar heard about this, he decided not to speak publicly to the common soldiers (in a military assembly). He did not think it was a good idea to discuss these matters in front of a crowd, as reports might reach the enemy. He was also afraid that his soldiers might refuse to obey orders. They might raise an uproar and cause some harm (mutiny, disobedience or the loss of political reputation). He therefore assembled his lieutenants, along with some leading members of the Gauls (trusted native supporters). He spoke to them as follows:

> My friends, I think we should debate our interests in private council, rather than public assemblies. In private, men set objectives that are very different from public declarations. In this setting we can choose the safest and most suitable course for us and impose the best measures on the wider community (Roman soldiers and their Gallic allies).
>
> But even in private discussions, men need to be strong and forceful to maintain their reputation. Now, those who do not engage in such affairs are thought to be safe (they avoid intrigue and political conspiracies). But a state that wants to hold power over other nations would quickly be overthrown if it did not follow these practices (plotting against enemies and opponents in private). These practices were not devised by mankind, for they are a principle of nature itself. They have always existed. They persist and will continue as long as there are men. But in this council do not choose what is of greatest advantage to yourselves, decide what is most credible and advantageous to all Romans.
>
> Consider that we have come here with many officers of high rank and status, the senators and *equites*. We have a great multitude of soldiers and an abundance of finance. We are not here for pleasure, or to neglect our duties. It is right that we should manage the affairs of our subjects and preserve the properties of our treaty-bound allies (the Gauls). We must repel any enemy who would seek to do them harm. In doing so we may increase our own possessions (seize plunder and conquer new resource-rich territories). (…)
>
> Consider our previous engagements with the Gauls and the Germans (the Cimbrian migration fifty years earlier). When we remained on our side of the Alps, they crossed over and ravaged a large part of Italy. Finally, we campaigned across this frontier and brought the war to them. We seized more of these territories, so that this war (by the Cimbri and Tuetones) was the only occasion when they brought their conflicts into Italy.
>
> These are the facts. If anyone declares that we should not wage war, then he is saying that we should not prosper, that we should not dominate others, that we should not be free and that we should no longer be Romans. You would not endure the presence of a man who said these things. You would surely consider killing him if he stood before you. (…)
>
> For what reason did the Roman people send us out here (to Gaul). Why did they send me immediately after my consulship? Why did they

elect me to hold a five-year command, a longer term than any previous appointment? And they equipped me with four legions. Surely it was not so that we might stand idle? (...)

Suppose one of you objects and says, 'What has Ariovistus done so wrong that he should not remain a friend and ally, but be declared an enemy?' Well, a man must defend himself against those who are harming him. He must also take action against those who intend to harm him and intervene swiftly before suffering any injury. This is better practice than waiting until harm is done and then seeking revenge.

It has been proved that Ariovistus is hostile to us. Look at what he has done. I contacted him on friendly terms and asked him to come and consult with us about present conditions. But he didn't come and he would not attend. What have I done that is unfair, unseemly, or arrogant? I merely summoned him as a friend and ally. But what great insolence and impiety he has demonstrated by refusing my request. There can be only two reasons for this refusal. Either he suspected that he might suffer some harm from us, or he felt contempt for us and wished us injury. Now if he felt any suspicion towards us, then he was clearly conspiring against us. For why would an honest man with good principles suspect others, unless it was already in his mind to do them harm? Or maybe he was motivated by the second cause, by disrespect. Maybe he merely looks down on us and insults us with his arrogant words. Well, what do you expect him to do in future actions? This man has shown you contempt in an unimportant matter for no great gain. He therefore must stand convicted from afar, both for his current intent and his foreseeable actions (what he might do in the future).

Ariovistus bade me come to him if I wanted anything from him. I urge you to consider this incident a significant matter. Perhaps someone speaking in defence of Ariovistus would say that he was hesitant, infirm, or fearful. But this is no excuse. He summoned me into his presence. This proves that he is defiant and determined to refuse our requests. Or perhaps he intended to make corresponding demands on us. Just consider the insolence and insult this course of action reveals. The proconsul of the Romans summons a man and he does not come. Then this very man summons the Roman proconsul – this man who is an Allobrogian (the Gallic word for a foreigner).

This is not a minor matter. He failed to obey me and then he summoned me. I am Caesar, but I am more than that. I am a Roman. I am the proconsul and I hold the fasces (the symbols of state authority). I have the power of state and I command the legions. It was not just me who was summoned (and demeaned), but all these aspects of Rome. Privately I have no grievance against Ariovistus, but he has spoken and acted against us all. For it is Rome that has received his retorts and suffers his scorn.

Suppose someone tells you that Ariovistus is listed among our friends and allies? Well, this is a reason for us to detest him with greater intensity. For not even our greatest and most resolute enemies would ever venture to do what he has done as a supposed friend and ally. It is as though he has taken these positions (of honour) merely to wrong us with impunity. We did not make a treaty with Ariovistus just to be insulted and plotted against. And it is not us breaking the agreement. For we sent envoys to him as a friend and an ally. And look at how he has treated us!

Ariovistus was well treated by Rome when he acted to benefit us, and he obtained what he sought (an alliance). But now he acts against our interests and such a person is rightly regarded as an enemy. Do not be surprised that I once looked after some of his interests in the Senate and the Assembly. For I am consistent in my purpose. I sought to honour and reward those who were good and faithful. But dishonour and punishment must be imposed on those who are evil and disloyal. It is Ariovistus who has changed his purpose. For he no longer makes fair and proper use of the privileges that we have granted him. Therefore, if we justly go to war against him, no one will dispute our cause.

Ariovistus is not invincible. He is not even a difficult adversary. We know this because we have overcome these people (the Germans) on previous occasions (such as the Cimbrian War). Some of these conquests were easily achieved and occurred only recently (German captives defeated in the Italian Slave Revolts). We can also gain further confidence from what we know about Ariovistus. He has never united his people or unified their armed forces. Even now he does not expect a serious war and he is utterly unprepared. His countrymen (Germans east of the Rhine) will not assist him, even if he makes them tempting offers. Who would choose to be his ally and fight against us, when they have suffered no injury from us? Instead, they should co-operate with us. They could remove a despotic ruler on their very borders and obtain a share of his territory from us.

Even if some of them (the German tribes) should band together to oppose us, they will not prove superior to us in any way. Omitting all other factors, we have greater numbers. Our soldiers are more mature, better experienced and have performed greater deeds. We have armour that fully encompasses our bodies, while our opponents are unprotected. Our military employs reason and organisation, whereas our rivals are unorganised and rush impulsively at everything. Do not fear the magnitude of their large physique, their great violence, or their mighty shouts (the *baritus* – war chant). For no voice ever killed a man and their huge bodies have the same hands as ours. With our hands we can impose greater injury because their large, unprotected bodies will be an easy target.

Their attack charge is a tremendous headlong rush. But they are easily exhausted, and the attack is effective for only a brief time. You have experienced this, and you have conquered men who fight in this manner (the Celts). I have outlined these concerns so that you will not be misled. You can be certain of victory. Numerous Gauls similar to these (German) people will be our allies in this conflict. So even if they did possess some terrifying advantage, we can match them with our allies (other North Europeans).

Consider what I have said and instruct the masses in these arguments (inform the Roman rank and file). Some of you may disagree, but follow my example and fight just the same. For I will never abandon the command that I have been granted by my country. (If all else fails) the Tenth Legion is all I require. And they would advance unarmoured through the flames of war if I called upon them to do so (absolute loyalty). So, the rest of you can depart now. And the quicker the better. I will not tolerate your presence here if it is for no purpose. You will not consume the public funds or claim the rewards of other men who undertake this endeavour. You will not take any share of the plunder acquired by others (the war loot distributed amongst successful troops).

At the end of this speech no one raised any objection. Some might have held the opposite view, but they agreed with Caesar and widely circulated what they had heard. They had no difficulty in persuading the soldiers to accept and obey (the new narrative). This was because some of the soldiers had been singled out by the general (the Tenth Legion). Caesar had always favoured the Tenth Legion and gave them special treatment. The soldiers of the Tenth wanted to fulfil Caesar's expectations, while the rest of the troops wanted to emulate the reputation of the Tenth.

091 Frontinus, *Stratagems*, 3.5.11 'On Determination'

Caesar prepared to fight the Germans, led by their king, Ariovistus. But his soldiers began to panic when the prospect of battle drew near. Caesar therefore called them to an assembly and announced that, if necessary, he would fight the enemy alone with only the Tenth Legion (his most dedicated soldiers). This was an honour that roused up the Tenth to unique heroism, while the other troops were overwhelmed by humiliation, since their own reputation for being courageous was in doubt (an incitement to action).

Details of the German Force

092 Orosius, *History*, 6.7

Later, the Sequani (a powerful Celtic tribe in eastern Gaul) threatened warfare by inviting a vast number of German warriors into the country. They were led by king Ariovistus who boasted that he might subjugate all the Gallic tribes with his invading forces. But Caesar was determined to overcome and defeat this threat. The Roman army was terrified by the vast numbers and ferocity of the invading Germans, but the enemy refused opportunities to fight for a long time.

The (Germanic) army commanded by Ariovistus included the Harudes, Marcomanni, Triboci, Vangiones, Nemetes, Sedusii and Suebi (a wide alliance of Germanic tribes).

Preparations for Battle

093 Plutarch, *Julius Caesar*, 19

Caesar announced that he would command only the Tenth Legion and march immediately against the barbarians. He asserted that the enemy were no better warriors than the Cimbri, and he himself was no worse a general than Marius.

The Tenth Legion sent a deputation to him expressing their gratitude, while the other legions reproached their own commanders. The entire army was now impetuous and eager for battle. They followed Caesar on the long march north and encamped about 25 miles from the enemy.

Caesar's arrival shattered the plans Ariovistus had made. The German king had not expected that the Romans would attack his people. He thought that their army would not be able to withstand the German assault and was amazed at the boldness of Caesar. He also saw that his own forces were disturbed by the sudden Roman presence.

094 Cassius Dio, *Roman History*, 38.47

Caesar ordered an immediate march against Ariovistus while the soldiers were still enthusiastic for war. He was concerned that any further inaction or delay would cause the troops to become despondent once more. The speed and suddenness of the Roman advance caused Ariovistus such alarm that he requested an immediate conference with Caesar regarding peace terms. However, no terms could be agreed. Caesar insisted on imposing all his demands and Ariovistus refused to obey these dictates. The war therefore began with both sides feeling highly apprehensive and uncertain. This anxiety and suspense was felt by the allies and enemies of both sides in this conflict. The people of these regions (eastern Gaul) understood that they would soon be subject to whoever was victorious (Romans or Germans).

The barbarians possessed superior numbers and were physically larger than the Romans. But the Romans had the advantage of military experience and armour. Caesar's methodical approach was offset by the fierce spirit of the Germans with their reckless and impulsive attacks. As a result, the two sides were evenly matched. Their enthusiasm, hopes and expectations were likewise in perfect balance.

095 Julius Caesar, *Gallic War*, 1.41–50

Caesar's speech changed the attitude of all the soldiers who now felt a great eagerness to serve. Through its tribunes, the Tenth Legion was the first to express its gratitude to Caesar, for the praise he had given them. They affirmed their complete readiness for immediate military action. As for the other legions, they made their tribunes and senior centurions give excuses to Caesar, explaining that the soldiers had not felt any genuine doubt or panic. They said that it was not their business to decide the plan of campaign, that decision belonged solely to the commander (Caesar). Caesar accepted these attempts to avoid blame.

Caesar had absolute confidence in Diviciacus (a leading Druid of the Celtic Aedui) who located a route that would take the Roman army through open terrain (avoiding ambush). But this meant a detour of more than 50 miles. As Caesar had announced, the march began on the fourth watch (soon after daybreak, based on three-hourly changes of the guard). On the seventh day of continuous marching, the scouts reported that the forces of Ariovistus were 24 miles away from the incoming Roman army.

When Ariovistus learnt that Caesar was approaching, he sent deputies to him. They announced that Ariovistus was now ready to do what Caesar had requested and participate in a direct discussion of terms. Ariovistus still believed that he could comply without risk, although the Romans had moved closer to his position. Caesar did not reject the proposal because it suggested that Ariovistus was returning to a proper frame of mind (conceding to Caesar and Rome) after previously refusing the request.

Caesar also began to hope that Ariovistus would abandon his obstinacy, once he knew Caesar's demands and the benefits that could be conferred on behalf of Rome.

The date agreed for the parley was five days later. Meanwhile, deputies were continually sent to and fro between the German position and the Roman camp (conveying messages and agreeing conditions). Ariovistus demanded that Caesar should not bring infantry with him to the encounter. He was afraid that Caesar would use treachery to surround and capture him. He insisted that each leader should come with an escort of horsemen, otherwise there would be no meeting. Caesar did not want the parley to be cancelled on that excuse, but he was not willing to entrust his safety to his Gallic cavalry (the foreign allies serving Rome). He therefore decided to take the horses from Gallic troopers and place soldiers of the Tenth Legion on these mounts. He had absolute confidence in this legion and if action was required, he would have an escort formed from the most faithful comrades. As the order was being carried out, one of the soldiers of the Tenth Legion made a witty remark. He said that Caesar was giving better than he had promised when he said he would make the Tenth Legion an escort for the commander-in-chief (a position of high honour). Now its soldiers were being made into a new 'Cavalry' (a position once formed from the Roman elite – the '*equites*').

The site chosen for the meeting was a large and level stretch of land on which there was a mound of earth. This place was equally distant from the camps of both Caesar and Ariovistus. Caesar stationed the mounted legion about 200 paces from the mound (500 feet). The horsemen of Ariovistus halted at a similar distance. Ariovistus demanded that they should address each other while on horseback, and that each leader should approach with ten companions. When they finally met, Caesar began his speech by reminding Ariovistus of the benefits he had been granted by himself and the Senate. The Senate had recognised Ariovistus as a 'king' and 'friend' (ally). They had also sent him lavish gifts. Caesar pointed out that few leaders received these privileges and they were people who had usually performed some great personal service (to the Roman state). Ariovistus had no right to seek an audience with the Senate, or claim these benefits. But he had obtained these rewards nonetheless, through the favour and generosity of Caesar and the Senate. Caesar also reminded Ariovistus how long-established and close the Roman relationship with the Aedui had been (as their main Celtic allies). Decrees by the Senate had been frequent, conferring distinction on the Aedui, who had continually sought the friendship of Rome and held the dominant power in Gaul. By tradition, the

Romans did not allow their friends and allies to lose territory, or influence. Instead, they favoured an increase in the power, dignity, and distinction of their 'friends'. Caesar asked Ariovistus why the Romans would allow their allies (the Aedui) to be robbed of their possessions. The Aedui held these possessions as friends and supporters of Rome. Then Caesar repeated the demands that his deputies had expressed to Ariovistus. Ariovistus was not to make war on the Aedui or their allies and he must return the political hostages. If he could not send any of his followers back to their homelands, then he must not allow any more Germans to cross the Rhine.

Ariovistus offered only a brief reply to these demands, but he spoke at length about his own good qualities (his right to rule and receive respect). He said that he had crossed the Rhine, not because of his own ambition, but at the request of Gauls who had summoned him. He had left his homeland and kinsmen in search of great rewards. The settlements they now occupied in Gaul had been granted to them. Political hostages had been offered with consent. The tribute he took was his by 'right of war', for these are impositions that all conquerors impose upon the conquered. He had not begun this war against the Gauls. They had commenced hostilities against him. All the tribal states of Gaul had come to attack him in a united camp, but their forces had been defeated and overcome in a single military action. If they wanted to renew this conflict in another engagement, then he was prepared to fight them again. But if they wanted to enjoy peace, it was unjust for them to refuse tribute payments previously consented to and delivered.

Ariovistus said that the friendship of the Roman state ought to be an honour and a security. He had sought this distinction with hope, but now it was being presented as a hindrance. If the Romans insisted that tribute was remitted and political hostages given up, then Ariovistus would refuse their 'friendship' as strongly as he had sought it. As for the German masses that he was bringing into the country, his objective was to protect himself, not to attack Gaul. Proof existed, for he entered this country only upon request, and the warfare he had engaged in was defensive, not aggressive.

Furthermore, Ariovistus entered and occupied this part of Gaul before the Roman people had arrived. The Roman army had never before crossed their borders to reach this territory, or strayed beyond their part of Gaul (Gallia Transalpina – the stretch of Roman-held territory on the Mediterranean coast). What business did Caesar have? Why did he come into our (German) sphere of occupation? This new 'Province of Gaul' belonged to Ariovistus and it was equivalent to the Roman one (Gallia Transalpina – Provence). It was not right for Ariovistus to give way to Caesar. Suppose Ariovistus had made an attack on Roman territory? (Would that be justified?) So likewise, the Romans were unjust in obstructing Ariovistus, within his own jurisdiction (Germanic Gaul).

Ariovistus also addressed Caesar's statement that the Aedui were considered 'brothers' of the Romans. He said he was not so 'barbarian' or 'ignorant' that he was unaware of recent Roman affairs. During the current campaign, the Allobroges or Aedui must have rendered assistance to the Romans (to enter this region). In recent disputes between himself and the Sequani tribe, the Aedui were actively supported by the Romans. Ariovistus had to suspect that, despite the pretence of friendship, Caesar had brought an army into Gaul for the purpose of destroying him. Therefore, Caesar must immediately depart and withdraw his army from this region. If he did not, then Ariovistus would regard him, not as a friend, but as an enemy. If he put Caesar to death, he would gratify many nobles and leaders of the Roman people (rival politicians). He knew this because he had received messengers sent on behalf of rival Romans, whose favour and friendship he could gain by Caesar's death. Right now, Caesar should depart and permit Ariovistus to continue uninterrupted in his occupation of Gaul. If he did this then Ariovistus could offer him a great benefit without any serious effort, or risk. Ariovistus could initiate any campaigns that Caesar wanted (a new military alliance with common aims).

Caesar spoke at length to explain why he could not give up his current purpose. He said that it was his principle, and the principle of the Roman people, not to abandon allies who deserved reward. Furthermore, he would not accept that Gaul belonged to Ariovistus, rather than to the Romans. The Arverni and the Ruteni had been subdued in a campaign by Quintus Fabius Maximus (in 121 BC). The Romans had pardoned them, rather than forming them into a province, or imposing tribute. If the issue of time was important, then the Romans justifiably held sovereignty in Gaul (they were there first and had obtained earlier victories). After these victories the Senate had ruled that (greater) Gaul should continue to observe its own laws. And if that decision was obeyed, then (greater) Gaul should be free (not subject to German dominance).

During the progress of this discussion, Caesar was informed that the horsemen brought by Ariovistus had moved closer to the mound. The Germans were now launching stones and darts at their Roman counterparts (a provocation). Caesar ended the discussion and began withdrawing his troops, but he commanded them not to unleash a single dart (short javelin) against the enemy. This was because he realised that an immediate fight between his mounted legion and the German horsemen would involve considerable danger. Even if they were successful, a report might circulate that he had surrounded and attacked an opponent during negotiations (a dishonourable action).

The ordinary Roman soldiers learnt how arrogantly Ariovistus had behaved at the meeting. He had forbidden the Romans from entering Gaul, his horsemen had attacked our troops, and his actions had wrecked any agreement. The army was therefore inspired with far greater eagerness and enthusiasm for battle.

Two days later Ariovistus sent deputies to Caesar. He said that he wanted to discuss with him some matters which they had not settled during their previous meeting. He asked Caesar to appoint a new day for further negotiations, or send one of his staff to negotiate. But Caesar thought that further discussion was purposeless, especially as some impetuous Germans had launched darts at the Roman soldiers (the enemy were eager for battle). He thought it would be very dangerous to send one of his senior staff officers across to Ariovistus. It would put that man at the mercy of ferocious Germans (conflict had become inevitable). Instead, he planned to send Gaius Valerius Procillus, the son of Gaius Valerius Caburus. This young man had exceptional courage and was polite and courteous. His father had been granted citizenship by Gaius Valerius Flaccus (a Romanised Celt), and Caesar selected him because of his loyalty and his knowledge of the Gallic language, which he could speak fluently from long-term experience. He was also someone that the Germans would have no reason to resent (no previous associations). He chose Marcus Mettius to accompany him, since he was familiar with, and friendly to, Ariovistus (from previous political engagements).

Caeasar instructed these men to ascertain the views of Ariovistus and report back on his intentions. But when Ariovistus saw them approach his camp he called out to his army, 'Why have they come to me? To spy?' So that when the Romans tried to speak, he had them seized and placed in chains.

That same day Ariovistus advanced and pitched his camp next to a hillside about 6 miles from Caesar's position. The next day he led his forces past Caesar's encampment and occupied a new position about 2 miles to the rear of the Roman army. This was to cut the Romans off from the supply routes that conveyed grain and other materials from the borders of the Sequani and the Aedui (up to their current position). For five consecutive days Caesar brought his own forces out in front of the Roman camp and kept them lined up in battle formation. This was to give Ariovistus a chance to engage the Romans in battle. But Ariovistus kept his main army in camp and engaged in daily encounters that only involved cavalry.

The Germans trained in the following form of combat. They deployed 6,000 horsemen supported by an equal number of very swift and brave infantry. These men had been specially selected from the entire force and each horseman was assigned one infantryman for personal protection. They worked together when engaging the enemy. If any serious difficulty arose (on the battlefield), the horsemen could withdraw quickly, or converge speedily. They could form up around any fighter who fell severely wounded from his horse. If a longer-range advance was needed, or a more rapid retreat, the infantry trained to support themselves on the manes of the horses to keep up the pace (they gripped the horses and were carried away at a gallop).

Caesar observed how Ariovistus remained within his encampment. Therefore, to prevent further interruption to his supplies, he selected a new spot for the Roman camp that was about 600 paces beyond the German encampment (a quarter of a mile). He marched to this site with his army arranged in a triple-line formation (battle ready). He ordered the first and second lines to remain armed, while the third began to entrench a camp (with ditches, ramparts and wooden palisades). As stated, this Roman camp was only about 600 paces from the enemy position (extreme proximity).

Ariovistus responded by sending a large force towards the Romans to intimidate them and prevent them from completing their entrenching work. This force included about 16,000 light-armed troops along with all the German horsemen. Caesar kept to his previous plan, ordering the two lines of Roman soldiers to drive back the enemy, while the third completed the entrenching work. When the camp was secure, he stationed a force of two legions and part of the auxiliaries within its perimeter. Then he marched his remaining four legions back to the larger camp (that they had previously occupied).

Acting on this preparation, Caesar moved his troops out of both camps the next day. His forces advanced from the larger camp and stood in formation to give the enemy the opportunity for battle. When the Germans did not come forth, Caesar brought his army back to their main camp about noon. Then at last, Ariovistus sent a part of the German forces to attack the lesser camp. Both sides fought vigorously until evening. Then at sunset, when many blows had been given and taken, Ariovistus led his forces back to the German camp.

The Romans questioned some German prisoners to discover why Ariovistus did not fight a decisive action. From these reports, Caesar discovered the reason. It was a custom among the Germans for their women to make divinations by casting lots to determine whether to engage an enemy force, or not (*sortes* – pieces of stone or wood marked with sacred signs). The women had declared that if the Germans fought before the new moon, some divine force would forbid them a victory.

096 Cassius Dio, *Roman History*, 38.48

While the two armies were encamped opposite one another, the barbarian women conducted divinations (foretelling the future by interpreting natural phenomena). Due to their predictions the women forbade the men to engage in any battle before the appearance of the new moon. Ariovistus always paid great heed to these pronouncements whenever he had to make decisions. Consequently, he did not attack the Romans immediately with his entire force, even though the Romans were already challenging him to battle. He only sent out his horsemen backed by a supporting contingent of infantry warriors. But even this force inflicted severe injury on the Roman army.

Afterwards Ariovistus became contemptuous of the Romans and seized a position overlooking their entrenchments (bank and ditch defences). In response the Romans seized and occupied another vantage point close to this position. Caesar withdrew his army from their fortified camps and kept them outside, drawn up for battle until noon. But Ariovistus would not engage the Romans until evening when they had begun to retire back into their camps. Then he attacked with such suddenness that his forces almost captured a Roman rampart. These outcomes were so successful that Ariovistus no longer paid heed to the warnings given by the women (the divinators).

097 Polyaenus, *Stratagems*, 8.23.4

Caesar did not think his forces were strong enough to directly engage Germans who were prepared and ready for battle. He therefore assumed a defensive strategy against them. But then he learned that the German augurs (who foretold the future) had forbidden their warriors to fight before the new moon appeared. He therefore seized the first opportunity to advance his army and attack the enemy. This is because he reasoned that the Germans would fight with less eagerness and ferocity if they were acting against the instructions of their augurs. The outcome met his expectations and, without any other advantage than this, the Romans gained a complete victory.

098 Plutarch, *Julius Caesar*, 19

The German war spirit was also diminished by the dire prophecies of their sacred women. These women were able to foretell the future by observing the currents and eddies in river streams. They saw signs amid the whirling water and forbade any German to join battle before the new moon cast its first light.

Caesar heard reports of these prophesies and saw that the Germans were subdued. He decided that it would be a good plan to attack them while they were disheartened, rather than wait for the full time to elapse. He therefore attacked their earth and ditch defences and assaulted the hills on which they were encamped. He provoked the Germans and incited their main forces to assemble and fight a conclusive battle.

The Battle of Vosges (58 BC)

099 Julius Caesar, *Gallic War*, 1.51–54

The next day Caesar left what he considered to be a sufficient garrison at each camp. Then, in front of the lesser camp, he posted all the allied troops in full view of the enemy. This was only a demonstration, because the total strength of his legionary troops was small compared to the total numbers of the enemy. Leading the legions himself, Caesar deployed the Romans in a triple line adjacent to the enemy's camp. At last, compelled by necessity, the Germans began moving their own forces out of the encampment. They formed up in their tribal groups with an equal interval (between the nations). These tribes included the Harudes, Marcomanni, Triboci, Vangiones, Nemetes, Sedusii and Suebi. There were wagons and carts in the German lines, so the fighters would be unable to flee. Their women took position on board the wagons and watched with tearful eyes as the men marched forwards. The women called out to them not to allow their families to be taken into Roman slavery.

Caesar put the quaestors (state magistrates) in charge of the legions alongside the legates (regular commanders) so that every man would have a witness for his valour (a greater chance of recognition, reward and advancement). He himself took position on the right wing of the Roman force, having noticed that the corresponding division of the enemy was less secure (the left wing of the German force appeared weaker). When the signal for battle was given, the enemy dashed forwards so suddenly and swiftly that there was no time for the Romans to launch javelins against them. Nevertheless, the Roman troops attacked the enemy with great fierceness. They threw aside their javelins and fought with swords at close quarters. But the Germans followed their custom and speedily formed into solid masses to resist the Roman sword attacks (shield walls). Many of our soldiers were brave enough to leap on the enemy defensive formations. They tore the shields from their hands, or dealt them wounds from above.

The left wing of the enemy's army was beaten and put to flight. But their right wing, by sheer weight of numbers, pressed heavily into the Roman battle line. Young Publius Crassus, who commanded the Roman cavalry, noticed this development. He could respond more quickly than the other officers who were occupied in the front lines of battle. He therefore moved his cavalry round to form a third line of attack to support our struggling troops. This restored Roman prospects in the battle and caused all the enemy to turn and run.

The enemy did not cease their flight until they reached the river Rhine about 5 miles from that place. A few of the Germans trusted to their own strength and tried to swim across the river. Others discovered boats that could take them across to safety, while Ariovistus found a skiff moored to the bank and escaped across the stream. Our cavalry caught and killed the rest of the enemy. Ariovistus had two wives, one a Suebian who had accompanied him from his homelands in Germany, the other a woman from Noricum (a territory in the Celtic Alps). She was the sister of King Voccio and had married Ariovistus in Gaul (a political alliance). Both of his wives were killed, and one of his daughters was also slain. But the other was taken prisoner by the Romans.

Gaius Valerius Procillus had been bound with a threefold chain (restraints on his wrist, ankles and waist) and was being dragged along by the Germans as his captors fled. Caesar himself was leading the pursuing cavalry that overtook this group. His rescue of Procillus gave Caesar as much pleasure as the victory itself. A most distinguished member of the Roman Province of Gaul had been saved, someone who was a close friend and guest of Caesar himself. This demonstrated to Caesar that his good fortune remained intact and consistent. Procillus said that on three occasions the Germans had cast lots in his presence to decide whether he should be immediately burnt to death, or saved for a later sacrifice. So Procillus owed his safety and salvation to the favour of the gods. Marcus Mettius was also located and brought safely back to Caesar.

When the news of this battle was reported across the Rhine, the Suebi who had assembled on the banks of the river began to return homewards. The tribes who dwell next to the Rhine perceived their panic, pursued them and killed a great number of Suebi.

Alternative Accounts of the Battle

100 Cassius Dio, *Roman History*, 38.48–50

On the next day, the Romans followed their usual practice and drew up their forces in full military array (an invitation for battle). And on this occasion Ariovistus led his full army forwards to attack.

The Romans observed the enemy emerging from their tents and advancing towards them. They responded by rushing forwards so that the Germans could not form a secure battle line. The Germans had special confidence in their ability to hurl spears, but the Romans charged with a battle cry and closed the distance so quickly that their opponents could not effectively launch their javelins. They pushed forwards into such extreme close quarters that the Germans could not even use their tall spears or long swords. The impacted barbarians were pushed, shoved, and forced to fight more with their bodies than with their weapons (punches against blades).

The Germans struggled to overpower the soldiers they engaged (heavily armoured Roman troops) and they could not easily knock down, or topple, those who withstood them (Romans pushing forwards in dense ranks). Many Germans even lost their short swords in the struggle and fought with their hands and their teeth. They dragged their opponents down, biting, tearing, and ripping at them. They used their greater strength and physique to overpower their Roman adversaries. But this practice did not cause any great loss in the Roman ranks. They continually pushed forwards into their foe. Somehow, Roman armour and skill matched the ferocity of the enemy attack. This struggle continued for a long time, and it was nearly the end of the day before the Romans prevailed.

The Romans had an advantage since they carried daggers that were smaller than Gallic swords and had steel points (short-range stabbing blades). The Roman soldiers were also better accustomed to long-duration combat and had far greater endurance than the barbarians. The Germans could not prolong the strength and fierceness of their attacks. The enemy were therefore defeated, but they did not flee the battle site. Instead, they collapsed into large, helpless, exhausted groups. Some of these groups included more than 300 fighters who stood with their shields raised on all sides. These formations were so solid and compact that the Romans could not successfully assault, or dislodge them. Thus, both sides became immobile and were unable to inflict further damage, or suffer additional harm themselves.

The Germans neither advanced against the Romans nor turned to flee. So, the Romans stood immovable on the battlefield as if stationed behind a battlement (a solid wall of shields). They had set aside their spears before the battle had begun, because they thought these weapons would be of no use in combat. The German shield walls were vulnerable since their warriors had no helmets, but the Romans could not use their short swords to strike at the heads of their opponents while they carried their own heavy shields (the Romans had to reach upwards and strike far above the height of their own head). Therefore, the Romans cast down their shields and rushed at the Germans with just their swords. Some charged into the enemy formations from a running start, while others dashed forwards and leapt into the shield wall as though they were scaling a tower. The Romans delivered a fierce array of blows into the huddled German masses.

Many Germans were instantly slain with a single sword thrust (to the face or throat). They were dead before they fell, but they were kept upright in the tightly packed closeness of their defensive formations. Most of the Germans died during this engagement, but some were driven back to their wagons. These men died with their wives and children.

101 Florus, *Roman History*, 1.45

The prospect of fighting these unknown people caused great alarm and concern in the Roman military camps. A great many soldiers began rewriting their wills and this activity was observed in the camp square (an activity involving witnesses and signed declarations). But (when the fighting began) the giant stature of their German enemies made larger targets for Roman swords and other weapons. The Romans therefore attacked with great resolve and the barbarians retreated into tortoise-like formations (testudo) formed by solid walls of shields. The Roman soldiers were so determined to finish the fight that they actually leaped on the top of the enemy shields to strike at the throats of the Germans with their swords.

102 Orosius, *History*, 6.7

The fighting was especially fierce, due to the battle formation adopted by the Germans. They formed a dense phalanx-like array of warriors clustered into large groups. The warriors were protected on all sides by interlocking shields and these formations could halt and shatter the advancing Roman battle line. But the most agile and daring Roman soldiers leaped over the front of the enemy 'testudo' shield walls (tortoise-like formations). They tore away the protecting shields like a man might strip scales (of a fish). Other soldiers stabbed at the exposed shoulders (and throats) of the enemy who were surprised by the sudden assault and had no protection on this part of their bodies. The Germans were horrified by this new danger and their formidable shield walls began to break apart as many warriors started to flee. The Romans pursued them across 50 miles of terrain and inflicted a mass slaughter that seemed to be endless. Afterwards it was impossible to estimate the number of Germans who had fought in that battle, or the vast numbers who were slain. Ariovistus seized a small boat and escaped across the Rhine to Germany, but he abandoned his two wives and both daughters, who were captured by the Romans.

103 Plutarch, *Julius Caesar*, 19
The German army was routed in this decisive engagement and Caesar pursued the survivors as far as the Rhine. The intervening ground, which stretched across a 50-mile plain, was strewn with dead bodies and the spoils of war. Ariovistus successfully crossed the Rhine with a few of his followers. But the German dead were said to have numbered 80,000.

104 Cassius Dio, *Roman History*, 38.50
Ariovistus fled with some of his horsemen. He abandoned his territory and headed for the Rhine. He was pursued, but not captured, and he escaped on a boat ahead of his followers (Germans escaping the conflict). The Romans overtook and killed many Germans fleeing to the river, but others were swept away in the stream (drowned in their panicked efforts to cross to safety). This was the end of the war.

Assessment of the Germans

105 Appian, *Gallic War*, 4.22
Caesar also defeated the Germans led by Ariovistus. These Germans excel all other peoples as they are physically the largest, and the bravest, and more savage than any others (nations). They do not fear death as they believe their spirit survives beyond this life. They are also capable of enduring extreme cold with the same forbearance as a warm environment. In times of scarcity, they can survive on simple herbs, while their horses graze from the (leaves) on trees. It seems that they have no restraint or patience in their battles. They do not fight in a strategic manner, or form themselves into any regular order (disciplined unit formations). Instead, they fight in battles with the energy and spirit of wild beasts. For this reason, they have been overcome by the strategies and endurance of the Roman army.

The Germans made a monstrous charge against the legions (commanded by Caesar). They pushed the legions back a short distance, but Roman ranks were not broken. The legions outmanoeuvred their enemy, defeated them, and slaughtered 800,000 Germans (possibly an error, an exaggeration, or the total German population subdued during the campaign).

Germanic Tribes Support the Belgae in Northern Gaul (57 BC)

After defeating Ariovistus, Julius Ceaser moved his armies north to supress the Belgic tribes in north-east Gaul. But the Belgae summoned assistance from Germanic tribes on the far side of the Rhine.

106 Julius Caesar, *Gallic War*, 2.3
Caesar suddenly arrived (in Belgica) with more speed than anyone had expected. The Remi (a pro-Roman Gallic tribe) reported (…) that all the other Belgic tribes were armed for war and the Germans dwelling on the opposite side of the Rhine had joined them in this purpose (opposition to Caesar).

Belgic Ancestry

107 Julius Caesar, *Gallic War*, 2.4
Caesar asked the Remi what (Belgic) states were preparing to fight, and what was their size and military strength. He discovered that most of the Belgae were of Germanic origin, and they had crossed the Rhine a long time ago. They had driven out the Gauls from this territory and settled there due to the fertility of the soil (in northern Gaul). They said that in past times, when the Teutoni and Cimbri had harassed Gaul, the Belgae were the only nation who had prevented them from entering their lands (120 BC). The Belgae still recalled these events, since it gave them great pride and authority in military matters.

Concerning their numbers (…) the Germanic tribes, including the Condrusi, Eburones, Caeroesi, and Paemani, were thought to have promised the Belgae some 40,000 warriors.

Belgic Similarity to Germans

108 Julius Caesar, *Gallic War*, 8.25
The Treveri (a Belgic tribe) differs little from the Germans in their barbarous habits. This is due to their proximity to Germany and their training in frequent wars. They never submitted to Roman commands unless compelled by the presence of an army.

Attack on the Aduatuci (descendants of the Cimbri)

The Aduatuci were said to be descendants of the Cimbri and Teutones settled among the Belgae in northern Gaul. They could raise perhaps 19,000 warriors to defend the territory (Julius Caesar, *Gallic War*, 2.4). As Germans they had the heritage of a wagon-building culture, but they settled among Gauls, who constructed giant wicker and wooden effigies of their gods.

109 Julius Caesar, *Gallic War*, 2.29–33

The Aduatuci were approaching with all their forces to assist the Nervii (against Rome). But when they learned the outcome of the battle, they halted their march and returned to their home territories. (Fearing attack) they abandoned their settlements and strongholds and gathered all their possessions at a single site that was well fortified by natural defences. This site was surrounded by the steepest rock faces with the only approach being an upward slope less than 200 feet wide. They had fortified this approach with an enormous double wall (an earthwork) crowned with very heavy stones and sharpened stakes.

The Aduatuci are descended from the Cimbri and Teutones, who advanced into Gallia Narbonensis and reached Italy. During this march, they set down the stock that they could not transport on the near side of the Rhine (west bank) and left 6,000 men in the area as a guard outpost. Afterwards, this remaining force fought repeated conflicts against the neighbouring tribes, sometimes on the offensive and at other times in defence. Finally, they concluded peace and established this territory as their new homeland.

When the Roman army arrived, the Aduatuci made frequent sallies from their stronghold and skirmished with the soldiers. Meanwhile, the Romans managed to erect a fortified rampart 15,000 feet in circumference around their stronghold. This siege enclosure had vantage points at close intervals, and it confined the Aduatuci entirely within their defended settlement. The Romans pushed mantlets into position (mobile timber screens), constructed an assault ramp, then built a siege tower. At first the Aduatuci laughed at and loudly ridiculed these large constructions, since they were far from their walls. The Roman soldiers were short statured compared to the huge physique of the Aduatuci (Germanic heritage). So, they mocked them, asking how such puny men could bring such a heavy construction up to their walls.

But when the Aduatuci saw that the siege tower was moving and approaching their walls, they became alarmed at this entirely unfamiliar and extraordinary sight. They sent envoys to Caesar calling for immediate peace and expressed the following opinions. They believed that the Romans must be waging war with divine assistance, for how else could they move such a massive construction forwards with great speed. They therefore submitted themselves and all their possessions to the power of Rome. They asked only for the mercy and kindness that Caesar had granted to other communities. Caesar deliberated whether to keep the Aduatuci armed and intact. Most of the neighbouring tribes had an animosity towards them, but envied their courage. If he removed their weapons, then the tribe would not be able to defend themselves (they would be dependent on Rome). They might be tortured and slain by men who were their inferiors (rival Gauls). No fate that the Romans could impose would be worse than this.

Caesar responded to the Aduatuci saying that they had done nothing to deserve his mercy. But he would preserve their political status because that was his usual practice. However, they must surrender before the approaching battering ram touched their wall. They must submit all their weapons to him and then he would act as he had done for the Nervii (a subdued Belgic tribe). He would consider the Aduatuci surrendered subjects of Rome and command the neighbouring peoples to commit no outrage or offence against them.

The envoys reported this to their tribesmen who agreed to perform his commands. A great quantity of weapons was cast from the wall into the outer trench until the heaps almost reached the height of the defences and the Roman siege ramp. The Aduatuci then opened their gates to the Romans and enjoyed the benefits of peace. But the weapons they had surrendered were only a third of their armaments as the rest of their military equipment had been concealed within the town.

That evening Caesar ordered all the Roman troops to leave the town and for its gates to be closed. This would ensure that the townsfolk did not suffer any outrage from the soldiers during the night. But the Aduatuci had expected the Romans to withdraw, or be less watchful, after their apparent surrender. They had previously formed a plan to retrieve the weapons they had earlier concealed. These included shields made of bark or plaited osiers (interwoven twigs) which were hastily covered with hides. During the third watch (first light) the Aduatuci suddenly surged from the town in full strength. They raced down the hills to our field works along a path with less of a slope. But Caesar had made arrangements and flares were lit to signal detachments from the nearest forts. The soldiers moved with great speed to the location (the perimeter siegeworks).

The enemy fought fiercely, as brave men in a desperate situation. Their one hope lay in their valour, but they fought on unfavourable ground against troops who could hurl missiles down upon them from ramparts and towers. Some 4,000 warriors were slain and the rest were driven back into the town. The following day the Romans broke down the gates of the town. There was no more defence for the occupants. The soldiers were sent in.

Caesar sold all the plunder stripped from the town in a single auction (sold to associations managed by wealthy Roman businessmen). The purchasers reported that 53,000 captives were included in the auction (to be sold on as Roman slaves).

Another Account of the Aduatuci Defeat (57 BC)

110 Cassius Dio, *Roman History*, 39.4

Meanwhile, the Aduatuci who occupied nearby lands had assembled to support the Nervii. This tribe was connected to the Cimbri both by kinship and temperament (a people of Germanic ethnicity and culture). But the Aduatuci were defeated before they could accomplish anything significant. They withdrew from their main settlements and established themselves in a single well-fortified town. Caesar assaulted this position, but the Romans were repelled and kept back for many days. The soldiers therefore began constructing siege engines. The Aduatuci gazed at their work, observing the Romans cutting wood and carefully constructing machines. They could not comprehend what was occurring and scoffed at the Roman efforts. Then heavy-armed soldiers climbed aboard these constructions (siege towers and battering rams) and the machines were advanced upon the enemy position. The Aduatuci became panic-stricken at this unfamiliar sight. They made gestures of surrender and prepared to offer provisions to the approaching soldiers. Some of the warriors cast their weapons down from the walls. The Romans climbed down from their machines and began to stand idly by as though they had won a victory (while surrender terms were negotiated). But by nightfall the Aduatuci had recovered their courage and they made a sortie out of their settlement. They planned to surprise and slaughter the Romans in the darkness. Caesar was managing their surrender, but he had prepared for this possibility. The Aduatuci attacked the Roman outposts from every side, but they were driven back. None of the surviving Aduatuci were permitted any pardon after this action (the betrayal of a truce). All the captives were immediately sold (into slavery).

Claudius Ptolemy's map (AD 150).

Claudius Ptolemy's map of Germania (AD 150).

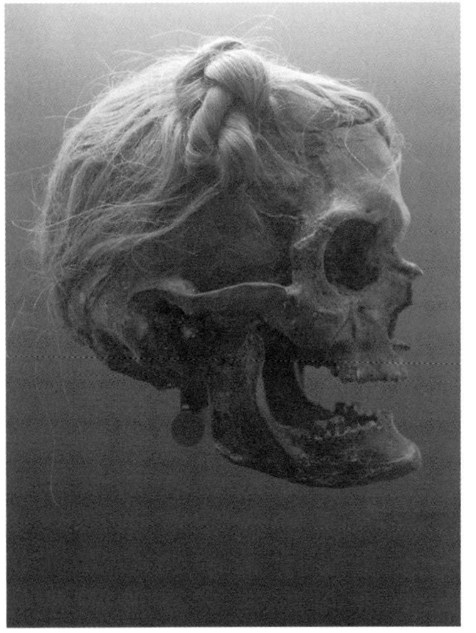

Skull of the Osterby bog body with a Suebian knot.

Roman pottery mask depicting a Germanic warrior (the 'Batavian' Mask, British Museum).

Left: Bronze figurine of a German depicted as a supplicant or praying (Bibliotheque Nationale, France).

Right: Bronze Roman figure depicting a captured German with his hands bound behind his back.

Head of a Suebic German depicted on the Czarnówko Cauldron. Bronze Roman cauldron discovered in a Germanic grave (AD 200).

Silver coins of the Emperor Augustus

Germanic Surrender (12 BC).

Denarius depicting a German presenting his child as a hostage to the Emperor Augustus (9 BC).

Silver coins of the Emperor Caligula honouring his father, Germanicus (AD 41–45)

Reverse of denarius coin: Triumphal Arch of Drusus Germanicus. The statue on the arch is positioned between trophies, each depicted with a bound captive at its base. Latin: *Devictus Germanis* (*DE GERM*) 'Conquered the Germans'.

Reverse: Victory Arch of Drusus Germanicus 'Imperator' (Supreme Commander).

Reverse: victory image formed from war trophies. Two Germanic shields, two pairs of spears, two war trumpets, and a *vexillum* (Roman military banner). Text: *DE GERMANIS*.

Lower part of the Gemma Augustea, a Roman cameo cut from onyx. The scene depicts the raising of a *tropaion* (victory monument fashioned from war trophies). Bound male and female figures are captured Celts or Germans.

Gilded silver roundel from a Roman military standard. The victorious general is Germanicus, or the future Emperor Tiberius, standing triumphant on a mound of Germanic captives, weapons and war trumpets.

Silver Roman skyphos (two-handled wine cup) possibly depicting the imperial prince, Tiberius, during his triumph of 8 BC. He carries an eagle-headed ivory sceptre and a laurel branch.

Roman silver drinking cup depicting Augustus and Drusus. The enthroned Augustus receives defeated barbarian chieftains offering their children as political hostages.

Roman silver drinking cup depicting King Priam of Troy appealing to Achilles for the return of his son Hector's body. Found in a Germanic chieftain's grave at Hoby, Denmark (first century BC). The Greek champion Achilles is depicted as Augustus and the cup was possibly a diplomatic gift.

Life-size Roman bronze statue of Germanicus discovered at Amelia, Italy. Germanicus died in AD 19, but the statue dates to about AD 40 (the reign of the Emperor Caligula). The breastplate depicts the Greek hero Achilles attacking Troilus, the youngest son of King Priam, outside the walls of Troy.

Marble Roman bust of a young German ('Arminius', in the Capitoline Museum in Rome).

Marble Roman statue depicting a Germanic woman, perhaps a personification of the country (Rome, second century AD) ('Thusnelda', currently installed at the Loggia dei Lanzi, Florence).

Cenotaph of Centurion Marcus Caelius. Killed by Germanic warriors during the Teutoburg massacre (AD 9). Monument from Xanten.

Silver Roman faceplate found at the Teutoburg Forest battle site.

Roman cavalry mask discovered at Hellvi, Gotland, Sweden. The eyes have been infilled, but one was damaged, perhaps to represent the Germanic god Oden.

Chapter Three

War Against the Usipetes and Tencteri (55 BC)

In 55 BC, Julius Caesar came into conflict with other German tribes who had crossed into Gaul. These population movements were caused by the Suebi expanding their territorial power in central Germania.

Power of the Suebi

111 Julius Caesar, *Gallic War*, 4.1

The Suebi are by far the largest and the most warlike Germanic nation. They are said to possess 100 districts and every year each one of these territories sends 1,000 men with weapons to participate in their wars (potentially 100,000 warriors). The kinsmen who remain at home maintain their own households and provide (sustenance) for their comrades absent on expeditions. The following year they themselves will take up arms to fight, while their returning comrades remain at home (managing communal resources and producing food). Consequently, their herds are not neglected while their skill and practice in war are continually maintained.

The Ubii are Threatened

112 Julius Caesar, *Gallic War*, 4.3

On the other side of their territory the Suebi border on the Ubii, whose state was once large and thriving. Compared to the other Germans, the Ubii are more sophisticated because they border the Rhine and are visited more frequently by merchants. They are also more accustomed to the manners of the Gauls, due to their proximity to these neighbouring peoples. In several wars, the Suebi made frequent attempts to expel the Ubii from the Rhineland, but were prevented due to their great population size and territorial extent. Nevertheless, they were able to make the Ubii tributary (taking regular payments of wealth and materials from them). This greatly reduced the reputation and power of the Ubii.

The Usipetes and Tencteri enter Gaul

113 Julius Caesar, *Gallic War*, 4.4

The Usipetes and the Tencteri were forced into the same condition by the Suebi (threat and oppression). For many years they resisted the power of the Suebi until they were finally driven from their territories. After traversing many parts of Germany, they came to the Rhine regions inhabited by the Menapii (Celts) who possessed territories, dwellings, and villages on either side of the river. But when this great multitude of Germans approached, the Menapii became alarmed and transferred their possessions and populations to the other side of the river. They then positioned guard forces on the Rhine to prevent the Germans from crossing.

The Germans tried every method to cross the Rhine, but they did not have sufficient river craft to cross in force. Attempts to cross by stealth were prevented by the armed guards of the Menapii. The Germans therefore pretended to leave the district and return to their own settlements and territories. The Menapii were informed by their scouts that the Germans had departed and without any concern, they returned to their villages beyond the Rhine. However, the Germans had merely moved three days' trek from the river. The German cavalry suddenly returned by undertaking the entire three-day journey in a single night. The returning Menapii were surrounded and slain and their river craft were seized. The Germans crossed the river before the Menapii on the far side of the Rhine were aware that they were under attack. The Germans approached their peaceful settlements, captured all their dwellings, and subsisted on their provisions during the rest of that winter.

114 Cassius Dio, *Roman History*, 39.47

The Romans had spent that winter in military camps established within friendly territory (the lands held by long-term Celtic allies). However, during this campaign season, the German tribes known as the Tencteri and Usipetes crossed the Rhine and invaded the country of the Treveri (a Celtic tribe centred on Trier). These Germans made the crossing because they were expelled from their homelands by the Suebi (a rival Germanic tribe), but they were also invited into the region by some of the Gauls (hoping to increase their manpower or political position).

The Romans Respond

Julius Caesar was still engaged in the conquest of Greater Gaul, when the Usipetes and Tencteri crossed the Rhine.

115 Julius Caesar, *Gallic War*, 4.1
The following winter (55 BC), Germanic peoples called the Usipetes and Tencteri crossed the Rhine River with a great number of men. They crossed the river close to where it empties into the sea. Their motive was that they had suffered attacks from the Suebi for several years. They were constantly involved in warfare, thereby prevented from engaging in essential farming.

116 Julius Caesar, *Gallic War*, 4.6
When Caesar learnt about this occurrence, he set out to join his army sooner than usual to avoid the development of a more serious war. Once he reached the army, Caesar realised that his fears had already happened. Several Gallic states sent embassies to the Germans, inviting them to leave the Rhine region and promising to provision them with everything they required. The Germans were encouraged by this prospect and roaming more widely, they entered the territory of the Eburones and Condrusi, who are dependants of the Treveri (a Celtic tribe). Caesar summoned the Gallic leaders, but decided to conceal what he had discovered. He calmed and reassured them, so that he could levy a force of (Gallic) cavalry to wage war against the Germans.

117 Julius Caesar, *Gallic War*, 4.7–9
Caesar provisioned his forces with grain and selected his cavalry. He marched directly towards the region in Gaul that the Germans were reported to have occupied (the west bank of the Rhine River). When he was only a few days' march from their location, he received official envoys from the Germans. They delivered this message:

> The Germans have not declared war on the Roman people, but we will not decline the opportunity to fight. If we are provoked, we will attack according to the ways of our forefathers. It is our custom to resist anyone who makes war upon us. We will not avert conflict by political appeals. We have been expelled from our country and it has not been our choice to come to this territory. If the Romans are inclined to accept our friendship, then we may be useful allies. Let the Romans assign us territories or permit us to retain the lands we have taken by force. Know

> that our tribe is inferior only to the Suebi. Not even the immortal gods are equal to our nation and there is nobody on earth we cannot conquer.

Caesar gave an appropriate reply, but ended his speech by stating that there could be no alliance between them if they remained in Gaul. It was not acceptable that men who had failed to protect their own territory should be occupying the land of another people. There was no land in Gaul available for distribution (to the Germans) without doing some injustice (to the current occupants). Besides, their people were simply too numerous to be placed in these lands. Nevertheless, if they wished they might settle in the territory of the Ubii (on the east bank of the Rhine). Envoys from the Ubii were currently with Caesar complaining of outrages done by the Suebi and requesting his help. He could issue the Ubii with orders to fulfil this scheme (and settle their land with new military allies).

The envoys said that they would report back to their own people and after considering the matter they would return to Caesar in three days. Meanwhile, they asked him not to move his military camp any closer to their position. Caesar replied that he was unable to grant this request. He had learnt that several days previously the Germans had sent a large division of cavalry across the Meuse River. This force was currently looting and foraging for grain in the territory of the Ambivariti (a nearby Gallic tribe). Caesar suspected that the Germans were proposing a delay because they were awaiting the return of this cavalry force.

118 Julius Caesar, *Gallic War*, 4.11

When Caesar approached within 12 miles of the enemy, the envoys returned to him as had been agreed. They met him as he was marching and urgently requested him not to advance any further. When they failed to attain this objective, they asked him to send orders ahead to the Roman cavalry who were proceeding in front of the main column. They insisted that the cavalry should be ordered not to engage with their forces. Meanwhile, they sought permission to send an envoy to the Ubii (suggesting they might relocate to the east bank of the Rhine). They announced that their envoy was seeking the sworn support of the Roman Senate and leading citizens of the Ubii. They were prepared to accept the terms Caesar was offering and only asked for an interval of three days in which to accomplish these aims.

Caesar thought that all these suggestions had the same purpose – a delay of three days to allow their absent cavalry to return. Even so, he announced that he would advance only 4 miles further that day to secure a water source. He instructed the Germans to assemble there in full strength on the following day, so that he could receive their requests. Meanwhile, he sent messengers to the prefects who had gone ahead with the entire Roman cavalry force. He ordered them not to provoke the enemy into fighting, and if they were themselves provoked, to withstand any assault until he reached them with the army.

The Roman Cavalry are Attacked

119 Julius Caesar, *Gallic War*, 4.11–12

The cavalry officers were not concerned as the Romans had 5,000 cavalry, compared with an enemy force numbering less than 800 horsemen. This was because many Germanic horsemen had crossed the Meuse River on a long-range foraging expedition and had not yet returned to their new territories. Furthermore, the Germanic envoys who had just left Caesar had requested a period of truce.

Nevertheless, the Germans immediately attacked the Roman cavalry, causing disorder in the forces. When the Romans stood firm, the German horsemen leaped from their mounts and attacked as infantry. They stabbed our horses in the belly, bringing down a great many of our cavalrymen. The Roman forces fled in such alarm that they did not halt the retreat until they reached our main army. In this encounter seventy-four Roman cavalrymen were killed.

Alternative Accounts

120 Plutarch, *Julius Caesar*, 22

When Julius Caesar returned to his forces in Gaul (in 55 BC), he discovered that a considerable war was occurring in the country. Two great German nations had just crossed the Rhine to seize the land. One of these nations was called the Usipetes, the other the Tencteri. Caesar fought against them both and described this in his *Commentaries* (*The Gallic Wars*). He says that the barbarians attacked the Romans while they were under a truce and engaged in a march (advancing). The Romans were not prepared for combat and with just 800 horsemen the Germans managed to rout Caesar's 5,000 cavalry.

121 Cassius Dio, *Roman History*, 39.47

When the German intruders learned that Caesar was in the region, they became alarmed and sent messages to him requesting a truce. They asked for lands to settle in Gaul, or at least permission to retain whatever they could seize (Roman non-intervention). When no terms were given, the Germans assured Caesar that they would soon return to their homelands (territories east of the Rhine). They therefore requested an armistice (continued non-aggression). This was honoured until a few Roman horsemen encountered a group of young German warriors. The Germans immediately treated them with contempt, as they had different opinions on the prospects of a fight. They halted the small Roman detachment, who were not expecting any interference or abuse, and began to harass them. Elated by this success, the German masses prepared for war with Rome. The German leaders resisted the move towards war and some of their senior men approached Caesar requesting a pardon for their actions. They claimed that the offence had been committed by only a small number of warriors. Caesar detained these German envoys with the assurance that he would soon give them his answer. Then he advanced with his army towards the main German encampment.

Political Opposition

There was political opposition to Caesar in the Roman Senate and concern that he was accruing too much military power. He had attacked Ariovistus, a former ally, and was now leading Roman forces into conflict with another foreign nation. But the attack by the German cavalry justified military retaliation.

122 Appian, *Gallic War*, 4.24 (from Constantine Porphyrogenitus, *The Embassies*)
One writer records that Cato (the Younger) proposed in the Roman Senate that Julius Caesar should be surrendered to the barbarians for this bloodshed (on former allies), perpetrated during negotiations. But Caesar wrote in his own commentary that, when the Usipetes and Tencteri were ordered to go back to their former homelands, they replied that they had sent ambassadors to the Suebians who had expelled them (from Germania). They claimed they were waiting for an answer before acting. But while these negotiations were pending, 800 of their horsemen attacked the Roman cavalry with such unexpected suddenness that they were forced to flee. The Germans sent another envoy to explain this violation of good faith, but Caesar suspected a similar deception and attacked before giving his answer.

The Romans Attack the German Camp

123 Julius Caesar, *Gallic War*, 4.13–15

The following morning, a large group of Germans consisting of royal chiefs and elderly men approached the Roman camp. They came with the same deceitfulness and subterfuge that they had previously practised. They said they wanted to explain the skirmish that had occurred the day before and exonerate themselves from any blame. The Germans said the engagement was contrary to what they had previously agreed and contrary to what they themselves had requested. They also sought to deceive Caesar by asking how they could obtain a further truce. But Caesar rejoiced that they had fallen into his power and ordered the group to be immediately detained. He then assembled his army outside the military camp, but ordered the cavalry to follow at the rear because he thought they had been intimidated by the recent skirmish.

Caesar divided the Roman army into three marching columns. They marched 8 miles in a short time and reached the enemy camp before the Germans could understand what was occurring. Alarmed by the speed of the arrival and the absence of their own leaders, the Germans did not have sufficient time to arm themselves or organise countermeasures. They were immediately confused. They could not decide whether to lead their forces out against the Romans, or to defend their camp, or to flee to safety somewhere else. Their dismay was evident from the tumultuous noise emerging from their camp.

Roman soldiers, agitated by the treachery of the preceding day, rushed into the enemy camp. Those Germans who were able to arm themselves resisted our men for a short time, fighting among their carts and baggage wagons. Since the Germans had left their homeland and crossed the Rhine with their entire families, the camp included infants and women. So, these people began to scatter and flee in every direction. Caesar therefore sent the cavalry to pursue them. When the German fighters heard the noise to their rear, they realised that their families were being slaughtered. They cast down their weapons and abandoned their battle standards. They fled out of the camp in the direction of the nearby river where the Meuse and the Rhine converge. A great many of the Germans were killed and those that reached the river threw themselves into the current as they despaired of any other escape. Overcome by panic, fatigue, and the turbulence of the river, they drowned.

The Romans were now alarmed by the prospect of a great a war, for it was reported that these Germans possessed a nation of 430,000 people.

But they returned safely to their own military camp with only a few men suffering serious wounds. Caesar had detained some of the surrendered Germans in the enemy camp and now offered these survivors the freedom to depart. But they dreaded revenge and torture from the Gauls whose lands they had attacked, so they expressed a desire to remain with the Romans. Caesar granted them this permission.

Slaughter

124 Cassius Dio, *Roman History*, 39.47–48
The Germans were not expecting any hostile move against them, especially as their senior men had recently gone to discuss terms with Caesar. They were living in tents and were taking their noonday rest when the Roman army approached. There were vast numbers of infantry warriors within the German encampment, but they did not have time to pick up their weapons. The Romans advanced and slaughtered them amid their wagons. Their women and children were shamefully scattered about the camp during the attack (this was an encampment formed from family groups – not a regimented military base).

Scale of Conflict

Caesar's figure of 430,000 'Germans' might have been an assessment of total Germanic manpower (Greater Germania from the Rhine to the Elbe). However, later writers took this estimate as a figure for the Usipetes and Tencteri.

125 Appian, *Gallic War*, 4.24a (from Constantine Porphyrogenitus, *The Embassies*)
It is believed that the German tribes, the Usipetes and the Tencteri, attacked the Romans with 800 horsemen and put to flight about 5,000 of Caesar's cavalry (55 BC). When they sent ambassadors to the Romans, Caesar took these men prisoner and made an immediate attack on these German tribes. They were so completely taken by surprise that 400,000 of the Germans were slaughtered.

126 Appian, *Gallic War*, 4.24b
The Germans attacked unexpectedly with a force of 500 Sugambri horsemen and forced 5,000 of Caesar's cavalry to flee. They subsequently paid the penalty for this action in their defeat. Caesar slaughtered 400,000 of the Usipetes and Tencteri, both armed and unarmed people.

127 Orosius, *History*, 6.8

Meanwhile, Caesar attacked the Germans who had crossed the Rhine in vast numbers and were about to bring all of Gaul under their control. These Germans are reported to have migrated with a population of 440,000, but Caesar eradicated almost all of them.

128 Plutarch, *Julius Caesar*, 22

Then the Germans sent envoys to Caesar, trying to deceive him a second time (a false truce). But Caesar thought it foolish to trust men who could not keep terms and pledges, so he detained the envoys and led his army against the barbarians (gaining a Roman victory).

Tanusius says that when the Senate voted sacrifices and public celebrations for the victory, Cato (a political enemy of Caesar) offered his pronouncement. He declared that Caesar should be delivered to the barbarians, for he had violated a sacred truce made in the name of Rome (the Germans had been allies). Delivering Caesar (for punishment) would purge the sacred violation and turn the curse onto one guilty man (the divine punishment incurred for harming a people who had not been formally declared enemies).

Among the Germans who had crossed the Rhine and entered Gaul, about 400,000 were slaughtered. The few who managed to make the journey back were received by a German nation called the Sugambri. This gave Caesar a cause for hostilities against the Sugambri.

Prospects for a Further Campaign

129 Cassius Dio, *Roman History*, 39.48

The German cavalry were not in the camp at the time and when they learned about the massacre they set out for their homelands (territories east of the Rhine). They crossed over and found refuge with the Sugambri (a tribe in north Germany).

Caesar sent messages to the fugitive Germans. He demanded their immediate surrender, but he did not expect any compliance. This is because the Germans beyond the Rhine are not afraid of the Romans, or inclined to follow their dictates. Caesar was therefore making these demands so that he would have an excuse to launch a campaign across the river. He was anxious to achieve something that none of his predecessors had ever accomplished. He could keep the (Germans) out of Gaul by invading their homelands.

As expected, the Sugambri did not surrender the horsemen. Meanwhile, the Ubii (a Germanic tribe) who lived in neighbouring territories and were hostile to the Sugambri, asked for Roman assistance. Caesar therefore constructed a bridge and crossed the Rhine.

Chapter Four

Caesar Campaigns across the Rhine (55–53 BC)

In 55 BC, after defeating the Usipetes and Tencteri, Julius Caesar led his legions across the Rhine.

130 Florus, *Roman History*, 1.45

It was not acceptable for German territories to offer refuge and protection to an enemy of Rome. Caesar therefore launched an attack across the Rhine.

131 Julius Caesar, *Gallic War*, 4.16

With the Germanic war (in Gaul) completed, Caesar thought it necessary to cross the Rhine. There were many reasons, but the most serious was that the Germans had found it easy to enter Gaul. Caesar therefore decided that the Germans should now become concerned about their own territories. He would achieve this by demonstrating that the Roman army could cross the Rhine and operate in Germany. His decision was also influenced by the knowledge that a large cavalry force belonging to the Usipetes and Tencteri had not been present at the recent military engagement. These horsemen had crossed the Meuse River to procure forage and plunder, so they had not been defeated alongside their kinsmen. Learning of these events (the Roman victory), they had recrossed the Rhine to enter the territory of the Sugambri (another Germanic tribe). They united with these Sugambri to pursue their cause.

Caesar sent ambassadors to the Sugambri demanding that they should surrender those who had made war against the Romans in Gaul. They replied:

> The Rhine is the boundary of the Empire held by the Romans. Did Caesar think it was unjust for the Germans to cross this boundary without his consent? Then he should not claim anything beyond it. Nothing beyond this boundary is subject to Roman dominion or power.

The Ubii was the only nation beyond the Rhine that had sent ambassadors to Caesar. They had formed an alliance with Rome and given over political hostages. Now they earnestly requested his assistance. They asked:

> that Caesar brings them military support because they are seriously threatened by the Suebi (the largest Germanic nation). Due to the politics of the Roman state, if Caesar can not intervene, then he should at least transport his army over the Rhine. This incursion would be sufficient to safeguard the Ubii and provide them with the prospect of further intervention. After the defeat of Ariovistus (the German war leader) at his last battle (on the Rhine) the fame and reputation of Caesar's army had become known to the most remote of the Germanic nations. If Caesar made the crossing, the Ubii could therefore feel secure under the fame and friendship of the Roman people.

For this purpose, the Ubii promised to provide the Romans with many ships for the river crossing.

Bridge over the Rhine

132 Julius Caesar, *Gallic War*, 4.17–18

Caesar resolved to cross the Rhine for the reasons stated, but he thought it was unsafe to cross using the borrowed native craft. Also he did not think this practice was consistent with his own military honour, or suited the dignity of the Roman state. Consequently, he decided to construct a bridge over the Rhine. This was an extremely difficult project due to the breadth, speed, and depth of the river. He nonetheless thought that the project had to be attempted because the Roman army should not be conducted across the river with the help of foreign powers.

This was his plan for bridge construction. Two wooden piles were driven into the riverbed in sequential rows 2 feet apart. Each pile was a foot and a half thick, sharpened at the base and cut to a height proportionate to the depth of the river. Mechanical devices were used to sink these vertical timbers securely into the riverbed. These ramming devices (pile drivers) embedded the timbers so that they sloped slightly in the direction of the river current. Caesar oversaw the construction of a second line of wooden piles about 40 feet further downstream. These posts were constructed and embedded in the same manner, but orientated to lean against the force and current of the river. Both parallel lines of posts were reinforced by beams 2 feet thick driven between the timber piles. These wooden reinforcements braced the construction by fastening both sides together with perpendicular supports. This structure was immensely robust due to the strength of the materials and the arrangement of the supports. The weight and force of the river current pushed the bridge supports into a stronger and firmer configuration.

These two lines of support beams were joined together by a timber platform running the length of the bridge. The intervening expanse was reinforced by further interconnected beams to form a complete frame. Further wooden piles were driven into the riverbed on either side of the bridge. These posts were positioned at an oblique angle to act as buttresses, reinforcing the structure against the flow of the stream.

Caesar was concerned that the barbarians might try to demolish the bridge by floating heavy tree trunks down the river, or sending craft downstream against it. Further beams were therefore sunk into the riverbed some distance upstream from the bridge. These defences would deflect and diminish any such attacks. The entire project was completed just ten days after timber began to be collected for the construction. Then Caesar led his entire army over the Rhine.

133 Plutarch, *Julius Caesar*, 22–23

Caesar desired further fame by being the first Roman to cross the Rhine with an army. He therefore began to bridge the river, though it was very broad, deep, turbulent and its currents inconsistent. Furthermore, the trunks and branches of trees carried downstream by the currents kept impacting and dislodging the supports of any bridge. Caesar ordered bulwarks made of great timbers to be fixed across the stream to break up and control the fierce currents. This bridge was truly a formidable sight, yet it was completed in just ten days.

Caesar enters Germania

134 Julius Caesar, *Gallic War*, 4.18–19

Caesar left a strong guard of soldiers at each end of the bridge he had constructed over the Rhine. He then advanced quickly into the territory of the Sugambri (a powerful Germanic tribe). While this occurred, he received envoys from several Germanic nations who requested peace and alliance with the Romans. Caesar responded in a considerate manner and instructed these people to provide him with political hostages. But the Sugambri were not among these tribes.

The Sugambri were preparing to flee their territories when the Romans began building their bridge. This tactic was on the advice of the Tencteri and Usipetes, who had been accepted into the Sugambri nation. Consequently, when the Romans approached the territory of the Sugambri, they realised that the land was abandoned. The enemy had departed with all their possessions and concealed themselves in forests and other wilderness regions. Caesar remained in their territories for a few days. He burnt all their villages and dwellings and cut down their entire grain crop.

Caesar then marched his forces to the territories of the Ubii (an allied Germanic tribe). He promised them his assistance if they were ever attacked by the Suebi (the dominant Germanic nation). He also learnt the following information from them.

The Suebi had been informed by their scouts that the Romans were building a bridge across the Rhine. They had held a council according to their custom and sent orders to all parts of their territory. The people were instructed to evacuate their settlements and transfer all the women and children into the woodlands, along with their possessions. All the men capable of wielding weapons were then to assemble in a single location. The chosen location was close to the centre of the territories held by the Suebi. The men had resolved to meet the approaching Roman army in this place and engage them in battle.

When Caesar learnt of these events, he reviewed his decisions. He had already achieved all the objectives he had crossed the Rhine to accomplish. His actions had struck fear into the Germans; he had taken vengeance on the Sugambri; he had also freed the Ubii from the immediate threat of invasion by the Suebi. In total, the Roman army had spent eighteen days operating beyond the Rhine. Caesar therefore thought that he had advanced far enough to serve both the honour and interests of Rome. He therefore returned into Gaul and demolished the bridge he had constructed over the Rhine.

Later Assessments

135 Florus, *Roman History*, 1.45

The Tencteri (a Germanic tribe on the Rhine frontier) brought further complaints to Caesar regarding other Germans (the powerful Suebic tribe living east of the Rhine). On this occasion Caesar took the initiative and crossed the Moselle (a tributary of the Rhine) using a bridge of boats. He headed towards the enemy and the Hercynian Forest (in central Germany).

The appearance of a Roman army on the far banks of the Rhine caused great panic and the entire (Suebic) population fled into marshes and woodlands.

136 Orosius, *History*, 6.9
After constructing a bridge, Caesar crossed into Germany and saved the Sugambri and Ubii (allied Germanic tribes) from a siege of their territories (by the Suebi). His arrival brought terror to the entire country and especially intimidated the Suebi, who were the largest and fiercest German tribe. According to information confirmed by many people, the Suebi possessed 100 cantons and districts (large territorial units). Caesar then destroyed the bridge over the Rhine and withdrew back to Gaul.

137 Cassius Dio, *Roman History*, 39.48
The Romans advanced into Germany, but discovered that the Sugambri had withdrawn to their strongholds and the Suebi were gathering to assist them (a more powerful tribe). Within twenty days Caesar had therefore withdrawn from the region.

138 Plutarch, *Julius Caesar*, 23
Caesar conveyed his forces across the river. No one ventured to oppose him, not even the Suebi, who were the foremost nation of the Germans. Instead, their population retreated into the deep forests with all their belongings.

Caesar therefore ravaged their country with fire (he burnt the abandoned dwellings). He gave encouragement to the firm friends of Rome (allied tribes), then having spent just eighteen days in Germany, he withdrew into Gaul. His next expedition was against the Britons, and this too was celebrated for its risk and ambition. Caesar was the first Roman to launch a fleet into the Atlantic Ocean, and cross the western sea with an army to wage his war.

Further Unrest in Gaul with Germanic Threat (winter 54 BC)

In 55 and 54 BC, Julius Caesar conducted military operations in southern Britain to subdue the tribes facing Gaul. His absence encouraged Celtic revolts in north-east Gaul and this threatened Roman supremacy.

139 Florus, *Roman History*, 1.45
Indutiomarus incited the Treveri (a Belgic population) to war and Ambiorix led the Eburones (a Gaulish-Germanic tribe). While Caesar was absent

from Gaul, these two tribes banded together and attacked his lieutenant general in the region. Dolabella (a Roman commander) bravely repulsed an attack by Indutiomarus and brought his severed head back to the military camp. But Ambiorix defeated the Romans with an ambush set up in a valley. Afterwards he plundered and killed forces led by the lieutenant generals Aurunculeius Cotta and Titurius Sabinus. No immediate vengeance would be taken upon this king (Ambiorix) as he evaded the Romans by passing back and forth across the Rhine (crossing between Gaul and Germany).

140 Julius Caesar, *Gallic War*, 5.55

During that winter, Indutiomarus (leader of) the Treveri (a Belgic tribe) sent envoys across the Rhine, promising large sums of money to the Germanic states (for their military support). They claimed that a great part of the Roman army had been slain and only a small force remained. But none of the German tribes could be persuaded to cross the Rhine. The Germans said that they had made the attempt twice, once in the war of Ariovistus, and then in the crossing of the Tencteri (both defeats). So, they would not test their fortune with a further attempt.

141 Julius Caesar, *Gallic War*, 6.2

After Indutiomarus was slain, the Treveri gave the chief command to one of his immediate kin (royal relatives). They continued their attempt to gain support from the neighbouring Germanic tribes by offering them payments. When the closest Germans refused, they tried more distant states until they finally found tribes who would support their cause. These Germans gave oaths to confirm their alliance and sent political hostages to secure the payments (the hostages guaranteed the good behaviour of the mercenary forces).

When Caesar received reports of these events, he realised that preparations for war were widespread. The Nervii, Aduatuci, and Menapii (Belgic tribes) had armed themselves along with all the Germans on this side of the Rhine (in Gaul). The Senones (a leading Gallic tribe) were also refusing his commands for assistance, as they were conspiring with the Carnutes and adjacent states (a full Gallic revolt). The Germans were now being induced (to enter this conflict) by frequent deputations of the Treveri.

Roman Fears (winter 54 BC)

In winter 54 BC, the Belgic chieftain Ambiorix surrounded a Roman military camp commanded by Quintus Tullius Cicero (the younger brother of the famous politician). The Roman garrison were led to believe that a large-scale Gallic rebellion was under way, supported by a vast number of Germanic mercenaries. They had to decide whether to remain in camp or withdraw from the region.

142 Julius Caesar, *Gallic War*, 5.27; 28–29; 41

(It was claimed) that a vast company of Germans had been hired (by the Gauls). This force had crossed the Rhine and would arrive in two days. (…)

Lucius Aurunculeius (a Roman officer) wanted to demonstrate that even vast numbers of Germans could be withstood and repelled by a series of well-entrenched territorial garrisons. They had already shown this by bravely withstanding the first charge of the enemy and inflicting many wounds on their attackers. (…)

Titurius argued against this view, saying that once larger numbers of the enemy arrived with German reinforcements, they would lose their opportunity to withdraw. Other disasters could be expected as the Roman garrisons in adjoining territories were overwhelmed. (…) The Rhine was close; the Germans were angered by Roman victories and aggrieved at the death of Ariovistus (circumstances of death unknown). The Gauls were insulted by the loss of their warrior renown, and incensed by Roman subjugation. Ambiorix must be acting with the certainty of success. (Titurius argued that) his plan (to withdraw) guaranteed their safety. For if there was no serious uprising, then they could reach the next legionary base without danger. But if the whole of Gaul was hostile and had formed a union with the Germans, then their only chance of safety required rapid action (immediate retreat). (…)

The leaders and chiefs of the Nervii (a Belgic tribe) claimed continued friendship with the Romans and were therefore admitted to talks with Cicero. They repeated the same arguments which Ambiorix had used against Titurius (urging the garrison to immediately withdraw from Belgic territory). The Nervii said that the Gauls were armed for war, the Germans had already crossed the Rhine; and the winter bases established by Caesar were being attacked.

German Warriors assist Gallic Rebels

143 Julius Caesar, *Gallic War*, 6.7–9

While Caesar was occupied, the Treveri (a Celtic tribe) collected a large force of infantry and cavalry. They prepared to attack Labienus with the one legion which had wintered within their territories (northern Gaul).

They were two days' march from his position when they learnt that two further legions sent by Caesar had arrived. So, the Treveri pitched their camp 15 miles from the Roman force and awaited the arrival of their German auxiliaries. (...)

The Treveri could not sustain their assault, and after the first charge they were routed and fled to the nearest woods. Labienus pursued them with his cavalry, slew a great number and seized many prisoners. A few days later he received the allegiance of the entire tribal state (surrendering to Roman power). This was expected, since the Germans who were coming to assist the Treveri had returned home when they heard of the rout. The kinsfolk of Indutiomarus, who had begun the revolt, followed him out of the territory (leaving Treveri territory for Germany). The position of chief was given to Cingetorix, who had remained loyal (to Roman interests) from the beginning. Meanwhile, Caesar crossed with his army from the territory of the Menapii into the lands of the Treveri (in north-east Gaul).

Alternative Account of Military Action by Labienus

144 Cassius Dio, *Roman History*, 40.31

In this period Gaul had become disturbed (by revolts), but Caesar restored order through warfare. Caesar and his lieutenants undertook many exploits, but I will describe only the most important incidents.

Ambiorix joined the cause of the Treveri tribe who were still angry after the death of Indutiomarus (their chief killed in battle). They formed a joint rebellion in this region (north-west Gaul) and sent for a mercenary force from the Germans (on the far side of the Rhine).

(The Roman commander) Labienus wanted to engage the enemy in battle before the German recruits could arrive, so, he invaded Treveri territory. The Treveri did not defend themselves immediately because they were waiting for reinforcements. They crossed a river to place a barrier between themselves and the Roman army, and then they remained quiet. Labienus therefore assembled his soldiers and delivered a speech that was intended to alarm his own men and encourage the enemy. He declared that they must withdraw to Caesar and safety, before the Germans came to reinforce the Treveri. Then he immediately gave the signal to his troops to pack up their baggage and depart. But when he had begun the return march, the events that he had expected, and planned for, occurred.

Labienus had delivered the information in a public address, so that the enemy might believe that the Romans were genuinely afraid and were making a hasty retreat. His speech was reported to the barbarians, who carefully took notice of events in the Roman camp. The Treveri rapidly crossed the river as quickly as possible and eagerly advanced against the Romans. Labienus met their attack while they were still scattered and disordered. The Roman counterattack terrified the foremost Treveri fighters who fled and caused disorder in the rest of their army. The enemy fled in panic, falling over one another and crowding together on the riverbank. Consequently, Labienus was able to kill many of them.

Second Crossing into Germania (AD 53)

After Ceaser suppressed the uprising in north-east Gaul, he decided that further military action was required across the Rhine.

145 Julius Caesar, *Gallic War*, 6.9–10

Caesar decided to cross the Rhine for two reasons. One reason was that the German tribes had sent warriors to the Treveri to fight the Romans. Secondly, he wanted to prevent Ambiorix from any retreat into their territories (Ambiorix – a hostile leader of the Belgic tribes in north-east Gaul). Once Caesar had made this decision, he set about constructing a bridge close to the place where he had crossed before with his army. The plan was well known and definite (following previous experience) and the work was accomplished in a few days due to the eagerness of the soldiers. Caesar left a strong guard in the territory of the Treveri to prevent the outbreak of any sudden disturbances. Then he led the rest of his forces across the bridge with the cavalry.

The Ubii had previously surrendered and given hostages to the Romans. Now to remove any doubt, they sent deputies to Caesar confirming that they had not broken faith. They had not sent any fighters to the territory of the Treveri (in the recent conflict). They begged and prayed for Caesar to spare them. Even if the Romans had developed a general hatred of the Germans, they should not be punished alongside the guilty. If Caesar wanted more hostages, then the Ubii promised to provide them. Caesar heard their case and ascertained that the German fighters (who had recently entered Gaul) had been sent by the Suebi. He therefore accepted the pleas of the Ubii and inquired about possible lines of advance into Suebi territories.

Within a few days the Ubii informed Caesar that the Suebi were gathering all their military forces into one place. They were ordering all tribes under their dominion to send fighters, both infantry and horsemen.

When Caesar heard these reports, he made new provisions for grain supplies and selected a suitable location for the Roman camp.

Caesar commanded the Ubii to bring in all their cattle and gather all the produce from their fields to be safeguarded within native strongholds. He hoped that the lack of provisions might disadvantage the (incoming) German force, which was not disciplined or trained (an enemy that lacked logistical organisation). He also instructed the Ubii to send scouting parties into the territories of the Suebi to ascertain their movements.

The Ubii carried out his commands and reported their discoveries after only a few days. They said that the Suebi had received more definite accounts of the Roman army and decided to withdraw. They had gathered all their forces, families, and allies in the furthest reaches of their country. The Ubii said there was a forest of immense size in this territory called Bacenis. It extended a long way into the country and formed a natural barrier that kept the Cherusci from raiding the Suebi, and prevented the Suebi from conducting similar offences against the Cherusci. The Suebi had decided to await the coming of the Romans at the edge of this forest.

Outcome of Second Crossing (53 BC)

146 Julius Caesar, *Gallic War*, 6.29

Caesar learnt from his Ubii scouts that the Suebi had withdrawn into the forests. He therefore decided to halt his advance, fearing that there would be a scarcity of grain because the Germans neglect this form of agriculture (the Roman army would rapidly exhaust their supplies).

Caesar decided to sustain German fears that he would return and that he still could interrupt the future movement of their forces. So, after he had withdrawn his army, he destroyed only 200 feet of the bridge. This was the furthest section of the structure where it reached the banks of Ubii territory. At the other end of the bridge (in Gallic territory) he ordered the construction of a tower that was four storeys high and posted a garrison of 12 cohorts (600 troops) to protect the bridge. He strengthened the station with considerable fortifications.

Overview and Assessment

147 Florus, *Roman History*, 1.45

This was not the only occasion on which Caesar crossed the Rhine. He entered Germany a second time using a bridge which he had constructed for this purpose. The alarm of the enemy was far greater on this occasion since this (more permanent) bridge seemed to be a yoke which made the river a Roman captive (like a beast harnessed for labour). Once again, the Germans fled into their woods and marshes rather than engage the Roman army. Caesar was bitterly disappointed, as no enemy remained in place to be conquered.

148 Cassius Dio, *Roman History*, 40.32

When many of the enemy escaped, Caesar took no further interest in them. His attention was instead focused on Ambiorix, since he kept moving to new locations and causing further harm to the Romans. The pursuit of Ambiorix caused Caesar a great deal of trouble and he was unable to catch him. He therefore launched an expedition against the Germans, alleging that they had wanted to help the Treveri. But he could not accomplish anything significant and was forced to rapidly withdraw. This was through fear of the Suebi (a large tribe in Central Germany).

Caesar enhanced his reputation by crossing the Rhine a second time. On this occasion he only destroyed parts of the bridge closest to the barbarians (the connection with the east bank). He also constructed a guardhouse on the remaining structure, as though he might return at any time and cross the river.

Caesar invites Germans to Plunder Rebel Territory in Gaul (53 BC)

Julius Caesar permitted the Germans to plunder the territory of the defeated Eburones.

149 Cassius Dio, *Roman History*, 40.32

Caesar was still angry at the successful escape of Ambiorix, so he permitted his (Belgic) homelands to be attacked and plundered by anyone who wished (rival Celtic tribes). The region had not been guilty of any revolt, but Caesar wanted to harm the chieftain. He publicly announced his decision in advance, so that numerous (native) warriors might assemble for the attack. Many Gauls and Sugambri (Germans east of the Rhine) assembled to plunder the land. However, the Sugambri were not satisfied with the spoils taken from Gallic territory and launched an attack on the Romans instead.

These Germans waited and watched until the Roman soldiers had left to seek provisions, then they attacked and tried to seize their camp. But the soldiers realised what was occurring and returned to rescue their comrades and kill many of the enemy. Afterwards the Sugambri became afraid of reprisals by Caesar and hurriedly withdrew back to their homelands. However, Caesar inflicted no punishment upon them, since winter was approaching, and Rome itself was in political turmoil. He dismissed his soldiers to their winter quarters and then went in person to Italy. He claimed that he needed to be in Rome to arrange the affairs of Cisalpine Gaul, but his real intention was to closely observe the events that were taking place in the capital.

Mounted Germanic Raiders (53 BC)

150 Julius Caesar, *Gallic War*, 6.35–37; 41

Reports reached the Germans on the far side of the Rhine that the Eburones (a Belgic tribe) were being pillaged and all (surrounding peoples) were invited to come and plunder their territory. The Sugambri, who live closest to the Rhine (on the east bank), selected 2,000 horsemen for this purpose. This was possible because they had accepted Tencteri and Usipetes (horsemen) who had fled (from Roman forces).

They crossed the river on boats and rafts, about 30 miles beyond the place where Caesar had built his bridge and stationed his garrison force. They intercepted and caught many Eburones who had scattered to flee their territory (after the Roman victory). The Germans also captured a great quantity of cattle which were highly sought after by the barbarians. They were tempted to advance further into Gaul as no distance or woodlands can halt these offspring of war and pillage.

The Germans asked their captives where Caesar was, and they learnt that the main Roman army had left the region. Then one of the captives said:

> Why are you pursuing such miserable and slender plunder, when you now have a chance to gain a far greater fortune? In three hours, you could reach Aduatuca, where the Roman army has concentrated all its stores. The garrison in that camp is so small that it cannot even man the wall and none of the soldiers dare to step outside their entrenchments.

The Germans seized this opportunity and stashing their plunder in a secret place, they headed for Aduatuca with the captive acting as a guide.

(Quintus Tullius) Cicero had been obeying Caesar's instructions for several days. He had carefully confined his troops to their military camp and not a single member of the support personnel had left the entrenchments.

But on the seventh day (...) he sent 5 cohorts (250 soldiers) to gather grain in the nearest fields. There was only a single hill between this foraging site and the military base. Other legionaries had been left at the camp due to illness, but they had now recovered enough to resume service. About 300 of these soldiers were therefore allowed to leave the fort. A large host of support staff also received permission to leave the encampment with a vast number of pack animals which had remained in the base (an opportunity to graze livestock).

By chance, the German horsemen arrived at the Roman encampment at this precise moment. There was a screen of woods on that side of the fort, so the riders were unaware of the Roman presence until they reached the perimeter. The traders encamped next to the ramparts did not have any opportunity to flee. Without halting their speed, the Germans immediately rode through the main gate of the Roman fort and burst into the inner military encampment. The surprised soldiers were not expecting any enemy assault. They were immediately thrown into confusion and the cohort on guard duty was scarcely able to withstand the first attack (possibly only 500 soldiers). The enemy then rushed around the perimeter of the camp searching for another entry. The Roman soldiers had difficulty defending the gates, but other entrances were impeded by the terrain or the camp entrenchments. There was confusion throughout the Roman camp as soldiers urgently asked one another what the cause of the sudden uproar was. But after the standards were raised (establishing unit formations) they did not know where their defensive actions should be directed.

Someone declared that the camp was already overrun, another insisted that the barbarians had arrived victorious from the destruction of the main army and its commander-in-chief (Caesar). The majority recalled superstitious beliefs regarding this place and remembered the disaster of Cotta and Titurius who had been killed in this same fort (a severe Roman defeat). These fears caused widespread panic, so the barbarians believed the reports of the captive that the Roman fort lacked a garrison (few soldiers appeared on the defences). The Germans decided to break through the perimeter, exhorting one another to seize this opportunity.

(...) when the Germans saw the Roman soldiers finally take position on the entrenchments, they despaired of storming the camp. They therefore retreated across the Rhine with the plunder they had deposited in the woods. But even after the enemy had departed, there was still great fear in the Roman camp. That night Gaius Volusenus reached the fort with the advance force of Roman cavalry, but he could not persuade the garrison that Caesar was really approaching, and his army was intact. Their minds were so filled with unreasoning terror that they assumed the Roman army was destroyed and only the cavalry forces had escaped the rout. They insisted that if the main army had been safe, the Germans would never have attacked their camp. This terror was only removed by the arrival of Caesar himself.

Germans in Roman Military Service (52–51 BC)

In 52 BC, the Gallic war leader Vercingetorix led a large-scale rebellion against Roman rule in Gaul. Caesar employed Germanic warriors in his military forces to defeat the rebels.

151 Cassius Dio, *Roman History*, 40.39

Meanwhile, due to Caesar's recent military failures, Vercingetorix (the Gallic war leader) felt increasing contempt for him. He therefore marched against the Allobroges (a Celtic tribe still loyal to Rome). While in the territory of the Sequani (another Celtic tribe), he managed to intercept the Roman general sent out to assist the Allobroges. The Roman force was entirely surrounded by the enemy, but it endured intact. They survived because retreat was impossible and there was no safety. The enemy had acted in an imprudent and careless manner due to their vast numbers.

Vercingetorix suffered a defeat in this engagement largely due to the presence of German warriors who were serving as allies in the Roman force. These Germans possessed mighty physiques and had an unstoppable enthusiasm for fighting. With strength and daring they broke through the Gallic ranks that encircled the Romans. After this good fortune, Caesar continued the conflict and besieged Alesia (Celtic oppidum settlement) where many of the enemy had fled for refuge.

Germanic Troops in Roman Service (52 BC)

152 Julius Caesar, *Gallic War*, 7.13

Caesar ordered the Roman cavalry to be brought out of camp to engage the enemy horsemen (Gauls). Then, when the Roman troops began to suffer in this combat, he sent 400 Germanic horsemen to reinforce them. It had become his practice to keep these Germans close to himself at the onset of any fighting (a rapid reaction force). The Gauls could not resist the Germanic charge and their cavalry suffered heavy losses as they fled back to their main army.

Revolt of Vercingetorix (52 BC)

153 Julius Caesar, *Gallic War*, 7.63; 65
The Treveri were absent from the (Gallic) war council because they were too distant from these events, and they were heavily endangered by the Germans. (…)

Caesar was aware that the enemy (Gauls) had a superior force of mounted troops. Also, since the lines of communication were now interrupted, he could not summon military assistance from the province (Gallia Narbonensis) or Italy. He therefore sent requests across the Rhine to Germany, asking the tribes that he had subdued in previous years for support. He asked for their cavalry and for infantry trained to fight alongside these horsemen. When they arrived he discovered that their horses were unsuitable for his purpose (horse breeds inferior to Gallic and Italian mounts). He therefore took the horses from the military tribunes, the *equites* (officer nobility) and the re-enlisted veterans. These mounts were then redistributed among the Germans.

The use of German Cavalry against the Gauls

154 Julius Caesar, *Gallic War*, 7.67
The next day the Gauls divided their cavalry into three divisions. Two of these divisions were deployed on the Roman flanks, while the third moved in front to obstruct their march. When Caesar realised what was occurring, he ordered the Roman cavalry to also form three divisions and charge the enemy simultaneously. Meanwhile, the main Roman force halted and the baggage trains were taken into the legionary ranks (for protection).

If the cavalry seemed to be in difficulty, or hard-pressed in any quarter, Caesar ordered the infantry to advance so that the army would move forwards in that direction. This deterred the enemy from pushing forwards in pursuit and encouraged the Roman cavalry to expect support.

Finally, the Germans (operating as Roman auxiliary cavalry) who were fighting on the right wing gained control on the top of the hill. They dislodged the Gallic cavalry from this position and pursued them as far as the river where Vercingetorix was stationed with his infantry forces.

During this pursuit, the Germans managed to kill a significant number of the enemy. When the rest of the Gallic cavalry saw what was occurring (on the right flank), they feared being surrounded. They fled the conflict and the Roman slaughter of the enemy took place in every direction. Three of the noblest of the Aedui were taken prisoner and brought before Caesar.

Roman Siege of Avaricum (major Gallic settlement)

155 Julius Caesar, *Gallic War*, 7.70

When the Romans were beginning the siegework, a cavalry encounter took place on a plain that extended across 3 miles up to a set of flanking hills (between the walled settlement and the Roman camp). Both sides engaged in a vigorous cavalry attack and when the Roman cavalry showed signs of being in difficulty, Caesar sent the Germans forwards (as rapid reinforcements). Then he positioned the legions in front of the Roman camp to counter any sudden charge by enemy infantry.

Due to the presence of the legions the Roman cavalry began to fight with greater confidence and the enemy started to flee. As they retreated through the narrow gates (of the defended settlement) the Gauls were hindered by their vast numbers and were crowded and crushed together in the effort. The Germans vigorously pursued them right up to the fortifications (the ditch, bank and palisades surrounding the stronghold). There was a great slaughter of the enemy and some of the Gauls abandoned their horses to cross the ditch and scale their own ramparts (to avoid the blocked gates).

Caesar ordered the legions posted in front of the ramparts to advance a short distance. The Gauls inside the fortifications fell into confusion, believing that a full Roman assault was imminent. They shouted the call to arms and there was panic in the settlement. Vercingetorix ordered the gates to be immediately shut in case the defenders tried to desert. After much slaughter and the capture of many horses, the Germans withdrew.

Gallic Attempt to Break the Roman Siege

156 Julius Caesar, *Gallic War*, 7.80

The combat occurred in full sight of everyone, so every deed that was noble or dishonourable was subject to full view (by Gauls on the settlement defences and Roman soldiers on the siegeworks). Both sides were incited to great courage in pursuit of praise, or fear of disgrace.

The fight was prolonged from noon almost to sunset. The outcome was uncertain until the Germans amassed their horsemen on one part of the battlefield to suddenly charge the enemy. The Gauls were routed, and their archers were surrounded and slain. Roman troops from other parts of the battlefield then pursued the retreating enemy right up to their own defences, giving them no chance to rally.

Failed Support for the Gauls

157 Julius Caesar, *Gallic War*, 8.7; 10

Caesar learnt that a few days earlier Commius the Atrebatian (a rebel leader) had left camp to gather support from Germans who were nearby in immense numbers. (…)

Commius now returned with some horsemen. He had a force of less than 500 cavalry, but the arrival of these Germans gave the Gauls some reassurance (prospect of further intervention).

Champion Contests during Siege

158 Julius Caesar, *Gallic War*, 8.13

There was no interruption to the daily combats which occurred in sight of both camps. These encounters usually took place at the fords of rivers and passages over the marsh. The fights involved the Germans that Caesar had brought over the Rhine to be intermingled with the cavalry.

On one occasion the Germans crossed the marsh in a large group. They attacked with great determination, slaying the few Gauls who stood their ground, then fiercely pursuing the retreating host. They caught some of the Gauls, engaging them in close-quarter fighting and wounding others at a longer range. A panic began which spread to the Gallic reserve force positioned some distance away. They were routed in a disgraceful manner, repeatedly abandoning favourable positions to escape back to their main camp. This sudden danger caused confusion amongst the whole enemy force.

Roman Ambitions are Frustrated (49 BC)

Julius Caesar addresses his soldiers in northern Italy before the outbreak of the Roman Civil War (49–44 BC).

159 Cassius Dio, *Roman History*, 41.30; 32

'Who is not outraged that those of us who bear the name "Roman" have to perform the deeds of Germans? Who will not grieve at the sight of Italy ravaged like Britain? It is an insult that we no longer exploit conquered Gauls. Instead, we devastate lands south of the Alps, as if we were hordes from Epirus (hostile Greeks), Carthaginians or Cimbri.

'We rightly give ourselves honours as the first Romans to cross the Rhine and traverse the ocean (entering Britain). But now we plunder our native land, which we once protected from the destruction of our enemies. We will receive blame instead of praise, insult in place of honour, loss instead of gain, and punishment instead of just rewards. (…)

'We have come here to assist and defend our outraged homeland. We would never have entered Italy as a hostile force if the homeland had not been in danger. For this action is forbidden by law. We should not have let our operations against the Germans and Britons go unfinished, for these regions should have been subjugated (added to the Empire).'

Germanic Troops in the Roman Civil Wars (49–45 BC)

Germanic forces remained in imperial service and fought for Julius Caesar in the Roman Civil Wars. In 49 BC, during the conflict in Spain, Julius Caesar guarded the river Ebro, to prevent supplies reaching his opponent Afranius. His army included Germanic troops who were confident at river crossings.

160 Caesar, *Civil War*, 1.83

Afranius deployed a double line consisting of five legions, with a third line including auxiliary cohorts. Caesar's battle line was also a threefold deployment, but the first line was held by four cohorts selected from each of his five legions. Next to them were the three reserve cohorts from three further legions. The archers and slingers were enclosed in the centre of this force, while cavalry protected the flanks. Both armies were in their battle array, but each commander kept to his purpose (campaign strategy).

Caesar did not want to engage in battle unless compelled to, and Afranius wanted to delay the defensive works being set up by his opponent (the blockade). The situation was therefore prolonged. This static battle array was maintained until sunset, when both sides finally withdrew to their own military camps.

The next day Caesar readied his forces to complete the defence works they had started. Meanwhile, the enemy approached a fording place on the river to see if a crossing was possible. When Caesar saw what was occurring, he ordered his light-armed Germanic troops and part of his cavalry to immediately cross the river and form defensive positions along the opposite banks.

Intervention in Egypt

In 48 BC, Caesar intervened in a royal dynastic conflict occurring in Ptolemaic Egypt. His forces included Germanic cavalry.

161 'Caesar' (Aulus Hirtius), *On the Alexandrine War*, 29

There was a narrow river with very high banks flowing into the Nile (a wide canal-like channel flanked by tall rampart-like sides). It blocked Caesar's path as he advanced his army towards the king's military camp (Ptolemy XIII). When the king learned that Caesar was using this route, he sent all his cavalry and a specially selected force of light-armed infantry, to prevent any crossing. These forces were ordered to engage Caesar at long range from the far banks (missile fire). This was an unfair engagement, since there was no opportunity for valour (for the Romans) and this action encouraged cowardice (caution and a military stalemate).

The enemy tactics enraged the Roman infantry and cavalry forces. They thought that this conflict against the Alexandrians could result in a permanent stalemate. But then, some scattered groups of German cavalry who were searching for places to ford the river, actually swam across the stream where the opposite banks were lower. Meanwhile, some of the legionaries managed to locate and fell some very tall trees. These trees were tall enough to connect both riverbanks (bridging the canal-like channel). The soldiers dropped the trees into place and quickly fashioned a causeway across the stream (using the trunks as supporting beams). The enemy were so terrified by the resulting attacks that they fled their positions. Almost all of them were killed and hardly any escaped back to their king.

German Unit changes Allegiance (Civil War, 44 BC)

162 Cassius Dio, *Roman History*, 46.37

Octavian gained authority over the German cavalry, along with the battle elephants, but these forces transferred their allegiance back to Mark Antony.

The Germans left the military encampment with the rest of the forces, but they roved ahead as if intending to engage any enemy that was advancing.

Then after a short distance they unexpectedly turned about and attacked the soldiers who were following, killing many of them.

Caesar as Dictator (44 BC)

Following his victory in the civil wars, Caesar planned the conquest of Germany (44 BC). The 'Expanded Empire' that might have been achieved through these conquests was depicted on Agrippa's World Map.

163 Plutarch, *Julius Caesar*, 58

Caesar's many accomplishments did not diminish his desire for new achievements and his great successes only fuelled his further ambitions. His passion for deeds and glory was constant, like a resource that was continually being consumed (such as fuel or food). When there was no one else to surpass, he sought to outdo his own past achievements, as if his earlier self were another rival to be outdone.

Caesar planned, then prepared, to lead a military campaign against the Parthian Empire (Iraq and Iran). After subduing them, he decided he would march around Hyrcania, the Caspian Sea, and the Caucasus, to invade Scythia by way of the Black Sea (circling the Pontic Steppe). Then he planned to seize the countries bordering Germania, then conquer Germany itself. Finally, on his route back to Italy, he would march through Gaul and so complete an entire circuit of his now expanded empire. His imagined enlargement of the Roman Empire would be bounded on all sides by the ocean.

Ambitions of Julius Caesar

Funeral Speech delivered by Mark Antony after the assassination of Caesar (44 BC).

164 Cassius Dio, *Roman History*, 44.42–43

'Before any of you knew that he was even at war, Caesar had conquered Gaul. He settled its political affairs so securely, that this region became a launching point for campaigns into Germany and Britain. Gaul is now enslaved to Rome, the very country that sent the Ambrones and the Cimbri against us (barbarian invasions of Italy). Gallic lands are now under the same forms of cultivation as Italy. Roman ships now sail, not just the Rhone and the Arar (the river Saône), but also the Mosa (Meuse), the Liger (Loire), and the Rhine, down to the ocean itself (North Sea).

'These were places that we had not even heard about, that we did not even know existed. But Ceaser conquered them for us. By his grand ambition and great determination, he made previously unknown places accessible and made unexplored regions traversable.

'But he provoked the jealousy of certain people (his political opponents) who also envied what you had obtained. And these people began a political uprising that forced him to return here to Rome before the proper time. For, if he had been allowed to continue his campaign, he would certainly have subdued all of Britain, together with the surrounding islands. Then he would have conquered all of Germany to the Arctic Ocean (Baltic Sea coasts). If so, the Romans would not have had territories and peoples at their boundaries (unconquered populations). Instead, their frontiers would have extended to the outer sea (Atlantic Ocean) and the open horizon.'

Chapter Five

Early Augustan Era (30–14 BC)

The Roman commander Octavian acquired supreme authority over the Empire in 30 BC. In 27 BC, he took the name Augustus and formally accepted the position of first emperor of Rome. During this period the Empire consolidated and expanded its European frontiers.

- **30 BC:** Romans defeat Bastarnae on the Danube frontier and resist German incursions across the Rhine.
- **25 BC:** Roman governor takes vengeance on Germans who kill traders crossing the frontier.
- **20 BC:** Roman commander Agrippa takes measures to halt German raids into Gaul.
- **16 BC:** Sugambri, Usipetes and Tencteri attack Gaul and defeat the Fifth Legion under the legate Marcus Lollius. Augustus prepares to lead the campaign.
- **14 BC:** Drusus the Elder receives military command in Gaul and begins construction of Rhine frontier forts.

Danube Region: The Romans subdue Moesia (30 BC)

In 30 BC, Roman forces defeated the Bastarnae, a Sythio-Germanic tribe who had crossed into Moesia, the Balkans south of the Danube.

165 Strabo, *Geography*, 7.3.17
Inland from the Black Sea (between the Dneiper River and the Carpathian Mountains) are the people of the Bastarnae. Their country shares a frontier with the Tyregetans and the Germans. They are therefore said to be part Germanic.

166 Cassius Dio, *Roman History*, 51.22–24
Octavian (Augustus) sent Marcus Crassus into Macedonia and Greece to conduct war against the Dacians and the Bastarnae. I have already stated who the Dacians were and why they had become hostile to Rome

(as a frontier tribal kingdom). The Bastarnae could be properly classed as Scythians (nomadic steppe dwellers) who had recently crossed the Ister River (the Danube) and subdued part of Moesia opposite their territory. Then they subdued the Triballi who occupy the neighbouring district and the Dardani who inhabit the Triballian country. They presented no challenge to Rome while they were engaged in these actions. But then they crossed the Haemus range and overran that part of Thrace belonging to the Dentheleti. These people were under treaty with the Romans, so Crassus intervened to defend their king, Sitas, who was blind. However, the main motive was to safeguard Macedonia (a well-established Roman province).

The arrival of the Roman army caused panic among the Bastarnae and they retreated from the territory without a battle. Marcus Crassus pursued them, gaining possession of the region called Segetica and invading Moesia. He ravaged this country, and his advance forces assaulted one of the Moesian strongholds. Thinking that these were Roman units acting in isolation, the Moesians made a sortie from their stronghold and repulsed them. But when Crassus deployed the rest of his army, the enemy were driven back, besieged, and the stronghold destroyed.

While Crassus was subduing the Moesians, the Bastarnae halted their retreat near the Cedrus River (the Tsibritsa) and waited to discover what might occur. But after conquering the Moesians, Crassus set out against the Bastarnae. The Bastarnae sent envoys to him requesting that he end his pursuit, since their people had done no harm to the Romans. Crassus detained the envoys and said he would give them an answer on the following day. He treated them kindly and made them drunk on wine, so that he could discover all their plans. The entire Scythian race is insatiable in their use of wine and will quickly drink themselves into a stupor.

During the night Crassus moved his army forwards to the edge of a forest and sent scouts through the woodland (a forest next to the Bastarnae camp). Reaching the far side of the trees, these soldiers were seen by the Bastarnae, who assumed they were an isolated force and rushed to attack them. As the soldiers retreated into the forest, the Bastarnae pursued them (abandoning the advantage they had as skilled steppe cavalry). Crassus then moved his main forces into the woods to kill all the Bastarnae they encountered and slay many others in the rout which followed (as the Romans reached the enemy camp). The Bastarnae found their escape hindered by their own wagons (encircling their position). Their desperate attempts to save their wives and children was also instrumental in their defeat.

Crassus personally slew the Bastarnae king Deldo. He would have dedicated Deldo's armour as *spolia opima* to Jupiter Feretrius ('Jupiter the

Striker') if he had been in supreme command (Octavian alone held this status). So ended this engagement (between Rome and the Bastarnae). Some of the remaining Bastarnae took refuge in a grove, but the Romans burned them out by setting fire to the trees on all sides. Some managed to reach a stronghold, but they were attacked and annihilated. Others who fled tried to swim across the Danube and were drowned. The remaining Bastarnae were scattered across the region. When a collection of survivors regrouped and seized a strong position, Crassus besieged them for several days without success. Roles, a tribal king of the Getae, offered his military assistance to destroy them.

Cessation of Serious Conflicts (29 BC)

167 Cassius Dio, *Roman History*, 51.20
The action which gave the greatest pleasure to Octavian (Augustus) was an order by the Senate to close the gates of Janus (temple of the twin-faced god of boundaries in Rome). This signalled the cessation of all foreign wars. (...) There were still armed enemies in existence including the Treveri (a Gallic tribe) who had summoned assistance from the Germans. There were also the Cantabri, Vaccaei, and Astures (hostile tribes in Hispania). (...) but these numerous disturbances in various regions were not important and did not have serious consequences. Therefore, the Romans of this period did not consider themselves to be at war.

Triumph of Octavian (29 BC)

168 Cassius Dio, *Roman History*, 51.21
On the first day of his triumph, Octavian celebrated victories over the Pannonians, Dalmatians, Iapydes, and their neighbours (regions south of the Danube). The celebrations also acknowledged successes against the Germans and Gauls. This is because Gaius Carrinas (the governor of Gaul) had subdued a revolt of the Morini and other (Belgic) tribes. He also repelled the Suebi when they crossed the Rhine to wage their war. (...) Carrinas celebrated this triumph alongside Octavian, because some of the credit also belonged to the supreme commander.

The Temple of the Divine Julius Caesar is Completed (29 BC)

169 Cassius Dio, *Roman History*, 51.22

Many forms of contest were arranged to mark the consecration of Caesar's Temple. (...) Vast numbers of wild beasts and tame animals were slain, including a rhinoceros and a hippopotamus. It was the first time these animals had been seen in Rome (brought from Egypt). (...) These beasts were imported along with Dacians and Suebi (war captives). The Dacians were a type of 'Scythian' who lived on both sides of the Ister (Danube). The Suebi were a German tribe living beyond the Rhine, but many people also claim this name (as a prestigious title among Germans). Both sets of captives fought as a crowd against one another (an arena battle between Germans and Dacians). (...)

These Dacians had previously sent envoys to Octavian, but when he refused their demands, they transferred their support to Mark Antony (his enemy in the civil war). Due to internal dissent, they had not provided Mark Antony with much assistance, but now they had been captured and were made to fight the Suebi. As expected, the whole spectacle lasted many days and there was no interruption to the schedule, even when Octavian became ill.

Augustan Policy

170 Cassius Dio, *Roman History*, 53.12

Octavian (the Emperor Augustus) declared he would not govern all the Roman provinces indefinitely in person. Weaker provinces were to be restored to Senatorial governance as they were peaceful and free from military commitments. Octavian retained the more powerful (militarised) provinces, recognising that their position was insecure and precarious. These provinces either had enemies on their borders, or had the capacity to begin a serious revolt. (...)

Octavian retained all of Gaul including Gallia Narbonensis, Gallia Lugdunensis, Aquitania, and Belgica. This included native Gauls and foreign peoples who lived in their country. Some of the 'Celts' (North Europeans) who we call Germans, had occupied all the Belgic territories along the Rhine and caused this region to be renamed 'Germany'. The southern part of this territory extended to the sources of the Rhine, while the northern parts reached the British Ocean (the provinces of Upper and Lower Germany – the Rhineland territories).

Augustan Propaganda

Roman poets portray the emperor subduing the main enemies of Rome including the Sugambri, who occupied the east bank of the Rhine.

171 Propertius, *Eulogies*, 4.6.78
I shall not describe how the Sugambri from their marshes were enslaved (Germanic tribes) or the dark-skinned kingdoms of Cephean Meroe were defeated (Nilotic kingdoms to the south of Egypt). Others can describe how the Parthians recently acknowledged their defeat with a truce (the Parthian Empire of Iran).

172 Horace, *Odes*, 4.5.25
Who fears the Parthians, or the Scythian hordes, or the rank German forests, while Caesar Augustus lives?

An Official Account

Augustus had his main political achievements inscribed on his tomb.

173 Augustus, *Achievements*, 32
The following kings sought refuge with me as suppliants: Tiridates of Parthia (29 BC), and later Phrates, son of King Phrates (25 BC), Artavasdes of Media (north-west Iran), Artaxares of Adiabene (a small kingdom in Mesopotamia), Dubnobellaunus and Tincomarus from Britain, Melo of the Sugambri (Rhineland Germany) (...).

Roman Action in Germany (25 BC)

174 Cassius Dio, *Roman History*, 53.26
About this same time, Marcus Vinicius (Governor of Gallia Belgica) took vengeance against Germans who had seized and slain Romans entering their country to trade. This achievement was credited to Augustus, granting him the title *imperator* (as commander-in-chief). For this and other victories, Augustus was voted a triumph (an award of the Senate). But he did not want to celebrate this achievement and instead a triumphal arch was erected in the Alps to commemorate the event.

Marcus Agrippa, the most Senior Roman Commander is sent to Gaul (19 BC)

175 Cassius Dio, *Roman History*, 54.11
Marcus Agrippa was then assigned a command in the Gallic provinces. The Gauls were quarrelling among themselves, but they were also being harassed by the Germans (tribal raids). Agrippa addressed these problems and then crossed into Spain.

Roman Knowledge of German Short-Battle Clubs (19 BC)

176 Virgil, *Aeneid*, 7.741
'They hurl their smaller missiles in the Teuton style, watched from the walls of Abella.'

177 Maurus Servius Honoratus, *Commentary on the Aeneid of Vergil*, 7.741
'Cateias' are Gallic weapons, but here they are said to be Teutonic. Some claim that this weapon was a short missile made from hardwood (a throwing club). It was a cubit in length (the length of a male forearm, from elbow to wrist) and was covered with iron studs. It was thrown at the enemy battle line (at close quarters) and recovered using a tether (twisted cord or chain links).

The Germans attack Gaul (16 BC)

In 16 BC, the Germans crossed the Rhine to raid Gaul and inflict a serious defeat on Roman forces.

178 Strabo, *Geography*, 7.1.4
Under their leader Melo, the Sugambri who live near the Rhine provoked a serious Roman conflict against Germany. Since this time other German chiefs have breached their terms with the Romans and created conflicts. The Sugambri grew powerful, were suppressed by Rome, then revolted a second time. By doing so they betrayed the political hostages given to the Romans and disregarded their own pledges of good faith.

Marcus Lollius is Defeated

179 Cassius Dio, *Roman History*, 54.20

During this era the greatest of the wars fought by Rome was against the Germans. This took the attentions of the (Emperor) Augustus away from the city (of Rome). It was reported that the Sugambri, Usipetes, and Tencteri had seized some Romans in their territories and crucified them. Then they crossed the Rhine and plundered both Germania (the Roman Rhineland provinces) and Gaul. The Germans had ambushed the Roman cavalry when they approached and pursued them as they fled. Then they caught Lollius, the governor of the province, in a surprise attack and defeated him. When Augustus learned about these events, he hurried to confront the enemy (with reinforcements). But he found there was no conflict to pursue in the region. The barbarians had discovered that Lollius was preparing to attack them, and the emperor was about to lead a campaign. They had therefore retreated to their own territory and were hoping to make peace (with Rome) by supplying political hostages.

For this reason, Augustus had no need to conduct further warfare and he spent the remainder of that year and the following year arranging other matters. This was the year in which Marcus Libo and Calpurnius Piso were consuls. The Gauls had suffered much due to the Germans and the actions of a man named Licinus (a corrupt Roman official engaged in extortion).

Roman Actions in 14 BC

180 Cassius Dio, *Roman History*, 54.25

Augustus now completed all the business which had occupied him in the provinces of Gaul, Germany, and Spain. He spent large sums of money in these regions, bestowing freedom (immunity from taxes) and citizenship on some communities, but removing these same rights from others. Then, leaving Drusus in Germany (as commander), he returned to Rome.

Chapter Six

Drusus and the Roman Conquest of North Germania (12–9 BC)

The Roman conquest of north Germania was commanded by a prominent member of the imperial family named Nero Claudius Drusus. Drusus was 26 years old when the campaign began. The conquest involved the following operations:

- **12 BC:** Operations across the Rhine (Usipetes and Sugambri). Alliance with the Frisii to navigate the North Sea. Roman army, perhaps two legions, embark by ship to the Ems River and subdue the Chauci (Lower Saxony).
- **11 BC:** Up to five legions ascend the river Lippe, defeating the Tencteri and Usipetes. Returning army defeats a Cherusci ambush at Arbalo. Garrisons left in Germanic territory, including perhaps Haltern (Aliso) in North Rhine-Westphalia.
- **10 BC:** Chatti and Sugambri attack Roman positions. The Marcomannic king, Maroboduus, relocates his followers south to Bohemia.
- **9 BC:** Led by Drusus, the Romans attack the Cherusci and reach the Elbe, erecting a trophy on the riverbanks (perhaps near Dresden).

Provocation

181 Velleius Paterculus, *History of Rome*, 2.97

Meanwhile, a disaster occurred in Germany under the legate Marcus Lollius (16 BC). Lollius was a man more eager for money than for honest action. He also possessed a vicious character that he tried hard to conceal. The loss of the eagle (battle standard) belonging to the Fifth Legion required a caesar (a senior member of the imperial family) to come from Rome to Gaul. Responsibility for this war was entrusted to Drusus Claudius, the brother of Nero (Tiberius).

As a young man Drusus possessed all the great qualities that nature could bestow and training could develop. It would be difficult to say whether his talents were better suited to a military career or the political duties of civilian life. His charm and good humour were unsurpassed, and he had a modest attitude when amongst his comrades, treating them as equals. His handsome physique was only surpassed by that of his brother (the future Emperor Tiberius).

182 Cassius Dio, *Roman History*, 54.32
Drusus had a similar experience (in Gaul). Since Augustus was absent (in Rome) and the Gauls were restless in their slavery (subjection to Roman rule), the Sugambri (Germans) and their allies resorted to war.

Drusus occupied the subject territory (in Gaul) ahead of the German attack. He sent for the leading men in the region (people who could lead an uprising) on the pretext that a (new) festival was to be held around the altar of Augustus at Lugdunum. This festival was still celebrated in the city up until recent times. Then Drusus waited for the Germans to cross the Rhine and when they did so, he drove them back.

Later Appraisal

The conflict escalated, leading to the Roman invasion, conquest and occupation of Greater Germania.

183 Florus, *Roman History*, 2.30
It would have been better if Augustus had not invested such great ambition and effort into conquering Germany. Its loss was a disgrace which far outweighed the glory of its acquisition. But Augustus knew that his adopted father Julius Caesar had twice entered Germany by bridging the Rhine. Caesar had sought hostilities against Germania, so Augustus wanted to make it a Roman province to honour his (adopted) father. This objective could have been achieved if the barbarians had tolerated our vices as much as they tolerated our authority.

Roman Expectations

The German war was occurring when Strabo was writing his geography.

184 Strabo, *Geography*, 6.4.2
The Romans took over Celtica (Greater Gaul) gradually over time, piece by piece. This included Transalpine and Cisalpine Gaul and Liguria (Celtic

territories extending across the Alps to northern Italy). Later the deified Julius Caesar, and afterwards the Emperor Augustus, conquered and secured all of Gaul through warfare. At present the Romans are conducting a war against the Germans using the Celtic regions as their base of operations. They have already brought glory to their homeland by winning triumphs over this enemy.

185 Cassius Dio, *Roman History*, 54.36
It was voted that the gates at the Temple of Janus Geminus should be closed, since all wars had ceased. But the gates had to remain open when the Dacians crossed the frozen Ister (Danube River) to plunder Pannonia and the Dalmatians rebelled against the extraction of tribute by the Romans. Tiberius accompanied Augustus into Gaul and from there he set out to bring the Dalmatians back under submission.

(Meanwhile,) Drusus harassed or subjugated the Germans, particularly the Chatti who had abandoned their own country. This was the land the Romans had approved for their settlement, but they now left to go and join the Sugambri.

First Campaign (12 BC)
North Sea Operations and Roman Advance to the Ems River

In 12 BC, Drusus campaigned against hostile German tribes on the far side of the Rhine. Then he used the Roman fleet to navigate the North Sea and conduct operations along the Ems River. These operations targeted the Usipetes, Sugambri, Chauci and Frisians.

186 Cassius Dio, *Roman History*, 54.32
Drusus then crossed over to the country of the Usipetes, passing through the riverine island of the Batavians (the northern Rhine frontier). From there he marched along the river to the Sugambrian territories, where he devastated much of their country. Then he sailed down the Rhine to the ocean and compelled the Frisians to join the Roman cause. Drusus crossed the Frisian Lake (coastal Netherlands) and invaded the country of the Chauci. But here the Romans experienced danger as their ships were grounded by the extreme ebb of the ocean (low tides). Drusus was saved on this occasion by the Frisians who had joined the Roman expedition as infantry. But their forces withdrew as winter arrived.

Operations against Usipetes, Tencteri, Chatti

187 Florus, *Roman History*, 2.30

Augustus placed his adopted son Nero Claudius Drusus in command of the German campaign. Drusus entered the region and conquered the Usipetes first. Then he overran the territory of the Tencteri and Chatti. As a victory monument, he erected a high mound to display the plunder and weaponry he had seized from the Marcomanni (perhaps a subset of the tribe that would flee south).

Second Campaign (11 BC) Romans Advance to the Weser and Fortress Established in Chatti Territory

188 Cassius Dio, *Roman History*, 54.32

When Drusus arrived in Rome in the consulship of Quintus Aelius and Paulus Fabius, he was appointed Praetor Urbanus. He received this position even though he already had the rank of praetor. At the beginning of spring, he renewed the war by crossing the Rhine and subjugating the Usipetes. He bridged the river Lupia (the Lippe) and invaded the country of the Sugambri. He advanced through this region to the territory of the Cherusci and the river Visurgis (Weser). Drusus was able to do this because the Sugambri were the only tribe in the region who had refused to join the alliance of the Chatti. Angered by the Sugambri, the Chatti had launched a campaign against them with their entire force. Drusus seized this opportunity to march across their territory unchallenged.

If he had not run short of provisions, Drusus would also have crossed the Visurgis. But winter was approaching and a swarm of bees had been seen in the Roman camp (a bad omen). Consequently, he did not advance any further and instead retired to friendly territory. Drusus encountered great dangers during this retreat as the enemy harassed the Romans constantly with ambushes. On one occasion they surrounded the Romans in a narrow pass and almost destroyed their army. The Germans would have annihilated them, except they had developed a contempt for Romans as though they had already captured them. They believed that all that was required was a killing strike (overconfident and incautious). The Germans therefore rushed into close combat with the Romans in a disorderly fashion. They received the greater losses in this engagement and afterwards they were no longer so bold. They remained at a distance, becoming an annoyance to the Roman soldiers, but refusing to come any closer.

Drusus scorned the enemy and established a fortified outpost at the point where the rivers Lupia and Eliso unite. He also set up a stronghold among the Chatti on the (far) bank of the Rhine. For these successes Drusus received triumphal honours and the right to ride into the city on horseback (as a military commander). He was also granted the right to exercise the powers of a proconsul when he finished his term as praetor. The soldiers gave him the title of 'imperator' by popular acclamation, just as Tiberius had received. But Augustus did not approve of this honour and instead claimed for himself the appellation 'imperator' from the exploits of these two men (as the supreme commander of the army).

Operations against the Cherusci, Suebi and Sugambri

189 Florus, *Roman History*, 2.30

On his next campaign Drusus simultaneously attacked the powerful tribes of the Cherusci, the Suebi and the Sugambri. These tribes had begun hostilities against Rome by capturing and crucifying twenty centurions. They performed this ritual in an oath-making ceremony to unite their people in a common cause against the Romans. They had been so confident of victory that they even reached agreement on how the plunder from their war was to be divided among the tribes. The Cherusci had chosen the horses, the Suebi claimed the gold and silver, and the Sugambri were allocated the captives. But the reverse occurred when Drusus defeated these nations. He seized their horses, herds, and precious necklets (Germanic torcs). This plunder was sold as the spoils of war alongside the captured prisoners.

Drusus occupied the newly seized territory. He installed Roman garrisons and guard posts along the Meuse, Elbe and Weser rivers. He established hundreds of forts, camps, and outposts along the Rhine. To safeguard these new territories, he constructed bridges at Bonna and brought a fleet to Gesoriacum (Bonn on the Rhine and Boulogne in northern France). Drusus also opened a route through the Hercynian Forest which had never been visited or crossed by any Roman. With these achievements Drusus established peace in Germania and altered the nature of its inhabitants. The country was transformed and made less hostile to humankind.

Fleet Operations in the North Sea and Baltic

190 Strabo, *Geography*, 7.1.3

The Elbe flows almost parallel to the Rhine and extends northwards to the great ocean (North Sea coast). This river must have a similar length to the Rhine. In the land between these two major boundaries there are other navigable rivers. They include the Amasias (the Ems) on which the Roman commander Drusus won an important naval victory over the Bructeri tribe.

191 Strabo, *Geography*, 7.1.3

Drusus Germanicus had subjugated most of the tribes in Germany, including those inhabiting islands along the northern coast. He had even captured the island of the Burchanis (Borkum) by besieging the shore.

192 Pliny, *Natural History*, 2.67

The greater part of the northern ocean (the Atlantic coast of Germany) was explored under the orders of the late Emperor Augustus. A military fleet sailed for this purpose around Germany to the promontory of the Cimbri (the Jutland Peninsula). Beyond this shore they observed a vast sea (the Baltic). They gathered reports of this expanse and reached a region in Scythia where the climate was excessively wet. The ocean must extend beyond this territory (further east) since there is a superabundance of moisture in the region (sea mists).

193 Tacitus, *Germania*, 33

Beyond the Angrivarii and Chamavi are the Dulgubnii and Chasuarii tribes. The lands are also occupied by several other tribes who are not so well known (northern Germany). The Frisii occupy territories approaching the Rhine (the Netherlands) and based on population size their tribe is divided into the Greater and Lesser Frisii. Their territory extends to the ocean and is flanked by the Rhine. This coast has vast lakes and sea inlets which have been navigated by Roman fleets. Roman ships have even ventured into the sea beyond this coast to reach another 'Pillars of Hercules' (the Skagerrak strait between Jutland and Norway). It is commonly claimed that Hercules once visited this country, but do we not ascribe every great work of wonder to this ancient demigod. The Roman commander Drusus was a daring explorer, but the ocean blocked his further progress and he could not find evidence of Hercules, or explore the seas beyond (the Baltic Sea). Since that era no one else has made the attempt and it is considered more pious and reverential to believe the actions of the gods, than to seek proof of them.

Summary of the Campaign (written in the AD 400s)

194 Orosius, *History*, 6.21

Later Drusus, the stepson of Augustus, was given command of Gaul and Raetia (the Celtic region of Switzerland). At this time all the tribes were moving like waves, either towards conflict, or to agreement of a permanent peace (mass political instability). Drusus subdued the largest and bravest of the tribes in Germany with his armies. The defeated peoples accepted peace terms and the conquest provided tranquility. The Noricans, Illyrians, Pannonians, Dalmatians, Moesians, Thracians and the Sarmatian Dacians were all subdued. The largest and strongest peoples of Germany were either overcome by different generals, or contained by the mightiest of rivers, the Rhine and the Danube.

In Germany, Drusus first conquered the Usipetes, then the Tencteri and the Chatti. Then he slaughtered the Marcomanni, almost eradicating their population (killed or displaced). Later, in a single battle, he overcame the bravest tribes, the Cherusci, Suebi and Sugambri. But his own forces suffered severe losses in this engagement against a strong and skilled enemy. The courage and fierceness of the Germans was revealed when the Romans advanced and found their women shut into a closed space behind their wagons (a wagon *laager*). In their fury these women used any and every implement that might serve as a weapon. When their efforts failed, they smashed the skulls of their infants on the ground and hurled the bodies at the Romans. They had murdered their own children and used their bodies as implements of slaughter.

Third Year: Romans Advance to the Elbe River (9 BC)

In 9 BC, Roman operations beyond the Rhine may have involved the defence of new forts, bases and military camps. By 10 BC, the Roman army was ready to advance again against the Chatti and Cherusci. These operations took Roman armies to the Elbe River.

195 Cassius Dio, *Roman History*, 55.1–2

The following year (9 BC) Drusus became consul with Titus Crispinus. But the omens that year were not favourable. Numerous buildings were destroyed by storms and thunderbolts, including the temples of many gods. Even the temple of Jupiter Capitolinus in Rome was damaged.

But Drusus paid no heed to these warnings. Instead, he invaded the country of the Chatti and advanced as far as the territory of the Suebi (tribes in inner Germany). It was difficult to traverse these territories and the Romans only defeated the attacking Germans after much bloodshed. From there Drusus entered the country of the Cherusci and crossed the Visurgis River (the Weser). The Roman army plundered everything in the region, advancing as far as the Albis (the Elbe). The Albis rises in the Vandalic Mountains (Riesengebirge) and becomes a mighty river before it empties into the northern ocean. Drusus wanted to cross this river, but he failed in the attempt. It is said that a woman of superhuman size approached Drusus at the river and commanded:

> Drusus, where are you rushing to reach with such eagerness? It is not your fate to see lands beyond here. Depart from this place, for your efforts and your life are nearly at their end.

It is marvellous that a deity should speak directly to a mortal man. I cannot discredit this account, for he ordered the army to set up trophies (marker monuments) before immediately withdrawing. The retreat was rapid, but Drusus died on the way from disease before the army could even reach the Rhine. The influence of the gods was seen in other incidents occurring just before his death. Wolves were seen prowling about the camp and howling in the night (animals associated with Romulus and Remus). Two unidentified youths were also seen riding through the midst of the camp (the Dioscuri or phantoms). The sound of unseen women was heard lamenting a death and shooting stars streaked across the night sky. So much for these events!

Augustus was not far from the campaign force (he was headquartered in Gaul). He therefore received news that Drusus was sick before he became gravely ill. He sent Tiberius to reach him as fast as possible (perhaps to assume command). Tiberius found Drusus still breathing, and when he died, he made immediate arrangements for the body to be conveyed back to Rome. Centurions and military tribunes carried the casket on the first stage of the journey to bring the body back to the winter quarters of the army (the Roman frontier). Then the foremost men of each city carried the casket through their district on the journey south to Rome.

Finally, the body of Drusus was laid in state in the Forum and two funeral orations were delivered. Tiberius pronounced a eulogy (spoken tribute to the dead) in the forum and Augustus gave his oration in the Circus Flaminius (a racetrack that could serve as an auditorium). Augustus had to give his eulogy outside the pomerium (the religious boundary of the city) because he had been on campaign. He could not perform the customary rites (thanking the gods) that were required to enter the sacred precinct. (The rites could not be performed while Augustus was observing a period of mourning.)

Afterwards the body of Drusus was carried to the Campus Martius by members of the equestrian order and some associates from senatorial families. Then it was committed to the flames (a funeral pyre) and the ashes were deposited in the sepulchre of Augustus (a marble mausoleum belonging to the imperial dynasty). Afterwards Drusus, together with his sons, received the title of 'Germanicus' (in recognition for subduing Germany). Further honours and statues were granted to his memory. A victory arch was built and a cenotaph erected on the banks of the Rhine.

196 Pliny, *Natural History*, 7.20

Tiberius made all possible haste to reach his brother Drusus who was gravely ill in Germany. He reached him by travelling day and night on the road in three stages, with each stage 200 miles long.

197 Valerius Maximus, *Memorable Deeds and Sayings*, 5.5.3

Drusus was now so faint and weak that there was little distinction between life and death. Nevertheless, he ordered the legions to assemble with their battle standards and go forth to greet his brother, proclaiming him 'imperator' (replacement commander). He also ordered a *praetorium* (command centre) to be constructed for him to the right of his own headquarters. Drusus made Tiberius take the titles of 'consul' and 'imperator', then just as he transferred this authority (political and military command), he finally succumbed to death. No example of fraternal love exceeds these actions, except perhaps the precedent of Castor and Pollux (legendry demigods).

198 Florus, *Roman History*, 2.30

Drusus died in Germania (in 9 BC, he fell from his horse near the river Elbe and suffered a lingering mortal wound). When the Senate heard that the brilliant young general had died, they acted without flattery to acknowledge his great merits. They bestowed unparalleled honours upon him and granted him a name derived from the province he had created. He received the family name 'Germanicus'.

Campaigns and Character of Drusus (12–9 BC)

199 Suetonius, *Claudius*, 1

Drusus was granted the offices of quaestor and praetor. He took command of the Raetian conflict and the war in Germany. He was the first Roman general to sail into the northern ocean and voyage beyond the Rhine (North Sea). He constructed a vast harbour for this purpose and built huge canals that still bear his name (the 2-mile long Fossae Drusinae, connecting the Rhine with the Yssel, permitting passage into the North Sea).

Drusus defeated the enemy in many battles and drove the Germans deep into the wild interior of their country. He did not cease his pursuit until an apparition appeared to him. The figure was a barbarian woman, larger than human size, who spoke to him in Latin. She forbade him to push his victory any further into Germany (beyond the Elbe).

Drusus received triumphal regalia for these exploits and the honour of an ovation in Rome (a lesser triumph, marking victory over inferior enemies). Immediately after his praetorship he was made consul and resumed his campaign. But Drusus died in his military camp, his summer base of operations. The site is considered cursed (by Fate).

His corpse was carried to Rome by the leading men of the free towns and colonies. There it was met and received by the scribal *decuriae* (attendants of the magistrates) and interred in the campus Martius.

But the army also erected a monument in his honour and each year on a stated day they made the 'ceremonial run' around this edifice (probably a procession in full armour). On the same day all the cities of Gaul mark this occasion with prayers and sacrifices. The Senate voted many honours to the deceased Drusus, including the erection of a marble arch on the Appian Way that was adorned with trophies. They also granted the surname 'Germanicus' (Defeater of Germany) to Drusus and all his descendants.

It is widely believed that Drusus supported the citizen masses (a popularist). In addition to his battlefield victories over the enemy he greatly desired to win the 'noble trophies' (*spolia opima* – trophies gained by killing an enemy leader in personal combat). He often pursued German leaders across the battlefield at great personal risk and he openly talked of restoring the old government (the Republic) when he inherited the Empire.

Grief over Drusus: Poetry Addressed to his Grieving Family

200 Livy, *Consolation to Livia*, 3

A youth is dead. A youth whose life followed a course that all might revere. He had great military skill and also greatness in peace (statecraft). He recently seized from the enemy their hiding places in the Alps (defeating Raetian bandits). He won renown sharing a military command with his brother (Tiberius). During this war he crushed the fierce tribe of the Suebi and the untamed Sugambri. He forced these barbarians to turn and flee and won for you, O Romans, an unprecedented triumph by extending your authority into new lands.

O mother (of this fallen youth), you were ignorant of the destiny that would befall him. You were preparing your vows of (safekeeping and success) to Jupiter and the armed goddess (Minerva). You planned to heap your gifts before our protector Mars (war trophies) and all those gods who it is right and dutiful to worship. As a mother, your mind was occupied with the sacred triumph (the victory celebrations her son would receive). Perhaps you were even thinking about the chariot (the centrepiece of the parade on which Drusus would ride). But now you must ready yourself for a funeral procession in place of a sacred triumph. For it is a funeral pyre that now awaits Drusus in front of the Temple of Jupiter. And this was the place where you pictured him safely returned. You cherished the joy you would feel as he stood there victorious (the triumphal general). (...)

What shall I say to you Antonia, most worthy wife of Drusus? Your marriage was a well-suited match, for your husband was a hero among youths and you were greatly beloved by him. With him you were a queen, a true offspring of the Caesars and equal to the wife of Jupiter (the matron goddess Juno). You freely consented to this marriage, his last and only love. You were his pleasant respite from weary toil. He died in your absence, but with his final words, as he lay cold with imminent death, he strove in grief to pronounce your name. Ill-fate has meant that you will not receive him back in the same form that he left, nor will he come back as the promised returnee (the triumphal victor). Your husband cannot return to tell you how the Sugambri were destroyed, or the Suebi turned and fled before the drawn swords of his soldiers. He cannot speak of the formidable rivers and mountains, or recite the names of all places and wonders he saw in that new world (the German wilderness). He returns to you cold, a lifeless corpse. He will lie on a funeral couch without you next to him. (...)

If our beliefs are real, then Drusus is in the Fields of Bliss (a benign afterlife). He will be welcomed by his honoured forefathers and the renowned ancestors of his mother's lineage (the men who formed the joint Julio-Claudian dynasty). He will ride radiant in a four-horsed chariot (the triumph he would have received on earth). In his imperial costume he will stand proud in this ivory vehicle, while the temples are decorated with triumphal garlands. His ancestors will receive the hero who bears the battle standards of Germania and the illustrious fame of consular command. They will rejoice in the new and well-earned title of their dynasty, which he alone seized in triumph from the conquered foe ('Germanicus' – conquerer of Germany). But they will scarcely believe that one so young was able to accomplish such great achievements in such a short time. Surely, they will think that a hero who performed so many mighty deeds must have been living for a long time. (…)

Drusus was the most prodigious of youths. While he lived, he was the greatest hope of the Roman people (for further conquest, prosperity and a stable succession). He held the supreme glory of the dynasty that produced him, but he was still mortal. Livia, you must have been concerned for your son's safety while he waged valiant wars. But life is bestowed to be used up and expended. And although living comes without 'interest payments', the final sum will be collected on that fated day (death). And fortune will ordain that day according to her own unjust decision. (…)

But the Power that recently brought you dreadful misfortune has often shown you great favour (Fate). You were born to an esteemed family, you were blest with two sons (Tiberius and Drusus), and the emperor, like Jupiter himself, made you his partner. Augustus returned safe to you after mastering the world and waging wars that increased Roman fortunes. The Neros (your sons) fulfilled all the hopes and prayers you could have had as a mother. Both of them held military commands and often routed our enemies. Recall the Isargus River in the Alpine valleys and Rhine streams discoloured by the dark stain of gore (battlefield blood). The voracious Danube, cowed Dacia, Armenia ready to flee and Dalmatia as a final supplicant. Apulia (southern Italy) seems far away, but the enemy in Pontus (the Black Sea) knew that Roman power was a short march away from them. The Pannonians were scattered across their mountain summits and the Romans entered that newly revealed German 'world'. These merits outweigh a single fault (his military glory surpassed his early death).

Drusus died far away, so you did not have to endure the sight of your son's eyes closing in death. This is not how the sorrow entered your troubled mind. You were forced to hear about his demise and your grief must have been preceded by fear and anxiety. Reports reached you about his long and perilous campaign, so sorrow did not immediately burst upon you, but apprehension led you gently into grief.

Portents from Jupiter gave further warnings of a bloody fate. Jupiter assailed three temples with his fire-bearing hand (lightning strikes). On a single night, Juno's shrine, the Temple of fearless Minerva and the sacred palace of the all-powerful emperor were struck. It also seemed that the brightest stars had fled from the sky and Phosphorus (the 'Morning Star') had drifted from its usual course. No one saw the 'Dawn-bringer' that night and daylight came unheralded by any star. This gave a warning of destruction on earth, as if a noble light had sunk below Stygian waters (a river boundary in the afterlife). (…)

Suppose Drusus could escape the misty shores of Acheron (the riverine barrier between life and afterlife). If the passage back was lawful, then he might proclaim the following words:

> Why count the years of life? I have lived to a greater extent than only my years will show. It is my deeds that you must count, and it is experience that constitutes 'age'. My life was filled with notable events, not years of delay. Let years of old age befall my foes (with chronic suffering). My forefathers taught me this, as did the 'Neros' before them who had shattered the Carthaginian multitudes. This is the lesson, taken from the ancestors of Caesar that I received through you (mother). My end and fate were therefore mine by right (death on campaign). My merits have granted me honour and my name is bestowed with titles. Read about my exploits as consul of Rome and as conqueror of Germany, a previously unknown world. Alas, I died, but it was in the cause of my country. My victorious temples are wreathed in Apollo's laurels (victory trophies).
>
> I have perceived the death rites of my own funeral and I have read the placards erected by the cities. That familiar and solemn march of men has occurred, accompanied by royal offerings. Those youths dutifully carried my corpse with great reverence and stood proudly beside my funeral pyre. I received praise from the sacred words of Augustus (the funeral speech) and drew tears from a deity. I do not need anyone's pity. Refrain from your weeping. Why grieve for me?

Chapter Seven

Tiberius in Command (8–7 BC/AD 4–6) Germania is Pacified

After the death of his brother Drusus, Tiberius took command in Germania. He fought two successful campaigns to pacify north Germania between the Rhine and the Elbe rivers. By 7 BC these territories were considered to be part of the Roman Empire, but most of the controlling military garrisons remained stationed along the Rhine (the major transport and supply route). When Tiberius was recalled, replacement commanders took charge of these forces. But a decade later a serious conflict occurred in north Germania, requiring Tiberius to resume command. These are the main events in this period:

- **8–7 BC:** Tiberius takes command and conducts two campaigns in Germania defeating the Sugambri. North Germania is considered conquered, and 40,000 Germans are resettled in Roman Gaul (west bank of the Rhine).
- **6 BC–3 BC:** Lucius Domitius Ahenobarbus is appointed commander in Germany. He crosses the Elbe with his army and constructs wooden causeways in territories between the Ems and the Rhine.
- **2 BC–AD 4:** Marcus Vinicius commands the five legions controlling Germany. An 'extensive war' begins.
- **AD 4:** Tiberius campaigns in north Germania. Canninefates, Chattuarii (Attuarii), Bructeri and Cherusci are subdued. Advance to the Weser and Lippe rivers.
- **AD 5:** Tiberius subdues the Cauchi and Langobardi. Roman fleet explores the north coast and rendezvous with the army reaching the Elbe River.
- **AD 6:** Tiberius prepares for the conquest of the Marcomannic kingdom in southern Germany (Bohemia). A total of twelve legions will converge from Germania, Illyricum and Rhaetia (Rhine and Danube territories).

Tiberius takes Command against the Germans (8–7 BC)

201 Velleius Paterculus, *History of Rome*, 2.97
It was largely Drusus who achieved the subjection of Germany and he spilled the blood of the Germans on various battlefields. But after only thirteen years (in high office) a cruel fate took away his life during his consulship.

The burden and responsibility for this war in Germany was then transferred to Tiberius. He conducted the war with his customary valour and good fortune and traversed every part of Germany in a victorious campaign. (The emperor) entrusted him with an army and as one of his main concerns was to preserve his forces, he did not suffer any great loss. Tiberius so completely subdued Germany that it was almost reduced to the status of a tributary province. He then received a second victory triumph and a second consulship.

North Germania is considered Conquered

202 Cassiodorus, *Chronicle*, 8 BC
Under these consuls, Gaius Asinius and Gaius Marcius, all the Germans between the Rhine and the Elbe surrendered to Tiberius.

Obstinate Sugambri

203 Cassius Dio, *Roman History*, 55.6
After a second period of ten years in power, Augustus launched a further campaign against the Germans. He himself remained in Roman territory, while Tiberius crossed the Rhine (entering Germania). All the barbarians, except the Sugambri, became afraid and requested peace. But their offers were declined because Augustus refused to finalise a truce with any of them until the Sugambri conceded.

The Sugambri had sent envoys, but the negotiations were so far from completion that Augustus arrested all the German representatives. Numerous distinguished envoys from Germany were sent to various Roman cities and many of them died during detainment. This is because the detainees became so greatly distressed at their confinement that they committed suicide. Afterwards the Sugambri remained subdued for a time, but they later gained revenge on the Romans for this misfortune.

Germans are settled West of the Rhine

204 Suetonius, *Tiberius*, 9

Tiberius conducted a war against the Raeti and Vindelici (Switzerland), then took command in Pannonia (south of the Danube). Finally, he fought in Germany. In the first of these wars, he subdued the Alpine tribes. In the second he defeated the Breuci and Dalmatians. Then in the third conflict (with Germany) he brought 40,000 surrendered people into Gaul and assigned them dwelling places near the (Roman) bank of the Rhine. Because of these exploits Tiberius entered Rome riding in a chariot to receive a victory ovation.

Augustus takes Credit

205 Suetonius, *Augustus*, 21

Augustus halted the Dacian invasions, slaying great numbers of them, including three of their leaders. He forced the (hostile) Germans back to the far side of the river Albis (Elbe). But the Suebi and Sigambri were an exception, for when they submitted to him, they were brought into Gaul and settled in lands near the Rhine. Other peoples caused unrest when a bridge collapsed, but they were also subdued (possibly a frontier river crossing).

Augustus conducted these wars through his generals, although he was nearby in some of the conflicts in Pannonia and Germany. He was not far from the fighting (the Rhine frontier). He managed operations from the cities of Ravenna, Mediolanum, or Aquileia (north Italy).

Lucius Domitius is given Command in Germania (4 BC)

206 Tacitus, *Annals*, 4.44

Lucius Domitius was chosen to be the husband of the younger Antonia, the daughter of Octavia (the older sister of the emperor). After taking command, he led an army across the Albis (Elbe), penetrating further into Germany than any Roman before him. For this achievement he gained triumphal honours.

Disturbances in Germany (AD 1)

207 Cassius Dio, *Roman History*, 55.10

As these events were occurring, there was an outbreak of conflict involving the Germans. While Domitius was governing the districts along the Ister River (Danube frontier), he intercepted the Hermunduri (a Germanic tribe). For some reason this population had left their own homeland and were wandering about in search of another territory. Domitius settled the Hermunduri in part of the Marcomannic territories (north of the Danube), then he crossed the Albis (Elbe). He encountered no opposition on the march (a military expedition) and made a friendly alliance with the barbarians on the far side of the river. He set up an altar to Augustus on the riverbank.

Afterwards, Domitius transferred his military headquarters to the Rhine (frontier). He tried to secure the return of certain Cheruscan exiles through his (political) contacts. When his efforts failed, the other barbarians began to regard the Romans with contempt (group defiance). This was the limit of Roman operations in that year. A war seemed imminent with the Parthians (the Iranian Empire), so no further attention was paid towards the Germans.

Tiberius resumes Command (AD 4)

In AD 4, the Emperor Augustus sent the imperial heir Tiberius north to further pacify Germania.

208 Cassius Dio, *Roman History*, 55.13

Later, when a German war occurred, Augustus was physically exhausted by old age and illness. He was incapable of campaigning, but due to circumstances and the persuasions of Julia (his daughter), who had been accepted back from banishment, he adopted Tiberius (as his heir). Tiberius was granted the tribunician power for ten years and was sent out against the Germans.

Campaign of AD 4
Suppression of the Chattuarii and Cherusci; Advance beyond the Weser; Military bases established on the Lippe River

209 Velleius Paterculus, *History of Rome*, 2.104–5

Tiberius did not remain long at Rome. As a champion and guardian of the Empire his presence was required in Germany. Three years earlier, in the governorship of your grandfather the illustrious commander Marcus Vinicius, an extensive war broke out (AD 1–4). Vinicius conducted this war with success in some regions, while other territories maintained an effective defence. Consequently, your grandfather was granted the ornaments of a triumph (title honours but not the full ceremonial event in Rome). He also received honorary inscriptions recording his deeds.

In this period, after I had previously filled the duties of the Tribunate, I became a soldier in the camp of Tiberius Caesar. Immediately after (Augustus) adopted Tiberius, I was sent with the commander to Germany as prefect of the cavalry. I was succeeding my father in that position, and for nine continuous years I served as prefect of cavalry, or as commander of a legion. I was therefore a direct witness to the remarkable achievements of Tiberius and in some minor way with my modest abilities, I assisted him. I do not think that any mortal man will ever again see the sights that I witnessed (on our outbound journey). Vast crowds gathered in Italy and the provinces of Gaul to see the commander once more. They gathered to congratulate him and celebrate their good fortune in being granted such a renowned leader. Tiberius had been a 'caesar' (an imperial heir) by virtue of his services long before he formerly received this title.

Words cannot express the feelings of the soldiers when they met their commander. Perhaps my account will scarcely be believed, but the soldiers wept tears of joy at the sight of him. They saluted him with great eagerness and rushed forwards hoping to touch his hand. They could not restrain themselves and cried out – 'Is that really you, commander?', 'Are you safe back among us?', 'General, I served with you in Armenia!', 'I fought for you in Raetia!', 'I received my battle awards from you in Vindelicia!', 'I got my military decorations from you in Pannonia!', 'And I was with you in Germania!'

Tiberius immediately entered Germany (AD 4). He subdued the Canninefates, the Chattuarii) and the Bructeri. He also subjugated the Cherusci tribe. Arminius was a member of the Cherusci and that man later inflicted a severe disaster on Rome (five years later, in AD 9). Tiberius then crossed the Weser River and entered the regions beyond. (Tiberius)

Caesar personally took part in every military operation that was either difficult or dangerous in this war.

Sentius Saturninus

210 Velleius Paterculus, *History of Rome*, 2.105

Tiberius Caesar placed Sentius Saturninus in charge of all the less risky expeditions. Saturninus had already served as a legate under Augustus in Germany and was considered a virtuous man capable of energy, action, and foresight. From his military training, he could endure the hard labours and duties of a soldier, but when there was time for leisure, he enjoyed relaxed and elegant pursuits (fine dining and high culture). His entertainments were sumptuous and jovial, rather than extravagant or indolent. But earlier in my work I have already written about the unique abilities of this illustrious man and his famous consulship.

That year (AD 4) the Roman campaign was prolonged into December to increase benefits derived from the great victory. The Alps were blocked by winter snows, but nevertheless, due to the affection he felt for his family (duties involving the imperial household), Tiberius Caesar returned to Rome. At the beginning of spring the defence of the Empire brought him back to Germany.

Campaign of AD 5
Cauchi and Langobardi submit; Advance to the Elbe; Roman Fleet explores the North Coast

211 Velleius Paterculus, *History of Rome*, 2.105–106

Before his departure, Caesar (Tiberius) had established his winter camp at the source of the river Lippe. This military base was in the core of Germany and Tiberius was the first Roman to establish a presence there.

By the gods! A great volume could be written about our achievements that summer under the generalship of Tiberius Caesar (AD 5). All Germany was traversed by Roman armies. Populations that had been almost unknown to Rome, even by name, were conquered. The tribes of the Cauchi were once again subjugated and the best of their warrior youth assembled in a seemingly endless mass. Their huge stature was evident and they were holding a strategically secure site. But all these Germans set down their weapons and were escorted by a gleaming line of our soldiers who took the flank and led them towards the tribunal of the commander. Once there they followed the example of their leaders and fell on their knees (surrendering to Rome).

The power of the Langobardi was broken (a tribal group in northern Germany) even though they had surpassed the other Germans in their savagery. Finally, something which had never been attempted or even hoped for before, was achieved. A Roman army complete with its battle standards was led 400 miles beyond the Rhine. This army reached the river Elbe, which flows past the territories of the Semnones and the Hermunduri.

The commander (Tiberius) had kept close watch upon the seasons and (when the weather permitted) he summoned a fleet to traverse the winding North Sea coast. Through a superb combination of careful planning and good fortune, this fleet crossed a previous unknown sea and sailed up the Elbe River (sailing further east than Drusus had attempted). After gaining victory over many tribes, the fleet reconnected with the land army commanded by Tiberius Caesar. They resupplied them with a great variety of provisions and materials.

North Germany is Pacified as far as the Elbe (AD 5)

212 Velleius Paterculus, *History of Rome*, 2.107

These were indeed great events, but I must mention a small incident. When we were encamped on the western bank of the Elbe, we could see the weapons of the enemy warriors glinting on the far side. It seemed that they might flee with every unexpected movement or manoeuvre of our vessels. Then one of the barbarians, who was very tall and elderly, approached the river. To judge from his clothing he was of high status. This man climbed into a canoe, made in the German manner from a hollowed log. On this strange craft he embarked from the far riverbank and manoeuvred out to the middle of the stream. From there he asked permission to land without harm on the shore that was occupied by our troops. He wanted to see Tiberius Caesar and he was granted this request. The German beached his canoe and was brought before Tiberius. He stared at the commander for a long time in complete silence. Then he said:

> Our young warriors must be insane. When you are absent, they venerate you as a divine being. But when you are present they fear your armies, instead of invoking your divine protection. With your permission I will speak and I will say, Caesar – today I have seen the gods that I once merely heard about. And in my life thus far, I have never hoped for, or experienced, a happier day.

The German asked for, and received, permission to touch the hand of Tiberius Caesar. Then he went back to his canoe and began his return crossing. All the way across he continued to gaze back at Tiberius until he had landed on his own bank (on the far side of the Elbe).

Tiberius Caesar was now victorious over all the nations and countries that he reached. His army was safe and undamaged. They had been attacked only once by an enemy who used deceitful tactics and had therefore suffered large casualties. Tiberius led his legions back to their winter quarters and returned to Rome with the same haste as in the previous year.

213 Cassius Dio, *Roman History*, 55.28

While these events were occurring, various commanders were also conducting expeditions against the Germans, especially Tiberius. Tiberius advanced to the river Visurgis (Weser) and later as far as the Albis (the Elbe), but nothing noteworthy was accomplished in these operations (regions pacified, but no new conquests).

Nevertheless, Augustus, Tiberius and Gaius Sentius (Saturninus), the governor of Germany, received triumphal honours for this campaign. The Germans, due to their fear of the Romans, had twice accepted truces. The Romans granted the second truce soon after the first was broken, because the Dalmatians and Pannonians were causing a great disturbance and (their imminent revolt) required immediate attention.

Description of a Frontier Fort

A governor named Arrian reviewed a Roman military installation for the Emperor Hadrian. It indicates the concerns of a Roman commander when establishing or maintaining forts in frontier regions.

214 Arrian, *Periplus of the Black Sea*, 9

A force of 400 select troops are quartered in the fort (at Phasis). Due to the nature of this site, this outpost seems to be very secure. It is positioned in a convenient location for the vessels that sail this way (along the Black Sea coast to the mouth of the river Phasis). In addition, a double ditch has been excavated around the wall of the fort. Both ditches are of similar dimensions.

The wall of the fort used to be an earthwork supporting palisades and timber towers. But now both the wall and towers are made of baked brick. Its foundations are very firm, and war engines have been installed (machines might damage weaker foundations due to recoil and reverberations). In summary, the fort is well protected against the danger of a siege and fully equipped to prevent any of the barbarians from even approaching. However, the mooring place for the ships must also be secured. Likewise, the whole area outside the fort is settled by military veterans, various merchants and others (families and supporting personnel). I therefore decided to construct another bank and ditch, extending from the double ditch that surrounds the fort as far as the river. This will enclose both the harbour and the houses outside the fort.

Plans for the Conquest of Southern Germany (AD 6) Assessment of the Marcomannic Kingdom

The Marcomannic kingdom dominated southern Germania. The Romans were able to install a Germanic ruler in the territory who had been raised in Rome, but his loyalties were dubious.

215 Strabo, *Geography*, 7.1.3
As a young man Maroboduus was sent to Rome (as a political hostage) where he enjoyed the favour of the Emperor Augustus. The Romans promoted Maroboduus as a king and returned him to Germany as ruler of the Marcomannic state.

216 Velleius Paterculus, *History of Rome*, 2.108
Nothing remained to be conquered in Germany except for the Marcomanni population (Bohemia, southern Germany). Their leader Maroboduus had instructed his people to leave their settlements (near the Danube frontier) and head inland to the clearings that were protected by the Hercynian Forest. Maroboduus was from a noble barbarian family. He was physically powerful and courageous, but he also had a superior intelligence (possessing an aptitude for strategic political thinking). He exploited internal disorders that occurred among the Marcomanni.

Either by chance, or by the impulsiveness of his subjects, Maroboduus gained a position among his people that exceeded that of an ordinary chieftain. He began to conceive an idea that he could form a definite empire and assume royal powers. To fulfil this ambition, he moved the Marcomanni far away from Roman power (the Danube frontier). He thought that by escaping the reach of the Roman military, he could develop his own population into an all-powerful regional force. Moving the Marcomanni towards (the Hercynian Forest), Maroboduus used warfare to reduce all the neighbouring tribes into subjugation, or else he brought them under his sovereignty by treaty.

Maroboduus also developed a company of guards to protect his new kingdom. Due to constant training, these men almost reached the Roman standard of discipline. Their existence placed Maroboduus in a position of exceptional power and made his kingdom a threat to our empire. His policy towards Rome was to avoid provoking any war, but at the same time he made it clear that he had the power and will to resist any aggression brought by the Empire. The envoys who Maroboduus sent to the Caesars sometimes presented him as a suppliant and at other times spoke as though he were their equal (holding royal power equivalent to an imperial prince). Soon individuals and entire tribes who had revolted from Rome found a safe refuge in his domains. So his kingdom became a rival of Rome with little concealment of its character.

Maroboduus increased his army to include 70,000 infantry and 4,000 cavalry. He trained this army through constant wars against neighbouring tribes, until it seemed that he was developing a force for some greater undertaking. His kingdom was to be feared because of its (geographical) position. (Greater) Germany was to the north and the main Marcomanni settlements faced this region. Pannonia (the Roman province) was to the south (across the Danube frontier), while Noricum was to the rear (Roman Austria, positioned to the south-west). The Marcomanni might suddenly attack in any one of these directions, so the kingdom of Maroboduus was dreaded (by all surrounding states). Even Italy was concerned by the growing power of Maroboduus, since the boundary summits of the Alps were less than 200 miles from Marcomannic territory.

Tiberius Caesar assessed Maroboduus and his domains. He decided to attack the region from opposite directions in the upcoming campaign year. Sentius Saturninus was ordered to lead his legions through the country of the Chatti into Boiohaemum (from the northern Rhine, south-east into Bohemia). This region (Boiohaemum) was the name of the main territory occupied by Maroboduus. As Saturninus advanced, he would cut a route through the Hercynian Forest which surrounded the region. Meanwhile, Tiberius would advance towards Marcomannic territory (heading north-east) from Carnuntum and the closest point in Noricum. The invasion force included the Roman army which was serving in Illyricum.

Chapter Eight

The Illyricum Revolt (AD 6–9) 'Fortune sometimes halts the plans of men'

Roman plans to conquer the Marcomannic kingdom (southern Germany) were interrupted by a major revolt in the imperial territory of Illyricum near the Danube frontier. This territory included Pannonia and Dalmatia and had only recently been added to the Empire. It had been forced to supply large amounts of men and materials to the Germanic war.

217 Cassius Dio, *Roman History*, 55.29

The people of Dalmatia resented Roman levies and tribute payments, but they remained pacified until other events provoked unrest. Tiberius made his second campaign against the Germans (in AD 6) and was joined by Valerius Messallinus, the governor of Dalmatia and Pannonia. Valerius led most of his army north to participate in this conflict.

The Dalmatians were ordered to send military contingents to this war, but once they had gathered their recruits, they suddenly realised the number and strength of their warriors. Urged by a man from the Desidiatian tribe named Bato, they revolted and defeated the Roman forces sent against them. The rest of the Dalmatian tribes also rebelled when they learned about this success. Then a Pannonian tribe called the Breucians joined the uprising under the leadership of another man also named Bato. They marched against Sirmium and besieged the Romans in that city (the district capital). (…)

When Tiberius learned about the revolt, he was afraid the enemy might invade Italy. He therefore returned from Germany with most of his army, while sending Messallinus ahead with a force to Pannonia.

Roman Preparations to deal with the Illyricum Revolt (AD 6) Military Manpower Shortages and Emergency Measures

218 Velleius Paterculus, *History of Rome*, 2.110–113

Fortune sometimes halts the plans of men, but at other times its merely delays the outcome. Tiberius Caesar had arranged his winter quarters on the Danube and brought his army up to a position only five days' march from the closest outposts of the enemy (the Marcomanni). Meanwhile, he ordered Saturninus to bring the legions into position (at the Rhine). They were ready and waiting a similar distance from the enemy (for a simultaneous attack). Tiberius arranged that the two armies would meet a few days later (after the invasion began) at a predetermined rendezvous site in the centre of enemy territory.

But due to the benefits of a long peace, the populace of Pannonia (the Roman province on the Danube) had become overconfident. Their military strength had also increased (manpower and resources martialled by Rome). When the Pannonians suddenly rebelled, Dalmatia and all the nations in that region joined the uprising. The glory (of new conquests) therefore had to be sacrificed for what was necessary (for defence). Tiberius realised that it was not a safe course of action to lead his army deep into the interior of a hostile country (the Marcomannic kingdom), while there was an enemy behind him (the Pannonians) that might attack an unprotected Italy.

The total population of the people and tribes which had rebelled against Rome was more than 800,000 (Pannonia and Dalmatia). The enemy could assemble about 200,000 infantry with military training and 9,000 cavalry were also being gathered. This was a large force acting on the orders of energetic and capable generals. One portion of the rebels decided to attack that part of Italy which was connected to Pannonia through the Nauportum and Tergeste route (eastern Alps). A second force headed east to overrun Macedonia (the Roman province to the north of Greece), while a third prepared to protect their homelands (Pannonia and Dalmatia). The chief authorities in this conflict against Rome were Batones and Pinnes acting as generals.

All the Pannonians had a knowledge of Roman military discipline and the Latin language. Many possessed both intellect and learning and were also familiar with Roman writings and, by Hercules! No nation had ever begun plans for an offensive war so swiftly after an uprising. The Pannonians quickly put their schemes into action. Roman citizens were overpowered and merchants were massacred. A large detachment of Roman veterans stationed in a region furthest from the commander were quickly exterminated with no survivors. Macedonia was seized by armed forces and everywhere devastation was inflicted with fire and sword. This caused such a great panic that even Caesar Augustus (the emperor), who was resolute and courageous after commanding in so many wars, became shaken with fear.

Roman levies were conducted in every district and all veterans were recalled to active service. The wealthy men and women were compelled to provide freedmen as soldiers in proportion to their income (robust slaves manumitted to serve in the army). Men heard Augustus say in the Senate that unless precautions were taken, the enemy might appear within sight of Rome within ten days. The military services of senators and *equites* were demanded and willingly pledged for this war. But all these arrangements would have been useless if Rome did not have the right man to take command. And so, as a final measure of protection, the state demanded from Augustus that Tiberius should conduct the war.

My abilities were modest, but I had an opportunity to take part in this glorious war. It was towards the end of my military service in the cavalry as a quaestor designate. I was not yet a senator, but I was given parity with the senators and tribunes elect. Augustus therefore entrusted me with a portion of the army. I led these divisions from the city of Rome to where Tiberius was assembling his forces. During my quaestorship, I had the right to be allocated a provincial command, but I was sent to Tiberius as a *legatus Augusti* (officer appointed by the emperor).

In the first year of the war, formidable enemy armies were drawn up for battle against us. But through the foresight of our general we evaded their combined forces. When they split into separate divisions, we routed them. Tiberius possessed such authority as a military commander that he could conduct the war with moderation and kindness when dealing with his troops (no harsh reprimands or punishments were issued). He also demonstrated great judgment in his placement of winter camps. The enemy was carefully blockaded by the outposts of our army and could not break through in any district. Consequently, their strength was gradually weakened through lack of supplies and by disaffection within their own ranks. (…)

O, Marcus Vinicius, now read my narrative of these events. This is the proof that Tiberius Caesar is as great a general in war as he is an emperor in peace. Under his command two Roman armies were united, the soldiers who had served with him (in Germany) and the troops (from Rome) coming to reinforce him. Ten legions were gathered together in one military camp along with more than 70 cohorts, 14 cavalry units and more than 10,000 veterans. In addition, a large number of military volunteers were present, along with the numerous cavalry sent by the Thracian king. No greater army than this had ever been assembled in one place since the civil wars. All the soldiers took pride in this fact and placed their greatest hope of victory in their vast numbers.

But Tiberius was a better judge of the situation. As he has done in all his wars, he rightly preferred efficiency to vast displays of force. He kept the newly arrived army in place for only a few days to allow the soldiers to recover from the march. Then he decided to send the reinforcements back (to Italy) since he realised that the combined army was too large to be properly managed and not well adapted to effective control. He escorted the returning divisions back (to Italy) with his own army, so the reinforcements would not try to engage the enemy and the enemy would not dare to attack them in defence of their own territories. This was a long and laborious march that involved great difficulties.

The German Command becomes an Illyrian War (AD 6–9)

219 Suetonius, *Tiberius*, 16

Tiberius was granted the tribunician power for a second term of three years and was assigned the duty of subjugating Germany. After presenting their directives to Augustus in Rome, the Parthian envoys (from the rival Iranian Empire), were sent to appear before Tiberius in his provincial command (Rhine territories).

However, when news of the revolt in Illyricum was reported, Tiberius was transferred to take charge of the new war (the Pannonian Revolt). The Illyrian War was the most serious of all foreign wars since the Roman conflict against Carthage. Tiberius conducted this war over the course of three years, commanding a force of fifteen legions and a corresponding force of auxiliaries. He met difficulties of every kind and managed to deal with a great scarcity of supplies. He was often recalled (to Rome), but maintained his command for fear that the nearby and powerful enemy might assume the offensive, if the Romans relented. Tiberius received a great reward for his perseverance, for he completely subdued and reduced to submission the whole of Illyricum. This territory is bounded by Italy and the kingdom of Noricum, by Thrace and Macedonia, by the Danube, and by the Adriatic Sea.

Victory in Illyricum: Disaster in Germany

220 Suetonius, *Tiberius*, 17

Events gave his achievement (the victory in Illyricum) a greater and more significant glory. For it occurred about the same time that Quintilius Varus perished with three legions in Germany. No one doubted that the victorious

Germans would have united with the Pannonians, if Illyricum had not already been subdued. Consequently, a triumph was voted for Tiberius and he received many high honours. Some also suggested that he received the honorary surname of 'Pannonicus', while others recommended 'Invictus' or 'Pius'. But Augustus vetoed the surname and confirmed his promise that Tiberius would be satisfied with the name he would receive at his father's death (adoption as successor to imperial power).

Tiberius himself postponed the triumph because the country was in mourning for the disaster inflicted on Varus. But he entered the city clad in the purple-bordered toga and crowned with a laurel (symbols of victory). Then he mounted a tribunal which had been set up in the Saepta, while the Senate stood surrounding him. There he took his seat beside Augustus who was positioned between the two consuls. Having greeted the people from this position, Tiberius was escorted to the various temples.

Chapter Nine

Massacre at the Teutoburg Forest and Aftermath (AD 9–13) Roman Withdrawal as Germania is Lost

The Roman commander Quinctilius Varus was appointed governor of a conquered and subdued Germania in AD 7. But while Roman armies were occupied in Illyricum, a chieftain of the Cherusci named Arminius began organising a major revolt in Germania. In AD 9, an army including three Roman legions was ambushed and massacred in the Teutoburg Forest by an alliance of Chatti, Cherusci, Sugambri, Usipetes, Bructeri and Angrivarii. These are the main events of this period:

- **AD 9:** Three legions commanded by Varus are slaughtered in the Teutoburg Forest. Two remaining legions, located near the Rhine frontier, manage to withstand the German assault. The Marcomannic king Maroboduus does not join the rebellion. Tiberius leads Roman armies north, from their victory in Illyricum, to protect the threatened frontiers.
- **AD 10:** Tiberius leads a Roman campaign into Germania, but cannot gain a decisive victory against an elusive enemy.
- **AD 11–12:** Tiberius is joined by his adoptive son Germanicus and conducts further campaigns into Germania, overcoming the Bructeri. No territories are reclaimed, and Tiberius is recalled to Rome.
- **AD 13:** Germanicus is appointed commander of the Rhine forces including eight legions (one-third of the Roman army).
- **AD 14:** Death of the Emperor Augustus and succession of Tiberius.

221 Florus, *Roman History*, 2.30

But it is more difficult to retain provinces than to create them. New territories are won by military force, but they are secured by justice. The Roman victory was brief, for the Germans had been defeated rather than conquered. When Drusus was in command the Germans had respected our moral qualities more than our military power.

After the death of Drusus, the Germans began to detest the extravagance and pride of Rome. They thought these attitudes were as abhorrent as the malice displayed by Quinctilius Varus. Varus had the audacity to convince an assembly and issue a legal edict against the Chatti. He thought he could restrain the violence of barbarians by the rod of a lictor (a symbol of office) and the proclamation of a herald.

But for a long time, the Germans regretted how their swords were rusting and their horses were idle. They saw toga-wearing Romans in their country (civilians) and experienced laws more oppressive than military force. So, the Germans seized their weapons and once again prepared for war under the leadership of Arminius.

222 Velleius Paterculus, *History of Rome*, 2.117–18

I will briefly describe the origins and character of Varus to explain these events. Publius Quinctilius Varus was descended from a political family that was famous, rather than aristocratic. He had a mild personality and quiet character, but he was not quick in decision-making or in physical action. Varus was more accustomed to the leisure of the camp headquarters rather than actual military combat. He demonstrated avarice in office, especially when he served as governor of Syria. It is said that he entered this rich province a poor man, and departed a rich man by leaving the province poor.

Varus was placed in charge of the Roman army in Germania (the recently conquered territories between the Rhine and Elbe). He believed that the Germans had lost their fighting spirit and that they were men only in their bodies and voices. He thought that a people who could not be subdued by military force might be made subject to legal rulings. With this attitude he accepted his posting in the very centre of Germania and governed it as though he were among a people who were enjoying the full benefits of peace. Instead of conducting military campaigns in the summer months, Varus sat at his tribunal. He wasted his time holding court and following the proper details of legal procedure.

But Germans possess a great ferocity combined with a scheming mentality. This attitude is difficult to understand, unless people are familiar with them. The Germans are a race of innate liars and under Roman occupation the tribes exaggerated a series of fictitious lawsuits against one another. They provoked each other with unnecessary legal cases and then feigned false gratitude when Roman justice intervened to settle escalating disputes.

This gave the impression that their savage character was being softened by a previously unknown process (legal arbitration by Rome). It seemed that German quarrels, usually settled by warfare, were now being mediated by law. Varus was so convinced by this process that he neglected his military responsibilities. He began to see his governorship more like the role of a city praetor (a civic official) who administers justice in the forum. He forgot he was general in command of an occupying army in the depths of Germania (enemy territory).

223 Cassius Dio, *Roman History*, 56.18–19

I will describe events which took place in Germania during this period, as important details have been omitted from other narratives.

The Romans did hold territories in Germania, but they did not inhabit all regions. They occupied districts that had been subdued and these territories had winter camps for soldiers and the foundations of cities. At these sites barbarians were adapting themselves to Roman customs. They were beginning to hold markets and arrange tribal meetings in peaceful assemblies. But the Germans had not forgotten their ancestral customs, their native ways, or their old means of independence. And they had not forgotten the power derived from warfare.

Under careful Roman supervision the Germans were gradually neglecting, then dismissing, their native customs. They were unperturbed by gradual alterations in their lifestyle, becoming a different population without appreciating any change. But when Quinctilius Varus became governor of the province, he tried to increase the pace of change in Germania. In addition to his standard duties, Varus began to use direct administration to interfere in the affairs of subject nations. He issued orders to the Germans as though they were actual slaves and he extracted money from their communities as though they were entirely subject to Rome.

The Germans were in no mood to submit. Their leaders longed for their former ascendancy and the masses preferred their accustomed conditions in place of foreign domination. But the Germans did not openly revolt against the Empire. They saw that there were numerous Roman soldiers posted near the Rhine and many garrisons within their country. So, the tribes tolerated Varus and pretended to do everything he demanded of them. But they led him far away from the Rhine into the land of the Cherusci and the Visurgis (the Weser River).

The Germans behaved in a peaceful and friendly manner to convince Varus that they would live submissively without the presence of soldiers. Consequently, Varus did not keep his legions together in a unified force as would be expected in a hostile country. Instead, he distributed the soldiers across the province. He sent many of them to guard and reinforce outlying communities that he believed were vulnerable, or helpless. The Germans had requested these garrison movements, saying they were needed to guard various districts, apprehend bandits, or escort convoys carrying provisions.

Arminius

224 Velleius Paterculus, *History of Rome*, 2.118

At this time a royal leader emerged from among the German nation. He was a young nobleman named Arminius, the son of Segimer. Arminius was courageous in action, mentally alert and possessed an intelligence far superior to ordinary barbarians. These attributes were clear from his appearance and mannerisms, for his eyes glimmered with a fierce intellect.

Although still a young man, Arminius had accompanied and assisted the Roman forces on many military campaigns. He had therefore been granted equestrian status (an award of second rank Roman nobility). But he used his position and the negligence of the Roman commander as an opportunity for treachery. Arminius astutely realised that an unwary man is quickly overpowered and defeated. Most disasters begin when a victim, with a full sense of security, encounters an unseen danger.

At first Arminius admitted only a few kinsmen into his conspiracy against Rome. But later many joined his cause and shared his intentions. He convinced them that the Roman military could be crushed. He was so certain of this, and so resolved to act, that he even set a date for the deed.

The plot was revealed to Varus by a loyal German nobleman named Segestes. Segestes urged Varus to immediately seize and imprison the conspirators, but Fate had other plans for him. It was as though his mind's eye was blindfolded (he could not comprehend or act on the information he received).

Sometimes a divine force impairs the judgment of a man condemned by Fate to a terrible destiny. It will, by wretched means, ensure his fate and thwart any evasion of his destiny. When some chance brings hope, another accident or intent will emerge that redirects the man back towards his preordained end. This is what happened to Varus. He refused to believe the information Segestes brought to him. Instead, Varus judged the loyalty of the leading Germans by their apparent friendship towards him. He took this to be a real measure of merit and an indicator of truth. But it was the only news of the plot that Varus was to receive. There was no time for a second warning.

Forewarned

225 Tacitus, *Annals*, 1.55

Arminius caused the uprising in Germany, and Segestes tried to reveal that a rebellion was being organised. At the final banquet before the military campaign (the expedition through the Teutoburg Forest) he had urged Varus to arrest him (Segestes), Arminius and all the other chiefs. Segestes assured the commander that the German masses would not attempt any uprising if their leaders were removed. Their arrest would give Varus an opportunity to assess the accusations and determine who was innocent. But Fate had Varus slain through the weapons of Arminius.

The Traitors

226 Cassius Dio, *Roman History*, 56.19

Arminius and Segimer were the greatest instigators of the plot and the leaders in this war. Yet these men were constant companions to Varus. They were welcomed into military environs where the governor performed his duties and they socialised with him. Consequently, Varus was confident that these German leaders had no harmful intent towards him. He refused to believe anyone who suspected these Germans, or advised him to be on his guard. He rebuked those who warned him, calling them overexcited, or accusing them of slandering his friends.

The uprising began in the parts of Germany that were furthest from the authority of Varus. This was arranged so that the commander would march the greatest distance and be overwhelmed in regions that he considered to be friendly territories. The plotters hoped that Varus would enter the intervening regions without sufficient precautions, unaware that the surrounding population was hostile. This plan was successful.

The plotters escorted Varus as he set out for the furthest districts of Germania. But on the outward march they asked to be excused from further attendance, so that they could assemble allied forces. They promised to bring these Germanic fighters to the immediate aid of Rome.

March, Ambush and Annihilation

227 Cassius Dio, *Roman History*, 56.20–22

The mountains of Germania are split by ravines where the trees are densely placed and extend to a great height. From the time of their first campaigns the Romans had struggled to enter and cross the regions contained by these ranges. It was a difficult task to fell trees, construct roads and bridge territories (by building wooden causeways across marshlands). Now they had to perform these tasks while under attack.

Varus had the Roman army travel in a convoy containing many wagons and pack animals as though it were a time of peace. There were women and children accompanying the army along with a large retinue of servants. For this reason, the Roman force was advancing in scattered groups instead of a unified military column. Rain and violent winds further interrupted and separated the advancing force. The surface water made forest roots and logs slippery and treacherous for those who walked the route. Branches torn from the trees kept falling onto the path of the column, causing further delay and confusion.

The Germanic forces were already prepared and waiting. When their leaders arrived, they massacred the Roman detachments posted in their territories. Then they moved forwards to intercept the Roman army led by Varus, marching through the midst of a vast and almost impenetrable forest (the Teutoburg). As the German warriors approached the Romans, they suddenly revealed themselves to be armed enemies instead of subject allies. Then they wrought dreadful havoc on the Romans.

While the Romans were distracted by logistic (supply and terrain) difficulties the barbarians suddenly and simultaneously surrounded them on all sides. They knew the hidden trails and could emerge from the densest thickets of the forest. At first their warriors hurled their spear volleys from a distance. The unprepared Romans put up no defence and a great number were wounded. Seeing this, the Germans approached closer to the Roman lines.

The Romans were not advancing through the forest in any regular order and the soldiers were intermixed with wagons and unarmed people (women, children and attendants). The Roman response was therefore chaotic, as soldiers could not form into effective combat units. The Romans were also outnumbered by the Germans at the main points of attack. This meant that they suffered greatly in the fighting and could offer no effective resistance.

Various detachments of the army halted and formed defensible encampments. But it was a difficult landscape surrounded by wooded hillsides. They burned or abandoned most of their wagons and destroyed or salvaged everything else that was not necessary for their immediate survival. The following day, these groups reformed and advanced in better order and some even reached a large clearing. But this route re-entered the forest, so they had to endure further casualties.

The Romans suffered their heaviest losses while defending themselves from attacks in this forest. This was because they were forced to halt and form ranks in a narrow space (the trackway). In this environment the cavalry and infantry could not effectively charge, or even pursue the enemy. When they attempted these manoeuvres, they frequently collided with one another or crashed into tree branches.

When the fourth day dawned, the Roman army was still advancing through the forest. But on this day, there was another heavy downpour and further violent winds. The soldiers could not advance further or manage to keep effective formation. Their equipment was waterlogged, and their bows and javelins were of minimal use (due to slippery ground and the water damage to the tension of bowstrings). In these wet conditions the soldiers struggled to even hold their shields.

By this time the forces of the enemy had greatly increased. Tribes that had wavered in their initial support for the uprising had joined the fighting in the hope of gaining plunder. The enlarged Germanic horde could more easily encircle and cut down the Roman forces. Meanwhile, the Roman ranks had been depleted since many soldiers had perished in earlier fighting.

Varus and the leading Roman officers now feared that they might be captured alive, or killed by the Germans. They had already been wounded and now made a bold decision. This was shocking, but an unavoidable course of action. Varus and his commanders committed suicide (a self-inflicted sword thrust to the abdomen, chest or throat).

When news of this occurrence spread through the army the Roman soldiers despaired. Some who still had strength suddenly became despondent and stopped defending themselves. Others imitated their commander (and killed themselves with a self-inflicted sword thrust). Other soldiers threw down their weapons and exposed their bodies to the enemy. No one could escape by fleeing the scene of battle, no matter how much they tried to evade their fate. The Germans slaughtered every man and animal without fear of resistance.

[Text missing from the Roman account]

Another Account of the Massacre

228 Florus, *Roman History*, 2.30

Varus was so confident in the peace arrangements that when one of the Germanic chiefs named Segestes gave a report of the conspiracy, he completely dismissed it. Varus was utterly unprepared and had no fear of an uprising. Such was his certainty that he was actually summoning the German leaders to his tribunal, when they suddenly rose up and attacked him from all sides. They seized his military camp and the three legions he commanded were overwhelmed.

Varus ended his life with the same courage as Paulus displayed on the fatal day of Cannae (both generals committed suicide after suffering a major defeat). The slaughter that took place in the marshes and woods of Germania was unsurpassed. The retaliations inflicted by the barbarians were horrific and there were unbearable abuses. They directed the most severe punishments against the legal pleàders (those who practised or participated in Roman law). The Germans gouged out the eyes of some victims and cut off the hands of others. One captive had his tongue cut out and his mouth sewn shut. The barbarian held the severed tongue in his hand and cried out, 'Now viper – you have ceased to hiss!'

The soldiers hastily buried the body of Varus to honour his status as a former consul. But the Germans found the disturbed ground and disinterred his corpse. They also seized the battle standards and prized eagles belonging to the legions. They still possess two of these eagles, but the third evaded capture. The standard-bearer tore the eagle from the ground and carried the figurehead concealed in a cloak. He attached the eagle to his belt and submerged himself in the blood-stained marsh.

As a result of this disaster the Roman Empire, which had previously advanced beyond the ocean, was halted on the banks of the Rhine.

[*Modern Note:* the third eagle was retrieved by the Germans and kept by the Chauci. It was recovered by the Roman general Aulus Gabinius Secundus in AD 41.]

Heroic Fate in Roman Imagination

229 Crinagoras, *Epigrams*, 7.741

Cite Othryadas for the great glory of Sparta (the last surviving Spartan in the legendry 'Battle of 300 Champions'). Or, if records of other military deeds are required, mention that sea fighter Cynegeirus (the Athenian commander at Marathon who gripped the stern of a Persian ship while his hands were being hacked off). Now consider that Roman warrior lying half dead by a tributary of the Rhine. He endures many wounds, but when he sees the eagle of his dear legion seized by the enemy, he arises from amid the corpses of the slain. He kills the enemy who carries this standard and takes possession of it once more for the sake of his commanders. In death he has won for himself a demise that does not know defeat.

Signals in the Heavens

230 Marcus Manilius, *Astronomicon*, 1.898

Gleaming comets can threaten the earth. This (celestial sign) often foretells the approach of funerals lit by torches. Urgent and relentless prayers are given when nature is sick and men are destined for the grave. These signs foretell wars, fires and sudden upheavals when armed uprisings are conducted by treacherous foreign nations. For example, when the barbarians broke their agreements and set upon Varus, the commander in Germany, comets threatened, burning above the whole world, while Varus opposed the enemy until the very end. The plains of that country were stained with the blood of three legions.

Appraisal

231 Velleius Paterculus, *History of Rome*, 2.119

I will briefly outline the details of this severe disaster for Rome. It was the worst defeat in foreign territory that Rome had suffered since the invasion of Parthia by Crassus (20,000 legionaries were killed and 10,000 taken prisoner during the Roman invasion of Iraq). I have described the German disaster in greater detail in my other work, so here I will merely outline the worst occurrences.

The Roman army in Germany excelled all others in bravery. It was first among the Roman forces in discipline, energetic action and combat experience. These qualities were opposed by the negligence of their commander, the treachery of the enemy, and the cruelty of Fortune. The soldiers were not given the opportunity to fight in the manner they were accustomed to. They could not extricate themselves from the danger they faced, or overcome the great odds which opposed them. When the threat became present, some were even reprimanded for using their weapons and displaying the martial spirit of Rome. As the Roman army marched, it was hemmed in by great forests and marshes. The enemy launched multiple ambushes along this course to exterminate them. In the subsequent fighting almost all the soldiers were killed.

The Romans had once slaughtered Germans like cattle. The lives of these Germans had once depended on the wrath, or the mercy, of the Romans. But now the situation was reversed and the Romans were butchered by their attackers. The general had more courage to die than to fight. Following the example of his father and grandfather, Varus thrust his own sword through his chest and bled to death.

Command passed to the two prefects of the military camp, Lucius Eggius and Ceionius. Lucius acted valiantly, but Ceionius had base instincts and proposed surrender. He saw that the greater part of the army had been destroyed. He preferred captivity and death by torture, rather than a violent end in battle. A lieutenant of Varus named Vala Numonius also acted shamefully. Vala had been an unassuming and honourable officer throughout his service to Rome. But when the enemy attacked, he abandoned the infantry and fled with his cavalry squadrons in the direction of the Rhine. Yet Fate intervened to avenge his cowardice and Vala was killed as he deserted the legions.

The partially burned body of Varus was retrieved by the enemy. They further mutilated and mangled the corpse. Finally, they severed his head and sent it as a prize to Maroboduus (the king of the Marcomanni in Bohemia). Maroboduus (who was still allied to Rome) sent the remains to Augustus. Though Varus had caused a great disaster, the emperor ensured that his remains were interred with honour in his family tomb.

Garrisons in Forts

232 Frontinus, *Stratagems*, 4.7.8, 'Varius Maxims and Devices'
Caedicius was a first rank centurion who took command in Germany after the Varian disaster (AD 9). The Roman soldiers felt oppressed and were afraid that the barbarians might gather timber to stack next to their defences and burn down their camp. Caedicius therefore pretended to require fuel and sent out men in every direction to gather wood (a standard task ordered by centurions). By this means he removed the entire supply of easily felled trees that the Germans might acquire.

The Rhine Holds; Aliso is Surrounded

233 Velleius Paterculus, *History of Rome*, 2.120
Further honour should be given to Lucius Asprenas. At the time of the disaster Asprenas was serving as a lieutenant under the command of his uncle Varus. He was assigned two legions (the First Germania and Fifth Alaudae, stationed at Mainz in Germania Superior, on the southern Rhine frontier). When the disaster occurred (the Germanic and Gallic) tribes on the far side of the Rhine began to question their loyalty to Rome. But Asprenas acted with notable bravery and energetic decisiveness. He quickly marched his army north into Germania Inferior (the Lower Rhine territories) to strengthen and renew Roman alliances with these nations.

But some say that Asprenas also conducted improprieties while in office. He saved Roman lives by his swift actions, but he also dishonoured the dead. He misappropriated the military-held funds and property belonging to soldiers who died with Varus. He seized the inheritance of a slaughtered army for his own reward and pleasure.

The extreme valour of Lucius Caedicius also deserves recognition and praise. At the time of the disaster, Caedicius was prefect of the camp at Aliso (a Roman military colony on the Lippe River). The town was besieged by an immense force of Germans who could not be resisted or defeated. Caedicius remained vigilant and waited for his opportunity. Then he led a breakout force which fought its way free and escaped back to allied territory (the Roman-held Rhine).

Despite the disaster, it must be acknowledged that Varus was a person of good character and noble intentions. But his lack of judgement cost him his life and led to the destruction of a magnificent army. This army was not lost due to insufficient valour or ability. It was simply the lack of judgement exhibited by a single commander.

The Germans expressed their full and furious cruelty towards the Roman captives. But one young soldier named Caldus Caelius performed a heroic act to escape this horror. His actions were worthy of his ancestors and the noble lineage of his people. Caelius suddenly seized a section of the heavy shackles that bound him in chains. He struck his own head with such force that he died instantly from a wound that poured out blood and displaced brain matter.

Severed Heads

234 Frontinus, *Stratagems*, 2.9.4, 'Concluding a War after a Successful Engagement'

Arminius, the leader of the Germans, ordered the severed heads of those who were slain to be fastened onto spears and brought up to the fortifications of the enemy (horror and intimidation).

Withdrawal from Aliso

235 Cassius Dio, *Roman History*, 56.22

After the massacre, the barbarians occupied all the Roman strongholds in Germany except one (the fortress of Aliso under the command of Lucius Caedicius). The Germans were delayed at this site, so they did not immediately cross the Rhine and invade Gaul. The Germans cannot conduct sieges and the Roman defenders of Aliso deployed numerous archers against their attackers. They repeatedly forced back the German assaults and inflicted large numbers of casualties.

Meanwhile, the Germans learnt that the Romans had posted a large guard of soldiers at the Rhine frontier. Commander Tiberius was approaching them with a formidable army (urgent reinforcements). Most of the barbarians therefore abandoned the siege of Aliso, and any that remained at the site withdrew a considerable distance away to avoid sudden sorties launched by the defending garrison. The Germans blockaded the roads and watched them, so that the besieged Romans might be defeated through a lack of provisions.

The Roman garrison could remain in place while their food stocks were plentiful. But when no relief force arrived, the defenders began to experience hunger. They waited until a stormy night to escape the fortress. They managed to get past the first and second enemy outposts undetected. But the forces fleeing the base included women and children who became fatigued and fearful in the darkness and cold. They could not keep pace with the soldiers and kept calling out and pleading with them to come back.

All of them could have been killed or captured by the enemy, if the Germans had not been more interested in immediately seizing plunder. This allowed the most able of the soldiers to make it some distance away before the German outpost was alerted. Realising they had been discovered, the trumpeters sounded the signal for a double-quick march. The Germans mistook the noise for the arrival of a Roman army sent by Asprenas (the Rhineland legions) and halted their pursuit. The remaining Romans therefore escaped.

After the conflict, Asprenas was able to assist some of the Roman prisoners. Their relatives raised ransoms for their release and Asprenas arranged with the German tribes for the captives to be returned. This was done on the condition that these men would never again return to Italy (the shame of defeat could not be seen in the political capital).

Response in Rome

236 Cassius Dio, *Roman History*, 56.23

It is reported that when the Emperor Augustus learnt about Varus and the disaster he tore his garments in an act of public bereavement. He mourned the loss of so many soldiers and feared the consequences for the German and Gallic provinces (the Rhine and Gaul). He expected the Germans might immediately invade Italy and attempt an attack on Rome. There was no great mass of military-age citizens available for deployment and the allied forces had also suffered severe losses.

Nevertheless, Augustus prepared for war. Because few men of military age were willing to join the army, Augustus imposed penalties. Citizens who refused service were forced to draw lots. Every fifth man under 35 would have his property confiscated and would lose his citizen rights. Every tenth man over 35 would receive the same penalty. When the great mass of citizens refused to follow this practice, the emperor began ordering executions. Finally, he filled the ranks with veterans who had already completed their military service and freedmen (former slaves who received citizen rights). When these forces were assembled, Augustus placed them under the command of Tiberius and sent them urgently north to reinforce the remaining provinces of Germania (Rhine frontier).

At this time there were a large number of Gauls and Germans in Rome. They were staying in the city for various reasons and some serving in the Praetorian Guard (the military unit assigned to the emperor). But Augustus now feared that these people might become involved in an uprising against the Empire. He therefore ordered them to leave the city and sent his personal bodyguard (the custodes, an elite unit of German warriors) to certain islands (to remove them from politics). All unarmed Celts and Germans were likewise expelled from Rome.

This is how Augustus handled matters during the crisis. Normal political business was suspended and major festivals were not celebrated (avoiding mass gatherings where there might be public unrest or panic). Augustus later received information that some of the soldiers had survived the disaster in Germany. He also received news that the remaining German lands (the Rhine provinces) were securely held under Roman garrisons. When he heard that the enemy were not attempting to cross the river, his alarm diminished. He paused to reconsider his actions.

Reaction to the Varus Disaster

237 Suetonius, *Augustus*, 23

Augustus suffered only two severe and humiliating defeats. These were the loss of (Marcus) Lollius and that of (Quinctilius) Varus, which both occurred in Germany. The defeat of Lollius was more demeaning than severe (16 BC), but the losses caused by Varus were almost fatal to the Roman state (AD 9). In this engagement three legions were slaughtered along with their general, their officers, and all their auxiliaries.

When the news reached Rome, Augustus ordered a watch to be kept by night throughout the entire city to prevent outbreaks of unrest. He extended the terms of the provincial governors, so that allies might be kept loyal by experienced men they already knew. He publicly vowed to stage great celebratory games to Jupiter Optimus Maximus (the Roman chief god) if the condition of the Empire improved. This was something which had been done in the Cimbric and Marsic wars (threatened Germanic invasion of Italy: 113–101 BC; Roman war with the Italian allies: 91–87 BC).

It is said that Augustus was so greatly affected (by the Varus defeat) that he did not cut his hair or trim his beard for several months (a custom in Roman bereavement). Sometimes he would pound his head against a door, exclaiming: 'Quintilius Varus, give me back my legions!' Each year he observed the day of the disaster as a time of great grief and mourning.

Confused Summary of the Conflict

238 Orosius, *History*, 6.22

Tiberius, the stepson of Augustus, cruelly slaughtered and destroyed the Pannonians when they rose in a new revolt (AD 9). Then he immediately engaged the Germans in a further war. As conqueror, he seized 40,000 of them as captives. This was truly a great and formidable conflict waged by fifteen legions over a period of fifteen years (commands ranging from 8 BC to AD 8). According to the testimony of Suetonius, there had not been a conflict on this scale since the Punic Wars (Roman wars against Carthage in the third and second century BC).

In this period Quintilius Varus had treated the conquered Germans in an exceedingly haughty and acquisitive manner (the imposition of tribute and taxes). In response the Germans revolted and totally destroyed the three legions that accompanied him. Augustus was severely affected by this state disaster. In his great distress he would pound his head against a wall, crying out, 'O, Quintilius Varus, give me back my legions!'

Omens Reconsidered

239 Cassius Dio, *Roman History*, 56.24

It seemed to Augustus that a catastrophe as sudden and severe as the German disaster had to be due to the wrath of some divinity. This reasoning was reinforced by the portents which occurred immediately before and after the Roman defeat. These signs led him to believe that some superhuman agency had decided the events.

In Rome, at the Field of Mars (central district of the city), the Temple of Mars was struck by lightning. Many locusts flew into the city, but they were devoured by swallows. The peaks of the distant Alps seemed to collapse and expel great columns of fire. Numerous comets appeared at the same time and set the sky ablaze. Spear-like points of light streaked across the sky, heading from the north to fall in the direction of the Roman garrisons. Bees swarmed around the altars in the Roman camps and formed honeycombs around the stonework. A statue of Victory in the province of Germania, which had previously faced enemy territory, turned around to face Italy. In one instance a Roman camp fell into disorder and the soldiers began fighting one another in a futile combat. They believed the barbarians were suddenly amongst them seeking their eagle battle standards as well (these legionaries might have attacked foreign auxiliaries).

Tiberius Responds to the Crisis

At the time of the massacre the imperial prince, Tiberius, was still in command in Illyricum. He possessed a large, well-equipped and experienced army.

240 Velleius Paterculus, *History of Rome*, 2.117
(The Roman commander and future emperor) Tiberius had just concluded the war in Pannonia and the Dalmatian conflict. Just five days after this achievement he received the official reports from Germania. The dispatches revealed that Varus had been killed and his three legions slaughtered. Three entire divisions of cavalry and six cohorts had also been destroyed. But fortune had granted a small mercy in the timing of this terrible incident. The disaster had not occurred when Tiberius was occupied by other wars.

241 Velleius Paterculus, *History of Rome*, 2.120
When Tiberius heard about the disaster he rushed to assist Augustus. Tiberius was the constant protector of the Roman Empire and he urgently wanted to continue in this role. Augustus sent Tiberius to Germania (the Rhine frontier). When he reached Gaul, the commander reassured the provinces, relocated the armies to meet the danger, and reinforced the garrison towns near the frontier. The enemy threatened Italy with an invasion just like the Cimbri and Teutones (just over a century earlier). But Tiberius met and eliminated this threat with actions that emphasised his own greatness. He immediately took the offensive and led the Roman army across the Rhine to attack the enemy in their own homelands.

Tiberius conducted an aggressive war against the enemy at a time when the emperor was merely content to halt and resist further German hostilities. The campaign by Tiberius penetrated the very core of Germania. He reopened military routes, devastated enemy field systems, burned dwellings, and routed any forces that resisted the Roman assault. The Romans suffered no serious losses in these operations and Tiberius successfully led his troops back to winter quarters (in the Rhine regions). For these exploits he enhanced his reputation and received numerous awards of glory.

Tiberius leads Roman Campaign into Germany (AD 10)

242 Suetonius, *Tiberius*, 18–20

The next year Tiberius returned to Germany where he realised that the disaster inflicted on Varus was due to the general's rashness and lack of care. Previously, Tiberius had always demonstrated independent judgment and self-reliance in command, but now he took no action without the approval of a council. Contrary to his usual habits, he consulted with many advisers about the conduct of the campaign. He also took more scrupulous care than was usual.

When he was about to cross the Rhine (with his army), he reduced all the baggage to a prescribed limit. He began the campaign by standing on the riverbank and inspecting the loads of all the wagons, to make sure that nothing was taken except that which was permitted or absolutely necessary. Once he was on the other side of the river, he adopted the following practices (while campaigning in hostile territory). He took his meals sitting on the bare turf and often passed the night without a tent. He gave all his orders for the following day, in writing, as well as any commands for actions to be taken in sudden emergencies (precise and fixed instructions to senior officers). He added that, if anyone was in doubt about any matter, he was to consult him personally at any hour whatsoever, even during the night.

Tiberius imposed the strictest military discipline (on this campaign) and reinstated bygone methods of punishment and ignominy. He even degraded the commander of a legion for sending a few soldiers across the river to accompany one of his freedmen on a hunting expedition. Tiberius left very little to fortune and chance, but he entered battles with greater confidence after certain events (small omens). Sometimes when he was working late at night his lamp would suddenly, and without human interference, die down and go out. He used to say that he held great confidence in this sign, since both he and his ancestors had found this omen trustworthy in all their past campaigns.

Yet, at his very moment of victory, Tiberius narrowly escaped assassination by one of the Bructeri (a Germanic warrior posing as a Roman auxiliary). This man gained access to Tiberius from among his attendants, but he was detected due to his nervousness. Torture was then used to extract a full confession of his intended crime.

After two years Tiberius returned from Germany to Rome and celebrated the triumph which he had postponed (his victory in Pannonia). He was accompanied by his generals who received the triumphal regalia at his insistence. Before entering the Capitol (the civic centre of Rome), Tiberius dismounted from his chariot and fell at the knees of his (adopted) father (Emperor Augustus), who was presiding over the ceremonies.

Outcome (AD 10)

243 Cassius Dio, *Roman History*, 56.25

That year, Tiberius rededicated the Temple of Concord in Rome (goddess of harmony and social stability). He had his own name and that of Drusus, his deceased brother, displayed at the temple. (…) Then Tiberius, with Germanicus acting as proconsul, conducted an invasion of Germany. They overran large parts of the country, but they did not win any major battles because the enemy would not engage them in close-quarter fighting. Consequently, the commanders could not reduce the power of any tribe. They were also afraid of suffering a further disaster, so they did not remain long in any territories far beyond the Rhine. The commanders stayed in the (Rhine) region until autumn and even celebrated the birthday of Augustus there, by holding a horse race overseen by the centurions (23 September). Then they returned to Rome.

Three Years of Campaigns (AD 10–13)

244 Velleius Paterculus, *History of Rome*, 2.121–123

When Tiberius re-entered Germany he displayed the same heroic valour and received the same good fortune as his first campaign. He defeated the enemy force by expeditions on sea and land. Then he completed a difficult task in Gaul where dissensions had broken out among the Viennenses (a subject population). He settled these matters by restraint, rather than by punishment (negotiation rather than military force).

At the request of his (adopted) father Augustus, the Senate and Roman people decreed that Tiberius should have authority equal to the emperor among the army and in all the provinces. (…)

Tiberius had broken the power of the Germans in three successive campaigns. For this he should have received and accepted further honours (additional triumphs). Tiberius should also have been awarded a triumph for his skilled generalship after the disaster that Rome suffered under Varus – when Roman forces in Germany were crushed. For the commander ensured that these events reached an appropriate outcome sooner than expected (containment of the enemy and swift Roman retribution). Tiberius can be admired for engaging with extreme toil and danger (on military campaigns). But a greater attribute was his ability to keep within the bounds of acceptable honours.

But a crisis now threatened that caused great foreboding (the choice of imperial successor). Augustus had dispatched his grandson Germanicus to Germany to extinguish all remaining traces of the war. He was also about to send his (adopted) son Tiberius to Illyricum to strengthen the peace in regions just subjugated by the recent war (the supressed revolt).

Germania is Abandoned

The campaigns had secured the Rhine frontier, but the Romans did not permanently advance their forces or reclaim lost territories. North Germany was now an independent region.

245 Cassius Dio, *Roman History*, 54.36

Afterwards Tiberius and Drusus (his son) returned to Rome with Augustus, who had remained at Lugdunensis for much of the time to keep a watch on the Germans from a close distance. In Rome the commanders (Tiberius and Drusus) accepted the decrees that had been passed in honour of their victories and performed their political functions.

News Reaches the Poet Ovid in Exile

246 Ovid, *Tristia*, 3.12.47

It is rare for sailors to cross the sea from Italy and reach this harbourless coast. I would welcome anyone who could speak Greek, but especially Latin. Maybe someone will come who has sailed on a steady southerly wind as far as Propontis and the Straits (the Hellespont). Such a traveller could recount the latest news, passing on and sharing rumours and reports. I hope he can tell me about the triumphs celebrated by Augustus. He can reveal the prayers made to Jupiter in Rome, because rebellious Germany is at last suppressed and its sorrowful head has been held under the general's foot (Tiberius). Anyone who tells me all these things, these matters that I have regretfully missed, will be an instant guest in my house.

Tiberius's Triumph (an imagined account)

Ovid imagines the victory that Tiberius might have expected in Germany.

247 Ovid, *Tristia*, 4.2

Perhaps savage Germany has already been defeated and subdued like the rest of the world. Maybe the Germans have already fallen on bended knee to the Caesars. Maybe the high Palatine in Rome is decorated with garlands (victory celebrations). Perhaps smoky incense is crackling on the flames, while dark blood spurts over the earth as the axe-blow falls on the luminous sacrifice (a slaughtered ox). These gifts are given to the temples of the benign gods, prepared as offerings by the victorious Caesars, young Germanicus and Drusus (the son of Tiberius, named after his uncle). May their dynasty rule over this world forever!

The women give sacred offerings for the safety of their kin. Livia (the wife of Augustus) and those splendid women, Agrippina and Livilla (the wives of Germanicus and Drusus). They present offerings to the noble gods, leading other women, including the virgin Vestals who maintain the purified fires (the Roman hearth cult). The populace of Rome rejoices alongside the Senate and the *equites* (the lesser nobility) who I was recently a part of (before exile). But I will miss this communal joy, for I have been forced far away (exiled in Tomis). Only the faintest rumour travels this far out (to the Black Sea coasts).

All the people in Rome will be able to watch the triumph. They will read the names of enemy leaders and the seized settlements. They will see the captive kings with chains around their necks marching in front of garlanded horses. Some of the captives will have the down-turned expressions expected from defeat. But others will present a more terrible aspect, indifferent to their fate (furious defiance). Some spectators will ask for campaign narratives, facts and names. Others will answer them, although they themselves know little about the real events.

> That man up there displayed in the imperial purple was the enemy leader. There's his second-in-command. That wretched one with his eyes cast upon the ground once wore a very different expression (commanding

> warrior prowess). That fierce one has eyes that still burn with hostile fury. He was the instigator who planned the enemy battles. There is the traitor who hides his face in his shaggy hair (perhaps Arminius). He trapped our men in a treacherous place (the Teutoburg Forest). They say the person following him was their priest, who sacrificed Roman captives to their gods. But these 'gifts' to their gods were often refused (a lack of divine aid evidenced by Germanic defeats).

Those floats (decorated wagons) display representations of lakes and mountains (images of Germania and stylised campaign features). All the forts and rivers are depicted in scenes filled with fierce slaughter and an outpouring of blood. Drusus the Elder once earned his reputation there in that place. Now his fine son Germanicus is finally worthy of his father. The 'split horns' (ivory reliefs) decorated with sedge (flowering grasses) depict the Rhine stained with his blood (the mortal injury he received on the Elbe River). See how even Germany herself is led along by her loosened hair (a female captive dressed as a personification of the country). This sorrowful figure is seated at the feet of our conquering leader (the emperor or his adopted sons). She offers her proud neck outstretched to the Roman axe (threatened with execution) and her hands that once held weapons are chained.

O Caesar, you will wear the imperial purple required by custom, you will ride high above everyone in the victory chariot. The acclaim of the people will greet you as flower petals fall all along the route (confetti-like material thrown from high buildings). Then soldiers, with their heads wreathed in Apollo's laurel (victory awards) will shout in loud voices 'We triumph!'

You will often see the four horses (of his chariot) rearing up in response to the commotion, the chanting and acclaim. Then you will reach the citadel (the Capitoline Hill) and the shrines that will favour your prayers. And there you will offer the votive wreath to Jupiter.

I am in exile (far from Rome), so I must see all of this in my mind's eye. For my imagination still has a right to be in the place that was denied to me. My mind travels freely across great distances, moving swiftly through the heavens (to Rome). Then, I cast my eyes across the centre of the city (using imagination) and my spirit can find a place (in the crowd of spectators). There I will observe the ivory covered vehicles (chariots or wagons displaying carved scenes of conquest). So, for a short while, I will be back in my homeland.

Joyful people in the jubilant crowd will experience this true spectacle watching their emperor. But for me, this is only the product of my imagination. I am far removed from experiencing all this. Anyone from Italy rarely visits this distant world (the inner shores of the Black Sea). So, there are few who can describe the triumph that I long to hear about, and when I do receive the news, it will already be out of date. Nevertheless, whenever that day comes I shall be glad to hear of it. For on that day, I will forget my misery and the public experience (rejoicing) will surpass my private gloom (exile).

Questions about the Abilities of Tiberius

248 Suetonius, *Tiberius*, 21

I cannot accept that an emperor (Augustus), with the utmost judgement and foresight, acted without great consideration in this vital matter (appointing a suitable successor). In my opinion, Augustus assessed the merits and various faults of Tiberius, before deciding that his good qualities dominated. He therefore delivered an oath in public before the Roman populace announcing that he was adopting Tiberius as his successor (AD 4). This was said to be for the 'good of the country'. In several extant letters Augustus refers to Tiberius as a very capable general and 'the sole defender of the Roman people' (before Germanicus was old enough to receive high commands, AD 13). To confirm this view, I have included a few extracts from the imperial letters.

> Farewell Tiberius, most pleasing of men. May success go with you as you wage war for me and for the Muses (the patrons of arts and poetry in Greco-Roman culture).
>
> Farewell, may happiness not desert me (colloquial expression) if you are not the most pleasing and valiant of men, the most conscientious of generals.
>
> Dear Tiberius, I have only praise for the conduct of your summer campaigns. I am certain that no one could have acted with better judgment than you amid so many difficulties, including the apathy of your army. All those who were with you (on campaign) agree that this well-known quote could be applied to you: 'One man alone by his foresight has saved our beloved country from ruin' (*Ennius*, the *Annales*).
>
> If any matter occurs that requires careful thought, or I am vexed about anything, then by Jupiter the god of Truth, I seek assistance from my

dear Tiberius. The lines of Homer come to my mind: 'though flames rage around us, we will follow him, to return to our homes (safety), since his wisdom and knowledge are great' (Homer, *Iliad*).

By the gods, when I hear or read that you are worn out by constant hardships, my whole body shudders with sympathy. I urge you to spare yourself from this toil, because any news of your illness might finish your mother and me. It endangers the entire Roman populace who perceive you as their future ruler.

It does not matter whether or not I am well. What matters is your wellbeing.

I pray that the gods, if they do not hate the Roman populace, will preserve you for us and grant you perpetual good health.

Imperial Policy and Decisions

249 Suetonius, *Augustus*, 25

Augustus used to say: 'No battle or war should be undertaken unless the prospect of gain is greater than the prospect of loss. For men who pursue small advantages with great risk are like those who fish with a golden hook. For if the line snaps, then the loss of the investment is greater than all the fish they might have caught.'

250 Suetonius, *Augustus*, 21

It could be said Augustus never made war on any nation without just cause. He did not want to increase his dominion, or military glory, regardless of the cost (risking manpower and state wealth). In fact, he forced the chiefs of certain barbarians to take oaths in the temple of Mars Ultor (Mars the Avenger) asserting that they would faithfully keep the very peace they had requested (defeated foes made allies rather than subjects). He also tried exacting a new kind of political hostage from the barbarians. These were women and girls, since he realised that the barbarians would disregard pledges secured by male hostages. But all people were given the privilege of reclaiming their hostages whenever they wished. Those who often rebelled, or plotted treachery, received no worse punishment than having their hostages sold into slavery. But Augustus made it a condition that these former hostages should not pass their term of slavery in a country near their homeland, or be freed within thirty years.

Importance of Geography

251 Strabo, *Geography*, 1.1.17

It is quite evident that geography is useful in many important matters. Consider hunting, where a hunter in the chase is more successful if he knows the character and extent of the forest. Only someone who knows a region can securely pitch a military camp at its most advantageous location, set an effective ambush, or direct a successful march. The usefulness of geography is even more apparent in large undertakings where rewards of success are greater, and the impact of disasters caused by ignorance are amplified. (…) Proof of what I claim comes from recent Roman campaigns conducted against the Parthians (Crassus in 53 BC and Mark Antony in 36 BC). A further example is Roman campaigns against the Germans and the Celts, for these barbarians conduct skirmish warfare in swamps, pathless forests, and other wildernesses. In these conflicts they make the ignorant Romans believe that far away objectives are actually close. They also conceal routes and resources that the Romans might use to secure provisions and other necessities.

Final Instructions

Augustus died in AD 14, leaving the Empire to his stepson Tiberius. His final posthumous instructions were read to the Senate.

252 Cassius Dio, *Roman History*, 56.33

The third document contained an account of all military matters, the state revenues, public expenditures, the amount of money in the treasuries, and everything else concerning the administration of the Empire. The fourth document had injunctions and commands for Tiberius and for the Roman state (…) Augustus advised them to be satisfied with their present possessions (the existing frontiers). Under no conditions were they to increase the size of the Empire to any greater dimensions. Augustus warned that an extended empire would be difficult to guard (from internal threats and foreign enemies) and they would endanger what they already possessed. During his reign he had always followed this principle, both in speech (stated aims) and action (enacted policy). He could have made great acquisitions from the barbarian world, but he did not wish to do so.

Function and Expenses of the Empire

253 Tacitus, *Annals*, 1.11

Tiberius then ordered the document to be produced and read to the senators. This contained a description of all the resources of the state. This included the number of citizens and allies in the military, the size of the fleets, a listing of subject kingdoms, an account of the provinces, direct and indirect taxes, necessary expenses, and customary bounties (the Roman budget). Augustus had written down all these details in his own handwriting including this advice: 'the Empire should be confined to its present limits.'

Chapter Ten

Germanicus Campaigns across the Rhine (AD 14–16)

After the death of Augustus in AD 14, Tiberius was acknowledged as emperor. His stepson Germanicus retained command of the Rhine armies consisting of eight legions (one-third of the Roman army). This army was equally divided between the two zones of the northern and southern parts of the Rhine. These were the forces that Germanicus commanded, possibly in an effort to reconquer Germany. The main events in this campaign are as follows:

- AD 14: Death of Augustus. Roman Legions in Pannonia mutiny (three legions). A separate mutiny occurs in the North Rhine (four legions). Drusus the Younger restores the situation in Pannonia, while Germanicus regains control over the Rhineland forces.
- Germanicus assembles a force of perhaps 30,000 troops drawn from four legions (North Rhine). He leads an attack across the Rhine against the Marsi (upper Ruhr River). He engages the Bructeri, Tubantes and Usipetes on the return march to winter quarters at Castra Vetera (Xanten).
- AD 15: Germanicus mobilises eight legions (North and South Rhine). He commands 4 legions with 10,000 auxiliaries for an attack against the Chatti. He sacks their tribal capital Mattium and restores an abandoned Roman fort in enemy territory. Lucius Apronius directs projects connected with roadbuilding and bridges.
- Leading a fast-moving advance force, Lucius Stertinius recaptures the lost Nineteenth Eagle Standard from the Bructeri.
- Germanicus advances beyond the Ems and entering the Teutoburg Forest he locates the site of the Varus Disaster, where three legions were massacred six years earlier (AD 9). After burying the Roman dead, Germanicus pursues a Cherusci force led by Arminius.
- Meanwhile, Caecina Severus commands a further 4 legions and 5,000 auxiliaries advancing into territory between the Chatti and Cherusci (disrupting tribal alliances). Caecina repulses the Marsi, but on the return march his legions are endangered at the Battle of Pontes Longi. The Cherusci attack the legions as they are traversing a series of wooden causeways crossing treacherous bogland (Lower Saxony).

- Two further legions led by Publius Vitellius are endangered by tides and treacherous conditions on the return march along the north coast.
- Germanicus receives a plea for assistance from a pro-Roman Cherusci chief named Segestes. Roman forces rescue Segestes and his kinfolk from Arminius and the anti-Roman faction.
- **AD 16:** Gaius Silius attacks the Chatti. Germanicus leads six legions along the Lippe River to relieve a Roman fort besieged by the enemy. New barriers and earthworks are constructed between Castra Aliso and the Rhine.
- Once the fleet is assembled, the Roman forces advance in three divisions:
  1. Leading 20,000 soldiers, Caecina Severus attacks the Bructeri while advancing overland to the Ems River.
  2. Albinovanus Pedo takes command of the Roman cavalry to invade the land of the Frisians (north coast regions).
  3. Germanicus, in command of four legions, meets the Roman fleet at Lake Flevo (a Rhine River inlet). The legions are transported into Germany via the North Sea and upriver sailing along the Ems.
- A combined Roman force advances to the Weser. Germanicus defeats the Cherusci chief Arminius at the Battle of Idistaviso (Rinteln).
- Roman forces are attacked approaching a defensive embankment known as the Angrivarian Wall, but they rout the Germans.
- The Roman army returning by ship are wrecked by a storm and incur severe losses.
- Germanicus orders Gaius Silius to attack the Chatti with a force of 33,000 infantry and 3,000 cavalry. With a larger army he invades and devastates Marsi territory. A second lost legionary eagle is reclaimed.
- **AD 17:** Germanicus is recalled and celebrates a triumph in Rome.

Germanicus and the Rhine Command (AD 13)

254 Tacitus, *Annals*, 1.3

Augustus appointed Germanicus, the son of Drusus, to the command of eight legions on the Rhine. He also required Tiberius to legally adopt him, although Tiberius already had a son in the household who was a young man (Drusus the Younger). Augustus did this so that there would be several safeguards (in the imperial succession: potential rivals in the dynasty would be interconnected by social bonds).

There were no wars at this time except the conflict against the Germans. But this conflict was to eradicate the disgrace caused by the defeat of

Quintilius Varus and the loss of his army. It was not prompted by an ambition to expand the Empire, or any hope of an adequate recompense (no plunder or resources in the territory could match the loss of three legions).

Northern Legions Mutiny (AD 14)

In AD 14, there were eight legions stationed on the Rhine frontier and at least six legions on the Danube (Pannonia, Dalmatia and Moesia). At the death of Augustus, the three legions in Pannonia mutinied over low pay and poor conditions. Tiberius sent his son Drusus Caesar (Drusus the Younger) north to dictate terms and restore order. A Germanic bodyguard in imperial service was part of the protection force assigned to the imperial prince for this mission.

255 Tacitus, *Annals*, 1.24

Tiberius was careful to withhold and suppress any information concerning this serious disaster (in case the mutiny encouraged further revolts, uprisings or political insurrections). He sent his son Drusus to the region, accompanied by some leading men of the state. They had no definite instructions and were simply told to take suitable measures. Drusus was accompanied by two praetorian cohorts that were strengthened beyond their usual force by the addition of some specially selected troops. A considerable part of the praetorian cavalry joined the expedition, along with the best of the German soldiers who formed the emperor's personal guard.

The commander of the praetorians, Aelius Sejanus, accompanied Drusus to advise and direct the young imperial prince. Sejanus had great influence with Tiberius, and his father Strabo was closely involved with imperial power (as a praetorian prefect). Tiberius instructed Drusus and Sejanus to restore order either by punishing, or rewarding, the mutinous soldiers.

When Drusus approached the mutinous camp, the legions respected his rank and assembled to meet him in the usual display (of parade ranks). But they did not display their usual proud character, gleaning armour and glittering military trophies. Instead, the men assembled in uniforms marked by unsightly squalor and with expressions of grief and defiance.

The Rhine Command

Germanicus was the son of Drusus the Elder, the famous brother of Tiberius. His father had received the *agnomen* 'Germanicus' as a posthumous honour to acknowledge his conquest of greater Germany (12–9 BC). This name was adopted by his son Nero Claudius Drusus 'Germanicus'. In AD 14, Germanicus was 28 years old, the same age as his father had been when he had conquered northern Germany. He commanded eight legions, but after the death of Augustus he had to deal with a military mutiny involving half his forces (North Rhine). The troops demanded increased pay and reduced terms of military service, but unlike the Pannonian mutineers, they had no obvious leaders. His cousin, Drusus the Younger, successfully suppressed the Pannonian mutiny, but Germanicus used his own situation to launch a new invasion of Germany.

Speech by Germanicus to Mutinous Rhine Legions (AD 14)

256 Tacitus, *Annals*, 1.43

'Could you have chosen a new commander who would have avenged the death of Varus and his three legions? The Belgae offered you assistance, but may the gods never allow them to boast with (false) glory that they rescued Rome and quelled the tribes of Germany. I call upon the divine spirit of the deceased Augustus and the echoes of my father Drusus (the Elder) in the Afterlife. I invoke them, and I call upon these soldiers filled with shame to be fuelled by a new ambition. Let them eradicate the stain of civil strife with the destruction of a real foe (the Germans).'

Attack on Germany (AD 14)

257 Tacitus, *Annals*, 1.48–51

Germanicus concentrated his (loyal) forces and prepared vengeance against the mutineers. (…) At the given signal, they rushed into the tents and butchered the unsuspecting soldiers. Only those with secret instructions knew the extent of the planned slaughter.

Soon afterwards Germanicus entered the military camp and wept as he spoke (a performance of grief). He announced that the recent destruction of life was a remedy for the army (a purge to restore order). Then he commanded the bodies of the slain to be burnt (eradicating all trace of the dishonour). The army now possessed a savage temperament and was eager to march against an enemy as atonement for their former frenzy (the purge). It was felt that the spirits of their fellow soldiers could only be appeased by bloodshed. Their living comrades must expose themselves to enemy wounds and thus receive honourable scars.

Caesar Germanicus encouraged these sentiments among his soldiers. He ordered the Rhine to be bridged, and then led across 12,000 men from the legions supported by 26 allied cohorts (perhaps 13,000 auxiliary troops). They were reinforced by 8 squadrons of cavalry who had remained loyal throughout the mutiny (perhaps 4,000 horsemen).

The nearby Germans were exulted by the death of Augustus and the public mourning occurring in the Empire. This was a greater source of elation for them than military dissensions (the mutinies that threatened the legions). Germanicus ordered a forced march and his army cut their way through the Caesian Forest (probably part of the Black Forest). Then they reached and crossed the barrier which had been begun by Tiberius (an abandoned roadway or defensive network). The general established his main military camp at this defensive line. The front and rear were defended by entrenchments (bank and ditch defences) while timber barricades protected the flanks.

Germanicus then advanced through some forest passes that were relatively unknown. When the pathway divided, Germanicus was unsure whether he should take his army through the shortest route. This passage was not guarded by the enemy, but it was unexplored and seemed to cross more difficult terrain. He therefore chose the longer route for his advance and ordered urgent preparations for battle. Roman scouts reported that the Germans had conducted a grand banquet the night before and revelled in many festivities and games (festivals celebrated by bouts of heavy drinking and champion challenges).

Caecina (a Roman officer) was ordered to advance with some light cohorts to clear away any obstructions in the woods. The legions followed at a moderate distance. At nightfall, assisted by bright starlight they advanced through darkness. Unseen, the soldiers surrounded the settlements of the Marsi and began establishing a cordon to encircle the enemy. The Germans were asleep in their beds, or sitting around their tables ignorant of any danger. Their settlements had been formed in a careless and disordered manner and they had not posted any sentries. It seemed that they had no apprehension of war, but these were not a peaceful people. Their condition was due to recklessness and lethargy; the result of a populace still stupefied by the effects of alcohol (the drunken revelry after their festival).

Caesar Germanicus divided his eager legions into four columns to maximise the devastation he could inflict. The Roman army then ravaged an area 50 miles wide with slaughter and burning (destroying villages, farmhouses, crops and food stores). No compassion was shown to anyone, regardless of gender or age (women, children and the elderly were massacred). Everything, both profane and sacred, was destroyed including the so-called temple of Tamfana (probably a Germanic priestess or goddess).

This was a special gathering place for all the surrounding tribes, but the site was annihilated by the Roman army. The soldiers did not suffer a single serious wound in these engagements. They slaughtered an enemy that was half asleep, unarmed, or struggling to flee.

This slaughter provoked the Bructeri, Tubantes, and Usipetes. They gathered around the forest passes through which the Roman army was expected to return. Germanicus knew this and therefore prepared his army to fight as they advanced. The Roman vanguard was formed by the cavalry supported by some auxiliary cohorts, then came the First Legion. The baggage and supplies were in the centre, the Twenty-First Legion on the left, the Fifth Legion on the right. The Twentieth Legion secured the rear with the rest of the auxiliaries.

The enemy did not move until the army began to advance in marching columns through the woods. Then they began making light skirmishing attacks on the flanks and the vanguard units. Finally, their whole force charged the Roman rearguard and the light-armed cohorts were thrown into confusion by the dense mass of attacking German warriors. Caesar Germanicus rode up to the Twentieth Legion and addressed the soldiers in a loud voice. He cried out that the time had come for the soldiers to extricate themselves from the shame of mutiny. He commanded, 'Advance and speedily turn your guilt into glory.' Their courage was raised and in a single charge the Roman soldiers surged through the enemy horde. They drove the Germans back into open terrain and inflicted a great slaughter on their warriors. Meanwhile, the troops of the vanguard units emerged from the woods and reached the well-entrenched military camp (a secure defensive site). The return march to Roman territory was conducted without opposition and the army was led safely back to winter quarters. The confidence of this new victory had obscured the regretful past (the mutiny).

Divisions among the Germans (AD 15)

As the German tribes mobilised for war, a Cherusci chief named Segestes adopted a pro-Roman position in opposition to his kinsman Arminius.

258 Tacitus, *Annals*, 1.55

Segestes was dragged into the war by the unanimous will of his nation (compelled to fight alongside his kinsmen in the conflict against Rome). But his feud against Arminius was also heightened by personal motives. Arminius had abducted and wed the daughter of Sesgestes (Thusnelda), who was betrothed to another man. The son-in-law and father-in-law detested one another and a union that should have increased the bonds of friendship and alliance had therefore become an incitement to further anger.

Second Year: Campaign Escalates (AD 15)

Germanicus remained in command of the Rhine armies. The campaign was renewed the following year, bringing all eight legions into action (North and South Rhine).

259 Tacitus, *Annals*, 1.55–60
A victory triumph was decreed for Germanicus, although the war continued. Germanicus was heavily engaged in preparation for the summer campaign. He planned a sudden advance into the territory of the Chatti at the beginning of spring. There was now hope that the enemy might be divided between the treacherous Arminius, and Segestes who was loyal to Rome. (…)

Germanicus gave Caecina command of 4 legions and 5,000 auxiliaries. This force was joined by some hastily raised levies from the Germans dwelling on the west bank of the Rhine (Roman territories). Germanicus commanded an equal number of legions and twice as many allies (20,000 legionaries and 10,000 auxiliaries). He established a fort on the site of his father's entrenchments near the Taunus Mountains (a site used in 12–9 BC). Then he advanced quickly in marching order against the Chatti, leaving Lucius Apronius to direct projects connected with roadbuilding and bridges.

It was a dry season in Germany that year and the streams were relatively shallow. This was a rare occurrence in that climate, and it allowed Germanicus to conduct a rapid march without obstruction. But he was concerned that heavy rains might swell the rivers and impede his return.

Germanicus invaded the territory of the Chatti so swifty that anyone weakened by age or gender was captured or slaughtered (the elderly, women and children). The able-bodied men managed to swim across the river Adrana. They tried to resist the Romans as they began building a bridge, but they were forced back by missiles and arrows. Afterwards, they tried in vain to negotiate peace. Some took refuge with Germanicus, while the rest left their villages and home districts to disperse into the forests.

Germanicus burned down Mattium, the capital of the tribe, and devastated the open countryside (destroying farms and settlements). Then he marched his forces back towards the Rhine. But on this occasion the enemy did not dare attack, or harass, the rear section of the withdrawing Roman army. This had been their usual practice whenever the Romans conducted a planned retreat in good order. The Cherusci wanted to help the Chatti, but (the Roman commander) Caecina intimidated them by the presence of his army. The Marsi ventured to engage him, but they were repulsed in a successful battle.

Soon afterwards envoys came from Segestes, imploring the Romans for military assistance against his kinsmen who were redirecting their violence against him (a split within the Cherusci tribe). Segestes was hemmed in by his opponents, supporters of Arminius who advocated war. Among these barbarians a man who possesses greater courage and daring inspires more confidence, and gains more esteem, in times of violent unrest. Segestes had sent his son Segimundus along with the envoys, but the youth was reluctant to engage with the Romans due to his shame and guilt. For when the revolt occurred in Germany (AD 9), Segimundus had been serving as a priest at the altar of the Ubii (a site devoted to the imperial cult on the west bank of the Rhine). But when he heard about the uprising, he had torn apart the sacred garlands and fled to the rebels. Now, however, he hoped for Roman mercy as he brought his father's message (a plea for assistance). Segestes was graciously received and sent with a military escort to the Gallic bank of the Rhine (treated as a political hostage).

It was now worthwhile for Germanicus to march back into Germany with his army. A battle was fought against the besiegers and Segestes was rescued along with a large group of his kinsfolk and their dependents. Among them were some high-status women including the wife of Arminius (Thusnelda), who was also the daughter of Segestes. It was found that she exhibited the spirit of her husband (anti-Roman), rather than the sentiments of her father. She was not reduced to tears and did not speak in the tones of a supplicant. She folded her arms across her bosom and cast her eyes down towards her offspring (she was pregnant with the child of Arminius). Plunder seized during the defeat of Varus was also recovered from those who surrendered to Rome.

Segestes now presented himself (to the Romans) in person. He was dignified and resolute, recalling how he had once been a faithful ally of the Empire. He said:

> In the past I have shown steadfast loyalty towards the Romans. From the time that Divine Augustus granted me citizenship, I have chosen my friends and foes with a thought for your advantage. But I have not hated my homeland. Such traitors are detested, even by those they support.

> I have always believed that the Romans and Germans have the same interests, and that peace is better than war.
>
> I denounced Arminius to Varus when he led your army. Arminius ravished my daughter and violated your treaty (a joint enemy). But Varus was a negligent commander overseeing ineffective laws. I urged him to arrest myself, along with Arminius and his accomplices (the instigators of the revolt). I would gladly have died that night (wrongfully accused alongside the plotters) if I had seen Arminius cast into chains, or suffered the same fate at the hands of his supporters. But what followed has to be deplored rather than defended (the Germanic uprising).
>
> As soon as you give me the opportunity, I will demonstrate my commitment to the old order (Roman dominance). I favour peace over unrest, but not for any personal reward. I want to clear myself from any suspicion of treachery. I want to prove myself to be a worthy mediator for those Germans who choose repentance over ruin. I ask forgiveness for my son who acted in youthful error. As for my daughter, I admit that she was brought here by compulsion (seized against her will from her husband Arminius). Consider this. She bears the child of Arminius, but she owes her existence to me.

Germanicus gave a gracious response. He promised Segestes that he would protect his children and kinsfolk, offering him a place in the old province (imperial territory). Then Germanicus led the return march of the army and accepted the title of imperator from Tiberius. The wife of Arminius (Thusnelda) gave birth to a boy, who was brought up at Ravenna (north Italy). But afterwards they suffered a grievous insult, which I shall describe at the proper time (perhaps humiliated at the Roman triumph of AD 17).

The surrender and kind reception of Segestes became widely known. These reports were greeted with hope or grief, depending on the eagerness that individuals felt for war. Arminius already possessed a furious temper, and he was driven into a frenzy by the capture of his wife and the knowledge that his unborn child was condemned to Roman slavery. He dashed among the Cherusci, demanding, 'War against Segestes! – War against Caesar!' He taunted the Romans, saying:

> Noble is the father, mighty is the general. Brave is the army of great strength that carried off one weak woman. I have defeated three legions, three great commanders, but not by treachery. I do not wage war against pregnant women. I fight openly against armed men. The

> Roman standards which I hung up to the gods of our country can still be seen in the groves of Germany.
>
> Let Segestes dwell on that conquered riverbank (Roman Rhine). Let him see his son restored to his priestly office. The Germans will never accept the sight of the Roman rods and axes (*fasces* – symbols of imperial authority) or togas (the garb of Roman citizens) between the Elbe and the Rhine.
>
> Other nations are ignorant of Roman rule. They have no experience of the punishments and payments that we have resisted. The great Augustus was ranked among deities, but we have opposed and confounded his heir Tiberius. So, do not fear this inexperienced youth (Germanicus) who leads a mutinous army. Favour your homeland, your ancestors, and your ancient customs. Reject the rule of tyrants and the prospect of new Roman colonies. Do not follow Segestes into shameful servitude. Follow your leader Arminius to glory and greater freedom!

This language roused the Cherusci, but also incited the neighbouring tribes. Inguiomerus, the uncle of Arminius who had received the long-term respect of Rome, now added his support to the enemy (the anti-Roman faction). This increased the alarm felt by Germanicus.

Third Year: Bructeri attacked; Frisia overrun; Cherusci engaged

Germanicus remained in command to organise and lead a third campaign against the Germans. This time the Roman forces operated in three divisions.

260 Tacitus, *Annals*, 1.60

Germanicus decided to divide his forces so that the Roman assault would not surge into enemy territory from one single locality. He placed Caecina Severus in charge of 40 Roman cohorts (20,000 soldiers) and ordered him to distract the enemy by advancing through the territory of the Bructeri to the river Amisia (the Ems). He placed Albinovanus Pedo in command of the Roman cavalry and ordered him to invade the land of the Frisians (the north coast regions).

Meanwhile, Germanicus took command of four legions (the First Germanica, Fifth Alaudae, Twentieth Valeria Victrix and Twenty-first Rapax). These legions assembled and prepared to board the Roman fleet at the 'Lake' (Lake Flevo – a flooded region near the Rhine estuary to the North Sea). The infantry, cavalry and fleet all gathered in this region before beginning their simultaneous military operations. The Chauci (an allied Germanic tribe) offered military assistance and joined the conflict in support of Rome.

Eagle Standard Recovered; Site of the Teutoburg Massacre

261 Tacitus, *Annals*, 1.60–62

Germanicus sent Lucius Stertinius ahead with a fast-moving mixed force of soldiers. They immediately routed the Bructeri and began burning their settlements. During the carnage and plunder which followed, the soldiers found and recovered the eagle of the Nineteenth Legion. This was the battle standard which had been lost by Varus (in the Teutoburg Forest). The soldiers then advanced eastwards to the furthest frontier of the Bructeri nation. They invaded and devastated all the lands between the rivers Ems and the Lupia (the Lippe). This was close to the Teutoburg Forest, where the remains of Varus and his legions still lay exposed and unburied.

Germanicus was determined to see that the proper final honours were paid to these soldiers and their dead commander. His entire army felt a great compassion for their former kinsfolk, comrades, and friends. These fallen soldiers had suffered the full calamities that war inflicts on mankind. Germanicus therefore sent Caecina ahead with an advance force to reconnoitre the scarcely known forest passes. He was instructed to raise bridges over streams and put down wooden causeways on routes through treacherous wetlands. With these precautions in place the army approached the place of the Teutoburg massacre. They prepared themselves to witness the horrific and mournful scenes that would be sure to provoke appalling emotions.

The soldiers located the remains of the first camp which Varus had established on his march into the Forest. From its circumference and dimensions, they determined that this had been a base for all three legions. Further on, they discovered a partially fallen rampart encircled by a shallow ditch. This must have been where some shattered remnant of the army had made their final stand against the attacking enemy. The whitening bones of men could be seen in the centre of this clearing, revealing where individual soldiers had stood their ground, or attempted to flee. Bones were strewn everywhere between the camps, or piled into heaps. Fragments of weapons and the decayed limbs of horses were visible within the remains. Human heads had been nailed to tree trunks in a prominent display of savagery. Near the battle site, the Germans had dedicated sacred groves around barbarian altars. They had sacrificed Roman captives at these sites. In these ceremonies, tribunes had been immolated and first-rank centurions consumed in the flames.

Survivors of the disaster had accompanied the soldiers. These were men who had escaped from the battle or the captivity which followed. They pointed out locations where their officers had been killed or some other major event had transpired. This place was where an eagle was seized by the enemy, that location was where Varus received his first wound, here is where the commander surrendered to Fate and killed himself. They pointed to the rising ground where Arminius had appeared, urging his warriors onwards to fiercer action. The survivors showed where numerous gibbets had hung from trees to suspend Roman captives. They showed the pits and explained how Roman prisoners had been crammed into these confines. But they also described how an exultant Arminius had insulted the battle standards and eagles seized from the defeated Romans.

So, six years after the disaster, a Roman army once more stood on the site of this battle. Consumed by grief and anger, they began to collect the bones of the three legions for burial. Each man did not know whether he was interring the remains of a relative, or of a stranger. But he knew that all those he looked upon were the bodies of his kinsfolk and people who shared his blood. The wrath of the army rose higher than ever against the enemy.

Germanicus began the task and personally deposited a clod of soil on the first burial mound that the army was raising. This was a welcome honour for the dead and all present shared a common sorrow.

The Campaign Continues (AD 15)

262 Tacitus, *Annals*, 1.62

Tiberius did not approve (of Germanicus halting to bury the Roman dead). This could have been because he interpreted every act of Germanicus unfavourably (hostility towards his nephew). Or Tiberius thought that contact with the slain and unburied might make the army reluctant to fight and increase their fear of the enemy. A general invested with the augurs had responsibility for very ancient and sacred ceremonies (priesthood status involving sacrifices and the interpretation of omens). These powers should not be defiled by funeral rites (sacred contamination caused by close contact with corpses tainted by sacrifice to barbarian cults).

Germanicus pursued Arminius as he withdrew into a trackless wilderness. As soon as he had the opportunity, he ordered his cavalry forwards to scour the plains occupied by the enemy. Arminius ordered his warriors to assemble, but keep close to the woods (giving the impression of a force still in retreat). When the enemy suddenly turned around, Arminius gave the signal to forces concealed in forest passes to rush forwards and attack. As this newly revealed force charged the Roman cavalry was thrown into disorder. Germanicus sent some reserve cohorts forwards to support the cavalry, but they were forced to flee by the shock of the retreating troops causing even greater panic. The Romans were being pushed into a swamp that was perilous to soldiers unfamiliar with this landscape, especially as the terrain was well known to the triumphant attackers. Germanicus therefore sent his legions forwards in full battle array (heavily armoured infantry to support the auxiliaries). The enemy were terror-struck, and the confidence of the retreating Roman troops was soon restored. Both sides separated without advantage to either force (no decisive battle occurred).

Soon afterwards, Germanicus led his army back to the Amisia (the Ems). Then he withdrew the legions using the fleet which he had summoned to this location. He ordered part of the Roman cavalry to head for the Rhine and return along the sea coast (north Germany).

Battle at Pontes Longi (AD 15)

Four Legions commanded by Aulus Caecina Severus were almost destroyed marching back to the Rhine through bogland territories.

263 Tacitus, *Annals*, 1.63–67

Meanwhile, Caecina, who commanded his own division, was advised to return with all possible speed via a familiar route called the 'Long Bridges' (a series of wooden trackways over boglands). It had been constructed by Lucius Domitius (Roman commander in 4–1 BC). On every side of the walkways there were quagmires of thick clinging mud or perilous streams. Around the marsh there were woods extending up a gradual slope. But these uplands were now entirely occupied by Arminius and his warriors. They had rushed back to this position by a shorter route and outpaced the Roman troops who were heavily loaded with weapons and baggage. The Long Bridges were badly decayed through age and Caecina doubted if he could restore the wooden trackways at the same time as fighting back the enemy. He therefore decided to establish a military camp close by, so that some of his forces could repair the trackways, while others repelled the enemy attack.

The barbarians tried to break through the armed cordons (protecting troops) and attack the engineering parties (soldiers engaged in repairs). The Germans continually paced around the troops seeking for opportunities to attack. They repeatedly charged the soldiers, creating a massive noise from the combat and the continuing sound of the labour teams (chopping wood, hammering nails, shouting instructions).

Everything about this situation was unfavourable to the Romans. The site crossed deep swamps with insecure footing, becoming more slippery as they advanced through the bogland. The Romans were weighed down by their heavy coats of mail and they could not aim their javelins while standing in the water (slippery footing). But the Cherusci were familiar with the fens and practised at fighting in this terrain. Their huge bodies gave the Germans a physical advantage and their long spears could inflict wounds at a greater distance (compared with Roman short swords).

At last nightfall gave respite to legions badly shaken from this disastrous engagement. By contrast the Germans were unwearied due to their great success. Without taking any rest, they laboured that night to redirect all the streams which rose from the slopes of the surrounding hills, into the lands below. Consequently, the boglands were subject to further flooding and the completed portion of wooden trackways was entirely submerged. As a result, the labour required by the Roman soldiers was doubled.

This was Caecina's fortieth campaign, both as a subordinate and a commander. He therefore had considerable experience of success and danger and could remain completely fearless. He considered all the options, but could only devise one plan likely to succeed. This was to keep the enemy confined to the woods, while the wounded and the more heavily encumbered Roman troops could advance across the trackways. There was a short plain between the hills and the swamps along which an extended Roman battle line could be placed. The legions were now assigned positions along this expanse. The Fifth Legion were stationed along the right wing, while the Twenty-First formed the leftward stretch of this expanding battle line. The Twenty-First were to lead and protect the vanguard force crossing the tracks, while the Twentieth Legion were positioned to repel pursuers (forming the rear).

That night was restless (full of disturbances). The exuberant barbarians on the hills filled the lands below with the echoing sound of their war chants, intermixed with their savage shouts. The Roman soldiers in the encampment maintained dismal fires and uttered broken exclamations (curses and mutterings of complaint). They lay scattered about within their entrenchments (on patches of drier ground) or wandered from tent to tent in a wakeful, restless condition, rather than being watchful and alert. The sleeping general was appalled by a ghastly dream. In a horrifying vision, Quintilius Varus, covered with blood, was rising out of the marshes. Varus seemed to be calling out to him, summoning him to share his fate. But when Caecina would not obey the call, Varus stretched out his hand over the general. Caecina pushed it away in revulsion.

At daybreak it was discovered that the legions guarding the Roman flanks had abandoned their position. From panic, or from direct disobedience, they had moved on to occupy some open territory beyond the morass (firmer ground). Arminius was now free to attack (the soldiers crossing the trackways), but he did not immediately rush into combat against them. The baggage carriers were clogged in the mud of the fosses (flooded ditches and drainage channels next to the trackways). The accompanying soldiers milled around them in disorder. Even the battle standards (rallying points for unit formation) were set about in a confused array. Every soldier was acting in selfish haste, oblivious to the commands of their officers. At this moment Arminius suddenly ordered the Germans to charge, crying out again and again, 'Behold a Varus! The legions are ensnared once more in his fate!'

While speaking these words, Arminius led the German charge with a group of specially selected warriors (fearless and fast). They rushed through a column of Roman soldiers, inflicting wounds mainly on the horses. The horses staggered and slipped as the slick blood spilled onto the slippery marsh. They flung their riders off and began bolting in all directions, racing here and there, colliding with anyone in their path and trampling on the fallen.

A fierce fight began around the eagles (the sacred battle standards of the legions). The standard-bearers were struggling to hold the eagles aloft as missiles flew towards them (spears and slingshots). Yet the standards would not stand firm on the sodden ground.

While Caecina was sustaining the battle (issuing commands and directing troops), his horse was pierced (by a spear). It collapsed and the general fell from his mount. As the enemy were closing in on his position, the First Legion interposed (to save him). The greed of the enemy helped the Romans, for they halted the slaughter to plunder (supplies, equipment and wealth). Towards evening the struggling legionaries had managed to reach firmer ground (regaining the advantage). But this did not end their miseries. They still had to dig entrenchments and erect suitable earthworks (for a military camp). However, the soldiers had lost most of the tools they needed to dig earth and cut turf blocks (for earthen ramparts).

Now there were no tents for the ordinary soldiers and no provisions for the wounded (medical supplies, surgical tools, stitches and bandages). The soldiers shared out their remaining food and ate together while still soiled with mud and blood. They grieved and moaned in the darkness, believing the absolute black of that night was a terrible omen (foretelling their obliteration). Many thousands of men were afraid that they had only one more day to live (they were about to be overcome and slaughtered).

(That night) a horse happened to break free from its halter (head collar). It wandered wildly about the camp frightened by the noises it heard, until it suddenly dashed against some soldiers and knocked them over. A panic ensued, as the surrounding soldiers thought that the Germans had burst into the camp (and must already be among them). They all rushed to the gates. Most headed for the Decuman Gate as the safest route to flee (the rear gate). It was furthest from the enemy and therefore a safer option for escape.

Meanwhile, Caecina had ascertained that there was no reason for the alarm (the camp was secure and the enemy inactive). But he could not halt the (panicked) soldiers by any command, any reason, or even any threat of force. Finally, he thew himself onto the ground in front of the gateway and appealed to their pity. They would have to trample over the body of their commander in order to pass through the gate. The soldiers paused, giving the tribunes and the centurions time to convince them that their fear was a false alarm.

Caecina then ordered his soldiers to assemble at his headquarters (the centre of the camp). He instructed them to hear his words in silence. Then he reminded them of the urgent crisis they now faced. He said:

> Your safety now depends on your weapons and your capacity to fight. Act with sense and remain within these entrenchments. We must wait for the enemy to approach in the hope of suddenly overpowering them. Then there must be a mass retreat from this position towards the Rhine. If you flee now, you will cast yourselves into further forests and deeper swamps occupied by a more savage and determined foe. Instead, wait for victory, and you will gain glory and renown.

Caecina urged the soldiers to recall all they held dear at home and think about their own military honour. But he said nothing about the immediate disaster they faced. Next, he removed the horses belonging to the officers and tribunes. Beginning with his own mount, he had the animals handed over to the bravest fighters in the army (a choice based on ability rather than rank). These men were to charge the attacking enemy, to be followed by the infantry.

Pontes Longi: Final Attack (AD 15)

264 Tacitus, *Annals*, 1.68

The German horde were restless, but full of hope and eager for action. They were also encouraged by the conflicting opinions of their chiefs. Arminius advised that the Germans allow the Romans to abandon their current encampment (and continue their march). The Germans could then resume their surprise attacks against a disadvantaged enemy, bogged down in swampy and treacherous ground. But Inguiomerus was backed by chieftains with fiercer sentiments and views more in keeping with the character of barbarians. He wanted a direct and immediate assault on the Roman encampment. He thought that the Roman position could be easily stormed, and immediate success would secure more prisoners and a greater concentration of undamaged plunder (weapons, wealth and equipment).

The Germans attacked at daybreak. They trampled over the ditches, or flung wickerwork platforms across the gaps. Then they scrambled up the earthworks where Roman defenders were sparce, or paralysed by fear. When a large force of Germans had surged into the fort, a signal was given to the cohorts. Suddenly, war horns blared and battle trumpets sounded. Instantly, with a shout and sudden rush, the Roman soldiers charged the Germans, seeking to encircle the enemy and cut off their retreat. They taunted their foes, crying out that there were no woods or swamps here. The Germans would have to fight on equal terms on solid ground.

The sudden sound of trumpets and the gleam of weapons was an unexpected shock for the Germans. They had burst into the camp with great energy, expecting to destroy a few poorly armed men. They had been elated with the prospect of success, but this sudden reversal was so shocking that they were easily cut down by the Romans. Arminius and Inguiomerus fled from the battle site. Arminius was unharmed, but Inguiomerus suffered a severe wound. Their followers were slaughtered, and in their fury the Romans kept pursuing and killing until nightfall. When darkness had fallen, the legions returned to their camp. But more soldiers had suffered wounds and the troops were still distressed due to a lack of supplies. But their victory gave them the strength and sustenance they required (the benefit of vastly improved morale).

Rumours of Defeat (AD 15)

Actions by Agrippina the Elder, the wife of commander Germanicus.

265 Tacitus, *Annals*, 1.69

Meanwhile, a rumour had spread that the Roman army had been cut off (in enemy territory), and a furious German horde was approaching Gaul. Cowards prepared to destroy the military bridge crossing the Rhine (expecting a German invasion). But Agrippina intervened to prevent this shameful act from occurring. She was a woman with a heroic spirit and in this crisis, she assumed the duties of a general. She distributed clothes and medicines among the surviving soldiers who were destitute or wounded.

Gaius Plinius (Pliny the Elder), the historian of the *German Wars*, writes about these events. He records that Agrippina stood at the far end of the Rhine bridge bestowing thanks and praise on the returning legions. This caused the Emperor Tiberius great concern. He thought:

> This zeal must have a sinister purpose (insurrection). She is winning the support of the soldiers, but not against a foreign foe. She has assumed the role of a general, moving among the regiments, attending the battle standards, and engaging in bribery (giving awards and gifts to select soldiers). Her ambition is evident. She parades her son around in the uniform of a common soldier and asks for him to be called 'Caesar' Caligula. Agrippina now possesses more political power and influence than most military officers and generals. This woman has even quelled a mutiny which could not be halted by any direct imperial command.

These concerns were encouraged and aggravated by Sejanus (a senior imperial advisor). He understood the character and personality of Tiberius and wanted to foster his hatreds until the correct political opportunity arose.

Return of the Remaining Roman Forces (AD 15)

Two further legions were almost destroyed by natural forces on the north coast.

266 Tacitus, *Annals*, 1.70

The other legions had been taken aboard ships for the return journey (sailings via the German river systems down to the North Sea coast). Germanicus gave Publius Vitellius command of the Second and Fourteenth

Legions. He instructed him to march back via a land route (along the north coast). This allowed the returning fleet to more easily manoeuvre through a sea containing treacherous shallows that were exposed during ebb tides (extreme low tides).

At first Vitellius pursued his coastal route without interruption, as the shoreline was dry and the incoming waves were gentle. But after a while, due to the approaching season (autumn), the north wind began to blow with force and the sea started to swell and rise. His army was being buffeted and forced to deviate from their route. Much of the country was flooded and the seashore was barely distinguishable from the wider landmass. What seemed to be solid ground or shallow pools was in fact treacherous quicksand, or deep water. Men were swept away by the waves and pulled under by powerful tides and currents. Pack animals were drowned, but their lifeless bodies resurfaced and blocked the route of the army with their bloated forms.

The Roman units became intermingled in these confused crossings. In places the army had to wade across a coastal channel with only their heads above water. Those who lost their footing were swept away from their comrades to be drowned in the surf. The soldiers cried out mutual encouragement to one another to resist the force of the waves. In these circumstances there was nothing to distinguish the brave man from the coward, the wise from the foolish, or forethought from random chance. The same strong tidal power tested every man and swept across everything it encountered.

At last, Vitellius struggled onto solid ground and led his armies into higher terrain away from the seashore. They spent the night in this place, but without campfires and essential food (clothes were sodden and provisions were spoilt). The exhausted men lay on the ground with bare and bruised limbs. Their condition resembled the pitiful fate of men suffering a siege (no comfort or provisions). Here they had no opportunity for a glorious death. There was only destruction without honour (death from the elements).

At daybreak they viewed the surrounding land and pushed onwards to the river Visurgis (Weser) where Caesar Germanicus was waiting at the river with the fleet. A rumour had reached him that the land force had been entirely drowned. The legions then embarked on the ships, and due to that rumour, no one (in the Empire) believed they were safe until they had returned with Germanicus (to the Rhine bases).

The German Hostages

267 Tacitus, *Annals*, 1.71

Meanwhile, Lucius Stertinius (the Roman legate) had returned. He had been sent to receive the surrender of Segimerus, the brother of Segestes (Germanic leaders supporting Rome). He conducted the chief and his son to the district occupied by the Ubii (west bank of the Rhine near Cologne). Both men were pardoned (for their involvement in the Germanic revolt of AD 9). But there was a reluctance to fully forgive the son (Flavus) since it was said that he had insulted the corpse of Quintilius Varus.

Meanwhile, Gaul, Spain, and Italy vied to replace the losses suffered by the Roman army. They delivered weapons, horses, and gold, but Germanicus took only the mounts and the military equipment. Germanicus praised their zeal, but subsidised the soldiers from his own funds. He also tried to soften the impact of the disaster with various acts of kindness. He visited the wounded soldiers, examining their injuries and praising their acts of courage to raise their hopes and encourage their ambitions. This strengthened their loyalty to him and their enthusiasm for battle.

Assessment of the Land Campaign

268 Tacitus, *Annals*, 2.5

Germanicus was eager to complete his final victories in Germany and the loyalty of his soldiers increased his resolve. He pondered battle plans and carefully considered all the previous military reverses and successes that had occurred during his three years of command. He knew the Germans would be defeated on the battlefield if they fought in open combat. But their armed resistance was facilitated by woodlands and swamps, short summers, and early winters. His own troops were affected, not so much by wounds, as by long marches and injuries to their limbs (the strain of marching, the burden of equipment, the hard labour involved in clearing forests, constructing stockades, roads and causeways). The supply of new horses available in Gaul had been exhausted. The long baggage trains (required to resupply troops in Germany) were an easy target for ambushes and the unsuccessful defenders were left humiliated (unable to safeguard the supplies or inflict severe casualties on the attackers).

Preparing the Naval Campaign (AD 16)

269 Tacitus, *Annals*, 2.5–8

Germanicus therefore decided to conduct a campaign by sea, reasoning that this would be an easy route for invasion. The attack would be an utter surprise to the enemy and the campaign could progress quickly because the legions and their supplies could advance simultaneously. The cavalry would also arrive at the battlefront with their horses in good condition (not injured, lame or exhausted). The Roman army would suddenly appear at the river mouths and waterways that led into the very core of Germany.

Germanicus decided on this plan and sent Publius Vitellius and Caius Antius to collect the required taxes from Gaul (tribute, goods and materials). Silius, Anteius, and Caecina were tasked with constructing the fleet. A thousand sailing vessels were required, and these were quickly constructed. Some of the ships were narrow vessels with a shallow draft (long ships with a short vertical distance from waterline to keel – adapted for coves and river systems). Others had a deep stern and a broad centre so that they would be more stable when struck by ocean waves. Some of the ships were flat-bottomed, so that they could be run aground without being damaged (for landing military forces, equipment and supplies). Several ships had a rudder at each end so that the oars could be turned around and the vessel rowed to shore in either direction (specialising in speed and manoeuvrability where terrain or conditions were uncertain).

Many of the ships had decks on which missile-firing war engines could be conveyed (catapults and torsion machines that launched harpoon-like javelins). These top decks were also suitable for transporting horses and carrying supplies. The ships were equipped with sails as well as oars, so they could be rapidly moved and manoeuvred by the enthusiastic soldiers on board. It was expected that this would be an imposing and formidable sight.

The island of the Batavi (in the Rhine) was selected as the gathering place for the fleet because of its easy landing sites. It was conveniently located to receive the army and convey it across the river. The Rhine flows continuously in a single channel and only encircles small river islands before reaching the Batavi. Then in Batavian territory it divides into two rivers and keeps up its speed until both streams flow into the ocean. The western stream of the Rhine which lies closest to Gaul is broader and gentler. It is known as the Vahal by the people who occupy lands near its banks. The northern Rhine is also known as the Mosa River at the point where it empties into the ocean through a vast outlet.

While the Roman fleet was assembling, Caesar (Germanicus) ordered his lieutenant general, Gaius Silius, to lead a rapidly moving force against the Chatti (a Germanic tribe east of the Rhine). Meanwhile, Germanicus received reports that a fort on the Lupia was being besieged, so he led 6 legions to this location (over 30,000 troops).

Silius organised sudden raids against the Chatti, but he was only able to carry off small amounts of plunder. However, he was able to seize the wife and daughter of the Chatti chief, Arpus. Caesar Germanicus had no opportunity to engage the enemy besieging the fort, since they dispersed when they heard rumours of his advance. He discovered that they had destroyed the barrow recently raised in memory of Varus' legions and smashed the old altar erected by (Nero Claudius) Drusus. Germanicus restored the altar and led the legions in funeral games to honour his father (Drusus). But he did not think it was necessary to construct a new barrow (on the site of the Teutoburg massacre). All the country between the Aliso fort and the Rhine was thoroughly secured by new barriers and earthworks (walls made from banks, ditches and palisades).

By this time the fleet had assembled (at the island of the Batavi). Caesar Germanicus was therefore able to allocate supplies to ships and assign vessels to the legions and the allied troops. The fleet therefore advanced through the Drusus Canals (a network of Roman military canals connecting the Rhine delta to Lake Flevo and the North Sea coast).

Germanicus prayed to (the divine spirit of) his father (Nero Claudius) Drusus to give him support as he embarked on this enterprise. He had followed the example of his father and the memory of his counsels and achievements when he had begun this undertaking. He conducted the fleet successfully through the lakes and voyaged along the coast as far as the river Amisia (the Ems). But he made an error when he ordered the fleet to moor on the west bank of the river to disembark the troops. The fleet should have been sent up the river (to disgorge soldiers and equipment on both banks). Several days were therefore wasted in the construction of bridges before the soldiers could advance into the country further east.

Romans advance to the Weser
Angrivarii revolt, Arminius appears

270 Tacitus, *Annals*, 2.8–11

The cavalry and the legions crossed the first estuaries at low tide without fear or concern. But the auxiliaries, including the Batavians who followed them, crossed the same stretches as the tides were rising. They plunged recklessly into the water to display their skills in swimming. But the units became disordered and some of these men drowned. While Caesar Germanicus was measuring out his military camp, he was told of a revolt of the Angrivarii to his rear (a northern Germanic tribe). He immediately sent Stertinius with some cavalry and a lightly armed force to punish their treachery with fire and slaughter.

The Visurgis River (the Weser) flowed between the Roman position and the Cherusci (the leading enemy tribe). On its banks stood Arminius (the enemy war leader) with the other Cherusci chiefs. Arminius asked if Germanicus had arrived. When he received verification, he asked to speak to his brother surnamed Flavus, who was with the Roman army. Flavus was famous for his loyalty to Rome. He had even lost an eye when wounded a few years earlier while fighting in the service of Tiberius.

Flavus received permission to approach Arminius. Arminius had his guards move some distance away. He also required that the Roman bowmen arrayed across the far bank should move out of range. Then Arminius saluted his brother and the two men met (with the river between them). Arminius asked his brother about the scar which disfigured his face. Flavus told him about the injury and the battle site in which he had received the wound. Arminius asked him what reward he had received for this military service. Flavus spoke of increased pay, a necklet, a crown, and other military decorations (awards for gallantry). Arminius jeered at his brother for accepting such a meagre recompense for voluntary slavery.

A disagreement ensued. Flavus spoke of the greatness of Rome and the immense resources commanded by Caesar Germanicus. He said that the vanquished would soon suffer a dreadful punishment, but mercy was available to those who surrendered. He told Arminius that his wife and son (still held captive in Rome) were not being treated as enemies. In response Arminius reminded his brother of his duty to his fatherland and his ancestral freedom. He called upon the gods and homesteads of Germany. He spoke of the mother who shared his hope that Flavus would not desert and betray his people. Flavus might still rule amid his relatives and kinsfolk (as a free German).

Bitter words were spoken and an argument began. The outraged Flavus called for his weapons and horse. He might have charged across the stream to fight his brother, if Stertinius had not hurried up and put his hand on his shoulder to reassure and restrain him. Meanwhile, Arminius faced him across the river, making menacing gestures and challenging him to combat. Much of what he said was in Roman speech (the Latin language) since Arminius had served in our military camps as leader of his kinsmen (Germanic auxiliaries).

The next day the German army took up position on the other side of the Visurgis (the Weser River). Caesar Germanicus decided it was not good generalship to engage the enemy with legions, as bridges had not been constructed across the river (allowing rapid retreat or reinforcement). He therefore sent the Roman cavalry across the river using the nearby fords. These cavalry forces were commanded by Stertinius and Aemilius, who was one of the senior centurions. They attacked at widely different points in the German line in order to engage and distract their enemy. Meanwhile, the Batavian chief Chariovalda charged into the river where the stream was strongest (his auxiliaries crossing by swimming where an attack was least expected).

The Cherusci pretended to flee from the Batavians and led the auxiliaries into a clearing surrounded by forest paths. Then they suddenly attacked them from all sides. All who stood their ground were overwhelmed as the Batavians turned and fled, with the enemy fiercely pursuing them. The Batavians rallied in a compact mass and began to fight, some in close quarters and others by hurling missiles. They withstood the enemy's assault for a long time, with Chariovalda commanding his men to form a dense formation to resist the attacking warbands. He himself charged into the fiercest part of the combat and died when he and his horse were struck by a dense hail of enemy darts. Many noble chiefs of his nation died with him. The rest of the Batavians escaped peril by their own warlike efforts, or by the arrival of the Roman cavalry led by Stertinius and Aemilius.

Advance across the Weser

271 Tacitus, *Annals*, 2.12–14

When Caesar Germanicus crossed the Visurgis (Weser) he learnt from a deserter that Arminius had chosen a new battle site. The German tribes had assembled in a forest sacred to Hercules and were planning a night attack on the Roman military camp. Germanicus trusted this account since the watchfires of the enemy had been seen in this vicinity. Roman scouts crept close to the site and heard the neighing of horses and the murmur of a vast and boisterous war host. This was to be a decisive engagement and Germanicus wanted a means to determine the attitude and commitment of his soldiers. He knew that tribunes and centurions often reported what he would approve of, rather than what was true. Freedmen could not be relied upon because they had servile temperaments, and political friends were inclined to flatter a commander. A military assembly (a large-scale gathering and address of the soldiers) was also not the solution, since in these settings a few men can direct and lead the shouts of the masses. Germanicus needed a way to discover the inner thoughts and resolve of the soldiers. He wanted to hear the hopes and fears expressed in military quarters, but without being noticed.

At nightfall he visited the augury tent (the ritual centre of the camp where omens were taken). He left by a hidden exit, unseen by the sentries, and travelled through the camp with just one companion. Across his shoulders he wore the fur of a wild beast (to disguise his outline and appearance). Germanicus walked through the temporary streets of the camp. He lingered by the tents and overheard the men speak about his role and reputation as commander. One soldier praised his noble rank, while another commented on his physical prowess. They all agreed that he was resolute, gracious and displayed an even temper, whether jesting or dealing with serious matters. They acknowledged that they ought to repay him by displaying the utmost effort in battle. They would inflict a glorious slaughter on the enemy as vengeance for their treacherous violation of the peace (the German resistance to Roman rule).

While this was occurring, one of the enemy, who could speak the Roman language, suddenly rode up to the outer edge of the camp entrenchments. In a loud voice he cried out a message from Arminius. All deserters (German allies and auxiliaries) would receive wives, lands and 100 sesterces (1 gold aureus) per day of military action against the Romans.

This insult infuriated the legions. They cried out:

> Let daylight come, let battle begin. Our soldiers will seize the German lands and carry off their wives. Hail to this omen! The women and riches of the enemy will be our plunder.

About midday there was a skirmishing attack on the Roman camp. But there was no rash discharge of missiles (javelins hurled in anger or frustration). The cohorts were assembled in close array before the ramparts and there was no sign of carelessness (this was a disciplined army eager for combat).

That night Germanicus received a dream that gave him great confidence (a divine message foretelling the future). Germanicus dreamt that he was engaged in an animal sacrifice when some sacred blood spilled on his toga. In response, his grandmother Augusta presented him with a replacement toga that was far more splendid than his existing garment (indicating greater rank, position and honours).

Germanicus was encouraged by this omen and when he consulted the auspices, he found them favourable (the flight of birds across the camp or actual sacrifices). He called a military assembly and outlined what precautions were required before the impending battle. Germanicus explained:

> Roman soldiers fight well on flat plains. But if they use their skills correctly, they can also engage the enemy successfully in woodlands and forest passes. The huge shields and unwieldy spears of the enemy cannot be used effectively amid tree trunks and bushes. Manage the throw of your javelins. Make use of your close-fitting armour and short swords (superior protection and capacity to fight at extreme close quarters). Launch your javelins in dense volleys (to maximise injuries). Then strike at the face of your opponents with your sword points. The Germans do not have breastplates or helmets. Their shields are not strengthened with leather or iron (bands binding or reinforcing heavy wooden boards). Instead, their shields are osiers woven together (a lightweight wickerwork frame that could block missile fire). Or they carry a thin painted board.
>
> The front ranks of the enemy are armed with spears, but behind them the rest have only short blades or wooden weapons hardened by fire (wood desiccated by partial charring to produce a more durable material). The German physique is terrifying and formidable, but their strength is quickly spent and they cannot endure wounds. They will ignore their leaders and flee without feeling any shame for their disgrace. The Germans disregard the laws of gods and men when they succeed. But they tremble with fear when they suffer disaster.
>
> Perhaps you are weary from crossing such a large expanse of land and sea. You seek an end to this military service. Well, this battle prepares the way. The Elbe is now nearer to us than the Rhine and there is no war beyond that river boundary. Empower me and we will succeed. Follow me closely and faithfully, as I follow the course taken by my father (Nero Claudius Drusus) and my uncle (Tiberius). And we shall stand as conquerors in the same locations.

The soldiers greeted the general's speech with great enthusiasm and the signal for battle was given.

Speech by the Germanic War Leader Arminius The Cherusci choose a Battleground

272 Tacitus, *Annals*, 2.15–19

Arminius and the other German chiefs addressed their clansmen. They urged them to bear witness:

> These Romans are the most cowardly fugitives from the army of Varus. They are men who would rather mutiny than endure further wars. Half of them have backs covered with wounds (from fleeing battle or military floggings). The rest have been battered by waves and storms and now expose themselves to a foe that is full of fury. They enter a land of hostile deities, with no hope of any advantage. They came here on a fleet that crossed the trackless ocean. They hoped that their approach might be unopposed and their escape unpursued. But after they battle with us, these defeated men will have no need of winds and oars. Remember their greed, their cruelty, and their arrogance. We have one course and purpose. Fight to retain our freedom, or die before we are enslaved.

The Germans were roused by these speeches and demanded immediate battle. Their chiefs led them down into a plain named the Idistavisus which lay between the Weser and a nearby range of hills. Due to the curvature of the river and the protection of the adjoining hills, this plain varied in width. Behind the hills was a tall forest with thick branches rising to a great height. However, close to the forest floor the branches were sparce and there were clear spaces between the tree trunks (little undergrowth at ground level due to a thick forest canopy).

The barbarian army occupied the plain and the outskirts of the wood. The Cherusci assembled on the high ground where they could rush down on the Romans during the battle (the hillslopes facing the plain). The Roman army advanced in the following order. The auxiliary Gauls and Germans formed the vanguard. Then came the infantry archers, next the four legions and then Caesar Germanicus himself with two praetorian cohorts and some specially selected cavalry. The other legions followed with the light-armed troops, the mounted archers, and the remaining allied cohorts (a total force of perhaps 40,000 soldiers). The soldiers were ready and prepared to form a battle line based on this marching order.

The Cheruscan warbands were impetuous and charged down the slopes to attack the Romans. When Caesar Germanicus saw them move from position, he ordered the Roman cavalry to immediately charge their flank.

Meanwhile, Stertinius, who was leading the other squadrons, took a wide detour to attack the enemy from the rear. Germanicus had assured Stertinius that the main army would be fully engaged when this counterattack struck.

At this very moment an augury occurred which gave great encouragement to the Romans. Eight eagles were observed flying towards the woods (matching the number of legions in the campaign army). Germanicus saw the birds and cried out, 'Go! Follow those Roman birds, for they are the true deities of our legions.' At that moment the Roman infantry charged and the cavalry, which had been sent in advance, smashed into the rear and flanks of the enemy army.

A strange outcome occurred as the two columns of the enemy fled in opposite directions. The forces that were occupying the woodlands rushed into the open and those that had been assembled on the plains fled into the wood. Meanwhile, the Cherusci, who were between them, were dislodged from the hills. Arminius was easily identifiable among these fighters due to his shouts and gestures. Though he was wounded, he kept fighting alongside his warriors. The Cherusci charged into the Roman archers and were about to rout them when the cohorts of the Raeti and Vendelici (Alpine and Rhine recruits) and the other Gauls counterattacked.

Arminius and his fighters pushed through the Gallic cohorts. This took supreme physical effort and Arminius urged his horse forwards in a furious rush. It is reported that he smeared blood on his face so that he could not be easily identified within the melee. But he was recognised by some Chauci serving among the Roman auxiliaries, yet they allowed him to escape. Inguiomerus (an influential Cherusci chieftain and uncle of Arminius) was also permitted to escape the combat. This was either due to his own courage, or the disloyalty of the auxiliaries (refusing to pursue, then attack their countrymen).

The rest of the German army were slaughtered in every direction. Many were killed while desperately trying to swim to safety across the Visurgis River (Weser). They died in a hail of missiles or were drowned by the force of the current. Others were crushed when the riverbanks collapsed by the weight of men fleeing the battle site. In their desperate efforts to escape, some of the Germans climbed to the very tops of trees and hid themselves in the boughs and branches. They suffered an ignominious death when the Romans summoned archers to shoot them down for sport. Others died when the Romans felled the trees and the concealed warriors were smashed and crushed in the fall.

This was a great victory achieved without the Romans suffering significant losses. Men were slaughtered from the ninth hour in the morning until nightfall. An area 10 miles long was covered with discarded weapons and the slain bodies of the enemy. Amid the plunder seized from the site were the chains that the Germans had brought to the battlefield. They had expected the conflict to be such a sure victory for themselves that they had brought chains to bind their Roman captives.

Roman soldiers gathered on the battlefield to hail Tiberius as emperor (supreme commander). They raised a mound of earth on which they arrayed the weapons taken from the enemy. This display resembled a Roman trophy (a victory monument) and the names of the conquered tribes were inscribed beneath their weapons.

The sight of this victory monument caused the Germans greater grief and anger than the wounds they had suffered, or their sorrow for the dead, or their battlefield losses. Those who had been preparing to abandon their settlements and retreat to the further side of the Elbe now longed for battle and they prepared to fight. Common people and chiefs, both the young and the old, spread unrest and gathered to attack the Roman army.

Second Battle against the Cherusci; Angrivarii submit; Victory as far as the Elbe

273 Tacitus, *Annals*, 2.19–22

Finally, the enemy chose a battle site flanked by a river and enclosed by forests. The site was a narrow swampy plain and beyond the encircling woods, there were further marshlands. On one side of the marshes the Angrivarii had raised a broad earthwork as a tribal boundary between themselves and the neighbouring Cherusci. The Germans arrayed their infantry along this barrier and concealed their cavalry forces in the nearby trees. This deployment would allow the German cavalry to attack the rear of the legions as they entered the intervening forest (en route to the earthwork).

But Caesar Germanicus was fully aware of the enemy's position and their battle plans. He knew what could be observed, and what was concealed. He therefore prepared to use the enemy's stratagems to fulfil their own destruction. He assigned the Roman cavalry to his chief officer Seius Tubero and instructed him to occupy level ground. Germanicus then arranged the Roman infantry so that only part of this force would advance across the plain towards the forest. Meanwhile, a Roman subdivision would confront the visible section of the German army, clambering up the earthwork defences. This was a complex and difficult military operation (the planning, timing and co-ordinating of separate Roman attacks). Germanicus therefore led the Roman charge and left the further arrangements to his senior officers (giving them scope to act or respond as required).

The Roman soldiers who advanced across the level ground made good progress. But the forces who assaulted the earthwork were struck with many heavy blows from above and had to fight as though they were scaling a wall (clambering, climbing, striking upwards and defending against downward attacks). The commander realised how disadvantaged his soldiers were, and withdrew his legions a short distance from the earthwork. He then ordered slingers and artillerymen to discharge a dense volley of missiles into the defences to scatter the enemy. Spears were hurled from the engines (long-range field artillery – mobile catapults able to launch harpoon-like javelins). Any defenders who made themselves conspicuous (in acts of bravado) suffered the greatest wounds, and the Germans were driven back from the earthwork.

The Romans stormed the ramparts while Caesar Germanicus, accompanied by some of the praetorian cohorts, led the charge into the woods. The Romans now engaged the Germans in extreme close-quarter fighting. Both sides fought desperately to maintain their position and avoid retreat. To the rear of the Germans there was treacherous marshland, while the landscape behind the Romans was hemmed in by the river and the hills. Their only hope was valour, and a victory provided the only means for safety and survival.

The Germans matched the Romans in bravery, but they were beaten by the style of fighting and the weapons they used. They were a vast horde, but crammed into a confined space. They could not easily thrust, or withdraw, their long spears. In this close engagement, the German fighters could not make use of their faster reflexes or more agile bodies (unencumbered by armour and heavier equipment). The Romans fought with their shields pressed right up against their chests as they gripped their sword hilts and repeatedly stabbed. They struck at the huge limbs and exposed faces of the barbarians, and cut a passage through the enemy, slaughtering them as they went.

Arminius was less active in this combat. This was either because the Germans faced severe danger in battle, or Arminius had been partially disabled by his recent wound. By contrast Inguiomerus was seen on many parts of the battlefield dashing here and there (to encourage the fighters or escaping danger). He retained his courage until the fortunes of war had overcome the Germans.

Germanicus removed his helmet to be more conspicuous and noticeable to his troops. He did this so that his soldiers might hear, then heed, his appeals to continue the massacre by pursuing the fleeing enemy. He reminded the Romans not to take prisoners, as they wanted the utter destruction of these nations. It was the only way the war could conclude.

Later in the day, Germanicus withdrew one of his legions from the battlefield. He ordered them to begin constructing the entrenchments of a military camp. The rest of the army continued to pursue and kill the enemy until nightfall, when they were glutted by death (exhausted by the brutal combat). In contrast, the cavalry only managed an indecisive success against the enemy.

Caesar Germanicus publicly praised his victorious troops. The army raised a mound from the piles of captured weaponry and beneath this display an inscription was placed, reading:

> The army of the Emperor Tiberius Caesar has conquered the tribes between the Rhine and the Elbe. This monument is dedicated to Mars, Jupiter, and Augustus.

Germanicus added nothing about himself, since he feared the jealousy of the emperor and was aware that the achievement alone would be sufficient (praise and recognition).

Germanicus instructed Stertinius to continue the conflict by making war on the Angrivarii. However, the Angrivarii immediately surrendered and willingly accepted all Roman impositions and demands. They therefore received a full pardon from the Empire.

The Shipwrecked Fleet (AD 16)

274 Tacitus, *Annals*, 2.22–24

At the height of summer, Germanicus sent some of the legions back to their winter quarters via the overland route (marching back to the Rhine frontier). But most of the army boarded the fleet on the Amisia River (the Ems) and were conveyed downstream to the ocean. At first this fleet of a thousand vessels encountered calm waters. The only noise on the ocean was the sound of the oars, or the ruffled billowing of sails. But suddenly a mass of dark clouds swept in and a hailstorm began. The waves rolled violently against the ships and squalls battered the vessels from every quarter. The storm reduced visibility and steering became difficult. The terror-stricken soldiers had no experience of maritime dangers, and this distressed the sailors. The soldiers offered them clumsy assistance that confounded, or undid, the actions of the skilled crews (the soldiers were manning the oars).

After a while the storm abated, and the wind and waves shifted to the south. Then a huge line of rolling clouds appeared on the horizon above mainland Germany. This phenomenon seemed to emerge from the uplands and deep rivers of their country (as though it were a supernatural power). Then with a mighty blast, it struck the Roman fleet. It caught and drove the ships into the open ocean with frightful effect. They were shoved in a disordered array towards the terrifying frozen north (Scandinavia). Ships were pushed towards islands with steep cliffs, or onto perilous rocks and sandbars concealed beneath the surface of the sea. The crews escaped these hazards with difficulty, but when the tides changed to the same direction as the wind, their anchors could not hold. They were propelled further into danger, struggling to bale out the water that was swept across the decks. Horses, beasts of burden and baggage, were thrown overboard to lighten ships that leaked copiously through damaged hull planks.

This particular ocean is stormier than all other seas, and Germany is known for its terrifying climate. Yet the scale and uniqueness of this disaster exceeded every other tragedy. The Roman fleet was surrounded by hostile coasts (enemy territories). They had been swept into a vast and deep ocean thought to be limitless. Some of the vessels were swallowed up by the ocean (sunk and submerged). Many were wrecked on distant islands, where stranded crews found neither sustenance nor signs of life. They perished of hunger, or survived by scavenging the carcases of horses that had been washed ashore in the disaster.

The trireme bearing Germanicus was separated from the fleet and made landfall alone in the territory of the Chauci (allied Germans). Germanicus stood on the rocks and promontories of this shore, watching by day and night. Again and again, he would cry out that he was responsible for this ruinous tragedy. His friends and companions restrained him from seeking death in the same sea that had taken his soldiers (by mortally stabbing himself and falling into the ocean – the honourable suicide expected from defeated commanders). At last, the sea settled, and a favourable wind once more blew across the ocean. Gradually, the shattered vessels began to reappear and reach Germanicus. Some had only a few rowers still able to manage the oars. Others had repaired sails using their clothing to patch tears in the canvas. Some of the more powerful vessels were intact and able to tow smaller, more badly damaged craft. When they returned to Germanicus, after hasty repairs, he ordered them to re-enter the ocean and search the islands for survivors.

Many stranded soldiers were recovered during these operations. The Angrivarii, who had only recently accepted an alliance with Rome, were able to return several soldiers who they had ransomed from more distant tribes. Some of the survivors had been swept across to Britain and they were returned by the petty chiefs who rule that island. Every one of the men who returned from distant regions offered extraordinary accounts of their experiences. They described strange sights such as violent hurricanes, unknown birds, and marvellous sea creatures. Some of these animals had part-human forms, or were half beast-like (seals and walruses). Perhaps men had really seen these creatures, or maybe they were the product of terrified imaginations.

Poetry Inspired by the Disaster

The Roman commander Albinovanus Pedo wrote poetry inspired by the disaster. The work has not survived, but a passage was quoted by Seneca.

275 Seneca, *Suaseriae*, 1.15

Latin poets describing the Ocean have either been too vague or too detailed in their works. The exception is Albinovanus Pedo who writes with great spirit:

> They witness daylight, but the sun is left far behind. They are long exiled from the well-known limits of the world. They have dared to go into the forbidden, gloom-filled territories at the edge of creation to try and reach its farthest shores. Now they behold an Ocean which has monsters beneath its sluggish waves. On all sides are savage sharks and dogs of the sea. Crashing waves and wrathful billowing winds seize their ships, rising them high in the water and swelling them with fear. As their fleet is caught by swift winds they feel their ships impacting on a shoal. They are now doomed. The remorseless fates will mangle them, or deliver them to the wild creatures of the ocean.
>
> One man stands defiant on the high prow, straining, yet failing to see through the dark clouds of the storm. He discerns nothing. It seems as if the world has disappeared. He cries out the thoughts of his imprisoned soul: 'Where are we being taken by the storm? Daylight has fled from us. We are at the limits of nature and this abandoned world is shrouded in endless gloom. Should we be searching for nations who dwell beyond another sky? Is it possible there is a land out there that is not subject to these fierce storms? But the gods are calling us back. They have forbidden mortal men to see the edges of this world. We

are violating foreign seas and sacred waters with our oars. Why do we trouble the untouched dwelling-places of the gods?'

German Campaign Continues Attack on the Chatti; Entering Marsi Territory; Recovering the Second Eagle

276 Tacitus, *Annals*, 2.25–26

The reported loss of the Roman fleet gave the Germans encouragement to continue the war. It also provoked Germanicus to complete his conquest. He ordered Gaius Silius to advance against the Chatti with 30,000 infantry and 3,000 cavalry. He himself invaded the lands of the Marsi with a larger army, since Mallovendus, the chief of this nation, had recently surrendered to Rome. Mallovendus claimed that one of the eagles (battle standards) belonging to Varus' legions had been concealed in nearby woods (probably a sacred Germanic site). According to reports, the eagle was guarded by only a small hostile force. Germanicus immediately sent troops to the location to engage the enemy. Some of the soldiers appeared in front of the wood, and others assembled at the rear before entering the trees. Fortuna favoured both divisions and they successfully recovered the eagle.

Germanicus now acted with greater energy and advanced further into hostile territory. The Roman army laid waste to everything they encountered. They destroyed the livelihood of any enemy who would not engage, or could not be immediately defeated. The Romans learnt from prisoners that the German population was utterly panic-stricken and more fearful than they had ever been before. The Germans now believed that the Romans were invincible and could overcome all calamities. They had thrown away a fleet and lost the weaponry and equipment of an entire army. The shores of Germania had been strewn with the carcases of horses and of men, but still the Romans rushed to the attack with undiminished courage. The Roman military spirit seemed undaunted, and their campaigns continued with enlarged numbers.

The Roman soldiers were led back to their winter quarters with their morale restored (returning to permanent forts and bases on the Rhine frontier). The soldiers rejoiced that their disasters at sea had been alleviated by a successful expedition against the enemy. Their personal losses (equipment and funds) were compensated by the bounty that Germanicus offered (a financial reward presented as a gift for their military successes).

Praise for the Emperor Tiberius; Germanicus as Conquer of Germany

277 Velleius Paterculus, *History of Rome*, 2.129

Germanicus was well trained by the guidance of Tiberius. He learned the basics of military command from him and when these skills had fully developed, Tiberius welcomed him home as the conqueror of Germany!

Expectations Denied

278 Tacitus, *Annals*, 2.26

The Romans were now convinced that the Germans were demoralised and would soon negotiate a lasting peace (submitting to Roman rule). They thought that after another campaign season was launched the following summer, the war could be concluded (and territories from the Rhine to the Elbe added to the Empire). However, Tiberius repeatedly sent letters to Germanicus insisting that the general return to Rome to celebrate the triumph that had been decreed for his victories. The emperor advised:

> You have now had sufficient success and enough disasters. You have fought victorious battles on a great scale. But consider the losses which the winds and waves have inflicted. They are not your fault as a general, but they are still grievous and shocking.
>
> I, Tiberius, was sent nine times into Germany by the Emperor Augustus (as a military commander). But I achieved more from political diplomacy than from military operations. I secured the submission of the Sugambri by negotiation. By similar means I compelled the Suebi with their king, Maroboduus, to accept peace terms. The vengeance of Rome has now been satisfied (revenge for the Varus disaster). The Cherusci and the other insurgent tribes can now be left to their own internal feuds.

Nevertheless, Germanicus requested another year to complete his campaigns. In response, Tiberius increased political pressure by offering him a second consulship. Germanicus could not refuse this supreme honour, but the functions of this high office could only be performed in Rome itself.

Tiberius added that if the Germanic conflict must continue, then the military operations should be led by Drusus (the younger brother of Germanicus by adoption). There were currently no other enemies for the Romans to suppress and Germanicus should leave his brother Drusus the opportunity to win his own victory titles and triumphal laurels. Germanicus knew that this appeal was a pretence and Tiberius was secretly jealous of the glory he had acquired. Nevertheless, he did not delay. He left his command and hurried back to Rome.

Achievements of Germanicus

279 Cassius Dio, *Roman History*, 57.18

Germanicus acquired a great reputation from his campaign against the Germans. He advanced as far as the ocean, inflicting an overwhelming defeat upon the barbarians. He collected and buried the bones of those who had fallen with Varus and reclaimed the military standards (lost legionary eagles).

The Triumph (AD 17)

The monumental Victory Arch of Germanicus and Tiberius was erected in Rome in AD 16. Germanicus celebrated his triumph in Rome in AD 17.

280 Tacitus, *Annals*, 2.41

At the end of that year, an arch was completed and dedicated near the Temple of Saturn (in the Roman Forum). It commemorated the recovery of the eagle battle standards lost with Varus, (a victory) achieved 'under the leadership of Germanicus and the auspices of Tiberius'. (…)

On the 26th of May, in the consulate of Gaius Caelius and Lucius Pomponius, Germanicus Caesar celebrated his triumph. He proclaimed his victory over the Cherusci, the Chatti, the Angrivarii, and all the other tribes positioned west of the Elbe. There was a procession of plunder and captives, including the representation of mountains, rivers, and battles (paintings and tableaux conveyed on carts and carriages). Germanicus had been prevented from completing his war, so the conflict was now assumed to be finished. The public enthusiasm for the event was increased by the noble figure of the commander himself (Germanicus) with five children climbing onto his chariot (imperial offspring who would inherit and safeguard the Empire). For there was an unspoken fear in the populace, remembering the fate of his father Drusus after he too had brought great joy to the crowd (he died aged 30). They also recalled the fate of his uncle Marcellus (who died aged 20). These popular figures had been suddenly snatched away from the Roman people (dying young). Those that the populace adore often have a brief and unblest existence.

281 Strabo, *Geography*, 7.1.4

The Romans believe that distrust is the best tactic for dealing with the German tribes. For good faith and trust has caused the Romans the greatest harm. As an example, the Cherusci and their subjects violated their treaties with Rome. Three Roman legions, including their general Quintilius Varus, were destroyed in an ambush by these tribes.

But, they all paid the penalty for this action when the younger Germanicus won a great military campaign against them. Their renowned people were captured and led in triumph through Rome. This included the chief of the Cherusci, Segimuntus, son of Segestes. It also included Thusnelda, the wife of Armenius, the Germanic war leader who violated the treaty against Varus. Thusnelda's 3-year-old son Thumelicus was also paraded in the triumph. Armenius still leads the war against Rome. Other captives included a leader of the Cherusci named Sesithacus, son of Segimerus and his wife Rhamis. A daughter of the Chatti chief Ucromirus appeared in the triumph, along with a Sugambri chief named Deudorix (Theodoric), the son of Baetorix who was the brother of Melo.

Segestes, the father-in-law of Armenius, opposed his kinsmen when they decided to launch a war against Rome. At an opportune moment he deserted them to support the Empire. Consequently, he was guest of honour at the Roman triumph that celebrated the capture of his kinsfolk.

Prisoners from other plundered tribes were led in the procession including captives from the Caulci, Campsani, Bructeri, Usipetes, Cherusci, Chatti, Chattuarii, Landi and Tubantes. A priest of the Chatti named Libes was also led captive in that triumph.

Excuses

In AD 17, Germanicus was sent to the eastern provinces to confront a threat posed by the Parthians (the rival empire ruling Iraq and Iran). There he died of a mysterious illness, aged 34. The Emperor Tiberius did not conduct any further campaigns to reconquer Germany and the territory reacquired its independence.

282 Tacitus, *Annals*, 2.5

The Emperor Tiberius welcomed these political commotions in the east (disputes over the kingdom of Armenia). This was because it gave him a pretext to remove Germanicus from the command of the legions in Germany. Germanicus had become well known and respected by his troops (and therefore a potential rival for imperial power). Filled with animosity, his uncle Tiberius schemed to place Germanicus in command of new eastern provinces where he could be exposed to political treachery and other unforeseen disasters.

Death of Germanicus (AD 19)

283 Tacitus, *Annals*, 2.73

Some compared the death of Germanicus to the fate of Alexander the Great. Both men were the product of a noble heritage and possessed great dignity. They both died before greatly exceeding the age of 30, suffering a suspicious death in strange lands (it was rumoured that Germanicus was poisoned). However, Germanicus was always gracious to his friends and moderate in his personal demands. He was the husband to only one wife and produced only legitimate children. His martial ability matched that of Alexander, but he was never hasty or careless.

Germanicus suppressed Germany with his many victories, but he was prevented from fully conquering the country (due to opposition from Tiberius). If Germanicus had been given sole control over military affairs, or possessed the full powers of a ruler, then he would have fully matched the glory of Alexander (obtaining major conquests).

Status of Empire under Tiberius (AD 20)

Tiberius abandoned Roman prospects for reconquering Germany. The Rhine became a permanent frontier with two large, militarised zones along its west bank. These territories came to be known as Germania Superior (south or Upper Rhine) and Germania Inferior (north or Lower Rhine). Each of these 'German' provinces had a separate governor, ensuring that the Rhine armies were no longer under a single frontier command.

284 Tacitus, *Annals*, 4.4–5

Tiberius rapidly listed the legions and the provinces they had to garrison. I will include these details in my work as they reveal what military forces the Empire maintained in this era, what kings were our allies, and the previous extent of our domains.

The seas flanking Italy were guarded by fleets based at Misenum and Ravenna. The adjoining coast of Gaul was protected by warships captured after the victory of Actium and transferred in part to Forojulium. But the main military strength of the Empire was concentrated along the Rhine as a defence against the Germans and a safeguard against the Gauls. This force included eight legions.

Spain, which had been recently subjugated, was occupied by just three legions. Mauretania (the western seaboard of North Africa) was ruled by King Juba, who was granted this territory by Rome. The rest of North Africa was garrisoned by two legions, and two legions secured Egypt. Syria and the frontier extending to the Euphrates was maintained by four legions (the frontier between the Roman and the Parthian empires). (...)

The banks of the Danube were guarded by two legions in Pannonia, two legions in Moesia, and two legions in Dalmatia. The two legions in Dalmatia were positioned behind the other four legions due to the location of the territory (further south). These forces were quite close to Italy if military assistance had to be summoned.

Long-term Consequences

Tertullian contrasts the spread of Christianity to the Power of Rome (AD 200).

285 Tertullian, *Adversus Judaeos*, 7

Even today the Germans are not permitted to cross the Roman frontiers and Britons are separated by the great circuit of their ocean. The Moors and the barbarous Gaetulians are also contained by Roman power in their own regions. For the Romans have fortified their Empire with garrisons and legions, but they cannot extend their great might beyond the frontiers into neighbouring nations.

Chapter Eleven

Fate of Arminius and Maroboduus (AD 17–20)

In AD 17, the Emperor Tiberius abandoned Roman plans to conquer and subdue Greater Germania. The Rhine and Danube frontiers therefore became heavily defended border zones. But Roman intervention had destabilised the region and the Empire created further unrest by encouraging warfare between the Marcomannic kingdom (south Germany) and the Cherusci-led northern tribes. These political strategies were managed by Drusus the Younger, the son of Tiberius.

Warfare among the Germanic Tribes (AD 17–20)

286 Tacitus, *Annals*, 2.44–46

Drusus (the son of Tiberius) was sent to Illyricum to gain military experience and win the goodwill of the army (AD 17–20). The emperor thought that the young prince was being demoralised by luxury in the capital and required experience in a military camp. He also felt more secure (as emperor) if both his sons (adopted and biological) were commanding the legions (the main military forces).

Tiberius made a pretext for war from the appeals of the Suebi (the Marcomannic kingdom) who were imploring the Romans to help them against the Cherusci. The Romans had withdrawn (from Greater Germany) and they no longer feared invasion (across the Rhine or Danube frontiers). But the tribes in this country had acted according to their natural customs and began fighting one another as they competed for further renown. The strength of the two nations (Cherusci and Marcomanni) were equal and the valour of their chiefs was well matched. But some of the Suebi hated the title of 'king' adopted by Maroboduus and began to favour Arminius as a champion of freedom.

One side in the fighting therefore included the Cherusci and their allies. They were joined by the armed warriors of Arminius and by tribal fighters from the Semnones and Langobardi who revolted (from the Marcomannic kingdom) to follow him. These forces should have given the Cherusci an overwhelming superiority, but Inguiomerus (a Cherusci chief) left the territory with a troop of warriors to join Maroboduus. He did this because he was an aged uncle and he thought it was demeaning to have to obey the orders of his brother's young son (Arminius).

The armies formed up with equal confidence on both sides. This was not a force of irregular warbands gathered for the type of haphazard and uncommitted attack that is common among the Germans. They had assembled for the kind of prolonged warfare they had learned and developed through conflict with Rome. They were committed to remaining with the battle standards (no retreat), obeying the commands of generals, and each side had placed reserve forces in readiness (rapid reinforcements).

Arminius reviewed the entire battle line on horseback. He rode up to each warband, boasting how he had regained freedom (for Germania) by slaughtering the legions. The spoils and weapons stripped from the Romans were still in the hands of many of his warriors. Arminius called Maroboduus a fugitive who had no experience in battle. He said that Maroboduus had hidden himself away in the deepest recesses of the Hercynian Forest and then pleaded for a treaty (with Rome) with presents and embassies. Maroboduus was a traitor to his country, a satellite state of Caesar (the Roman emperors). He deserved to be driven out with the same furious rage that had extinguished Quintilius Varus. The Germans should remember the many battles fought to achieve the final expulsion of the Romans. These fights had shown who would claim success in this current war.

Maroboduus also boasted about his achievements and slandered his foes. He clasped the hand of Inguiomerus and cried out:

> This man in front of you embodies all the great renown of the Cherusci. All their successful actions were due to his guidance. Arminius is ignorant and self-absorbed to claim the glory that belongs to another man.
>
> He treacherously ambushed three legions lacking officers, and attacked a general unprepared for treachery. His actions have brought great harm to Germany and caused his own disgrace, because his wife and son now endure slavery (as captives of Rome).
>
> As for myself, I have been threatened by twelve legions led by Tiberius. Yet I preserved the unvanquished glory of the Germans. When the Romans departed, they saw me as an equal. I have made this matter our decision. We decide whether to fight with all our might against Rome, or accept peace without bloodshed.

These words roused the two armies, but the combatants had their own motives. The Cherusci and Langobardi were fighting to confirm their past glory and enhance their newly gained freedom. Their opponents (the Marcomannic forces) hoped to increase their dominion (within Germany).

The shock of this battle was unsurpassed (two vast armies charging full force into combat) and the outcome was even more uncertain. The right wings of both armies were routed. Further fighting was expected, but Maroboduus withdrew his camp to the hills. This was a sign that he lacked confidence. Gradually his forces began to desert, stripping his army of its manpower. He fled to the Marcomanni (the core of his kingdom) and sent envoys to Tiberius requesting military assistance. The emperor answered that Maroboduus had no right to invoke the aid of Roman armies against the Cherusci, for he had rendered no assistance to the Romans in their conflict with the same enemy.

Instability in the Marcomannic Kingdom

287 Tacitus, *Annals*, 2.62–63

Drusus Caesar gained further glory by creating political discord among the Germans. He urged them to complete the destruction of Maroboduus who was already gravely weakened (as ruler of the Suebic Marcomanni – a powerful south German tribe). Maroboduus had forced a young dissident nobleman named Catualda into exile. He had taken refuge among the Gotones (a Germanic tribe living east of the Vistula River) and now that fortunes of the king were declining, Catualda decided to return and seek his revenge.

Catualda led a strong force of warriors into the territory of the Marcomanni. By using corruption, he induced many of the nobles to support him (probably bribes and pay-offs). They suddenly surged into the palace and the adjacent fortress and seized the long-accumulated plunder of this Suebic realm. They also captured camp followers and traders from our provinces (Roman merchants and civilians associated with the frontier military). These men had freely left their various home territories in the Empire to do business in enemy lands. They had originally been attracted by profits, but became neglectful of their Roman origins.

Maroboduus was now utterly deserted by his supporters and had no recourse but to seek the mercy of the emperor. He crossed the Danube where it flows past the province of Noricum (the Roman frontier near Switzerland). Then he wrote to Tiberius, not like a fugitive or a suppliant, but as someone who recalled his past greatness. In former times Maroboduus had been a famous king who received offers of alliance from many foreign powers. But he had preferred the friendship of Rome and he still maintained this allegiance. Tiberius replied that he would be granted a safe and honourable home in Italy. He could remain there as long as he pleased and if future interests required his departure, then he was free to leave under the same protection by which he had come (a return to Germania).

However, the Senate disagreed (contradicting the emperor). It was argued that Maroboduus had been as dangerous to Rome as King Philip of Macedon had been to the Athenians (fourth century BC). He had been as formidable as King Pyrrhus (of Epirus) and matched the threat that the Seleucid King Antiochus presented to the Roman people (serious threats to Roman lives and power in the third and second centuries BC). This speech is still extant (a record of the Senatorial debate). It magnifies the political power that Maroboduus held and stresses the ferocity of the tribes under his rule. It emphasises the proximity of his former realm to Italy and describes the events that led to his overthrow and ousting.

As a result, Maroboduus was detained at Ravenna (a strategic imperial city in northern Italy). His possible return to power was used to threaten and menace the Suebi, if they failed to obey Roman dictates. But Maroboduus never left Italy and after eighteen years he was reduced to an old man. He had clung to his hopes too long and had lost his former renown.

Catualda had a similar downfall and did no better in the refuge he sought after defeat. Soon after he seized power, he was attacked by an overwhelming force of Herunduri (a tribe from the Elbe region) led by (their ruler) Vibilius. Expelled from his homeland, Catualda was received by the Romans and sent to Forum Julii, a Roman colony in Gallia Narbonensis (southern Gaul).

The barbarians who followed these two rulers into exile received different treatment. It was thought that these Germans might create disturbances if they were allowed to remain in the Empire and mingle among the Roman population. Therefore, they were resettled beyond the Danube between the rivers Marus and Cusus. This land was in the territory of a ruler named Vannius of the Quadi (a Germanic tribe on the mid-Danube that was still allied to Rome).

Offer to Poison Arminius

288 Tacitus, *Annals*, 2.88

I find it stated by some writers and senators of this period, that a letter from Adgandestrius, chief of the Chatti, was read before the Senate. Adgandestrius promised to kill Arminius, if some poison could be prepared and sent to him (possibly a specialist poison that mimicked death by natural causes). The reply returned by Tiberius was that the people of Rome avenged themselves on their enemies by military force, not by secret treachery. With this noble answer the emperor tried to liken himself to commanders of an earlier era who had forbidden, and even denounced, the poisoning of King Pyrrhus (280 BC).

Fate of Arminius

289 Tacitus, *Annals*, 2.88

The Romans had withdrawn (from Greater Germania) and Maroboduus had been expelled (from the Marcomannic kingdom). Meanwhile, Arminius tried to become king of his people, but faced opposition due to the independent spirit of his kinsmen. He was attacked by armed resistance and while fighting with intermittent success, he was killed through the treachery of his countrymen (in a plot or ambush).

Arminius had delivered Germany (from imperial rule). He had defied Rome, not during its early rise under the command of kings and generals, but he had resisted the Roman Empire at the very height of its power and glory. He had indeed fought indecisive battles, but he remained unconquered throughout the war.

Arminius lived thirty-seven years and possessed leadership (among the Germans) for twelve years. He is still the subject of songs recited by the barbarian nations (Germanic narratives). But he is unknown among the Greek historians who only admire the achievements of their own culture. Armenius should be better known among the Romans, for we often celebrate the past, but are indifferent to current affairs.

Political impact of Free Germany on Dacia (Carpathian Region, Romania)

290 Strabo, *Geography*, 7.3.13

The Getae and the Daci are now reduced to a nation that can only muster 40,000 fighting men and they have come close to yielding full obedience to the Romans. But they are not completely submissive because they place their hopes in the Germans, who remain enemies of the Empire.

Revolt of the Frisii (AD 28) Further Territorial Control is Lost

Tiberius' only son, Drusus the Younger, died suddenly of illness in AD 23. Later writers, including Tacitus and Suetonius, claim that he was the victim of a plot by the praetorian prefect Sejanus. Afterwards, Tiberius, now aged 63, withdrew from political affairs in Rome. Meanwhile, on the north coast beyond the Rhine, the Frisii rebelled from imperial rule.

291 Tacitus, *Annals*, 4.72–74

That same year (AD 28) a people beyond the Rhine known as the Frisii broke the established peace with Rome. They went to war, not because they were frustrated at being subject to the Empire, but because the Romans became excessively greedy in their demands for tribute. Since they had limited resources (the Roman commander) Drusus (the Elder) had imposed only a moderate tribute on the Frisii. They were expected to provide ox hides for military purposes (an essential material for campaign tents, durable sacks for produce, flasks for water and wine, sandals for soldiers, bridles, saddles and straps for cavalry horses and pack animals).

No one had ever seriously considered the size or thickness of the ox hides required to fulfil this tribute, until Olennius was appointed the leading centurion to oversee the management of the Frisii. Olennius insisted that the hides of wild bulls (giant aurochs) should be the standard measurement for all future hides to be supplied (multiplying the size of the tribute). This imposition would have been difficult for most people, but it was intolerable for the Germans. The wild beasts in their forests are giant animals, while their domestic cattle are diminutive. When the Frisii could not fulfil the quotas, they were made to pay with their lands (forfeiting valuable frontier farmlands). Then they paid with the bodies of their wives and children whom they had to offer in bondage (members of their community entering voluntary slavery).

When their angry objections and protests increased and the Romans still offered no respite, the Frisii sought a solution by war. The soldiers appointed to collect the tribute were seized and gibbeted (nailed dead or dying to gallows in a public execution). Olennius realised what was occurring and fled to a fortress named Flevum which guarded the shores of the ocean (North Sea facing Britain). There was a large force of Romans and supporting allied troops in this outpost.

When Lucius Apronius, the propraetor of Germania Inferior (North Rhineland), learned about the revolt, he summoned the legionary veterans from Germania Superior (southern part of the Rhine frontier). These soldiers were accompanied by some specially selected auxiliary infantry and cavalry forces. The armies from both provinces were then conveyed down the Rhine to attack the Frisii. The Frisii abandoned their assault on the fortress of Flevum to defend their homelands. Apronius began constructing sturdy roads and bridges over the estuaries that led into Frisian territory. These were designed to facilitate the passage of heavy troops (armoured legionaries).

Meanwhile, Apronius located a ford that provided an alternative route of attack. He ordered the cavalry of the Canninefates (a subject Germanic tribe) to cross at this location, along with all German infantry serving with the Romans. They were instructed to outflank the enemy and attack their forces from behind. But the Frisii were already in battle array and ready to repel this crossing.

The Roman assault was conducted by auxiliary cavalry with the legions held in reserve as a supporting force. Firstly, Apronius sent forwards three light cohorts of horsemen. Then he added reinforcements including two further mounted units. Finally, he committed all the cavalry to this frontal attack. The combined cavalry force should have been sufficient to overcome the Frisii, but only if they attacked in a single unified charge. But as they came forwards at intervals, they failed to restore confidence in the troops being pushed back. Instead, they themselves were caught up and carried away in the panicked retreat.

Apronius had entrusted the rest of his auxiliaries to Cethegus Labeo, the commander of the Fifth Legion. Labeo realised that the auxiliary forces were now in peril and sent urgent messages to Apronius asking for the immediate intervention of the legions. The soldiers of the Fifth Legion surged into combat and drove the enemy back in a fierce engagement. Their actions saved the auxiliary cohorts and the cavalry who were exhausted by their efforts and their wounds. Many tribunes, prefects, and first-rank centurions died in this battle. But after this engagement, Apronius did not attempt any further vengeance against the Frisii.

Soon afterwards, the Romans learned from deserters about other killings (that had occurred during the uprising). It was reported that 900 Roman soldiers had been slaughtered in a wood called the Braduhenna. These men had resisted and fought for two days before being massacred. In another instance, a group of 400 Romans took refuge in the homestead of a soldier named Cruptorix. Fearing betrayal and capture by the enemy, these men died by mutual slaughter (they consented to be killed by their comrades, or committed suicide).

The Frisian name thus became famous across Germany (for gaining independence and inflicting losses against the Empire which were not avenged). Tiberius kept the Roman losses a secret, as he did not wish to entrust anyone with the war (the senior military command). The Senate did not care if Romans suffered a great dishonour on the extreme frontiers of the Empire. Everyone in Rome feared the regime and sought safety in sycophancy (false praise offered to avoid political persecution). And so prominent men were asked their opinion on other subjects. They decreed an altar to Clemency and an altar to Friendship (pacification and appeasement), and around these shrines they placed statues of the Emperor Tiberius and Sejanus (the praetorian prefect acting as the main administrator of the Empire).

Chapter Twelve

Germania in the Reign of Caligula (AD 37–40)

Caligula (Gaius Caesar) was born in AD 12. He was the son of Germanicus and the nephew of Tiberius. As an infant, he was present in the Rhine military camps of his father (AD 14–16), alongside his mother, Agrippina the Elder. He became emperor after the death of Tiberius in AD 37. This family heritage may have influenced his ambitions for Germany.

Caligula seems to have planned military operations across the Rhine. These events occurred in about AD 40, when the emperor was 28 years old. This was the same age that his father, Germanicus, and his grandfather, Nero Claudius Drusus, were when they subdued Germania as far as the Elbe.

Loyalty of Rhine Troops

292 Suetonius, *Caligula*, 9

Gaius gained the affectionate nickname 'Caligula' (a military half-boot) from soldiers, since (as an infant) he was raised in their military camps wearing the dress of a common soldier (a miniature uniform). Reared in these communities, he won the great love and devotion of the soldiers (as the son of their commander, Germanicus). This is evidenced by their behaviour in the threatened mutiny which occurred after the death of Augustus (AD 14). In this instance the mere sight of Gaius calmed their urgent anger. They insisted that he was immediately removed from danger and sent for protection to the nearest town (placed under civic authority). Then they became remorseful and pressed in upon the carriage, halting the vehicle and begging to be spared this disgrace (the suggestion that any soldiers might murder members of the imperial family).

The Bridge (AD 39)

The Emperor Caligula constructed a vast pontoon bridge at Baiae (near Portus Julius, the base of the Western Imperial Fleet in Italy). It was possibly an experiment in engineering for a German campaign involving a large-scale river crossing. Soil and horse dung were placed on pontoon decking to calm horses brought across (convincing the animals that they were still on solid ground).

293 Suetonius, *Caligula*, 19
Caligula bridged the gap between Baiae and the harbour at Puteoli which was about 3,600 paces (over 3 miles) across. He brought merchant ships to the site and anchored them in a double line. Then he heaped soil upon the decking of the bridge which was furnished like the Appian Way. He rode back and forth across this bridge for two successive days. (…) Many believe that he was trying to rival King Xerxes who gained great admiration for bridging the much narrower Hellespont (480 BC, during the Persian invasion of Greece). But others say that Caligula was trying to cause fear in Germany or Britain by creating these stupendous engineering works.

Mention by Jewish Envoys

Jewish envoys from Alexandria visited the Emperor Caligula in AD 39. They mention animal sacrifices to the emperor.

294 Philo, *Embassy to Emperor Gaius* (Caligula), 45
'We sacrificed to you three times. The first was when you succeeded to the Empire, the second time was when you recovered from that terrible disease that affected the whole world. Our third sacrifice was made in the hope that you might obtain victory over the Germans.'

The Rhine Expedition (AD 39)

295 Suetonius, *Caligula*, 43
Caligula had only one experience with military affairs and warfare. He had gone to Mevania to visit the river Clitumnus (a scenic site in central Italy). While there he was suddenly reminded of the need to recruit more men for his bodyguard of Batavians. He therefore decided to leave urgently for an expedition to Germany (a forty-day journey to the Rhine frontier).

Without delay he ordered legions and auxiliaries from all regions to assemble (on the Rhine frontier). Levies were conducted everywhere with the utmost strictness (new military recruits were selected and demanding specifications imposed). Every kind of provision was sought and gathered on an unprecedented scale. Then the emperor commenced his march north.

He advanced with such haste and speed that the praetorian cohorts were forced to place their standards on pack animals, even though this defied all precedent and custom (the battle standards were sacred relics that had to be carried by chosen troops, not packed away like ordinary equipment). (…)

The emperor established his camp (at the frontier). To demonstrate his vigilance and strictness as a commander, he dismissed in disgrace all the generals who were late in bringing auxiliary forces from various places. He reviewed his troops and discharged many of the chief centurions who were well experienced, but seemed too old (for active service). Some of these soldiers were only a few days away from completing their full military term (twenty-five years), but he dismissed them due to their age and apparent infirmity.

Expedition from Rome (Caligula AD 39)

296 Cassius Dio, *Roman History*, 59.21

Gaius (Caligula) set out for Gaul, supposedly because the hostile Germans were causing unrest. But in reality he wanted to acquire and exploit the wealth of Gaul and Spain. The emperor did not openly announce his expedition beforehand. Instead, he visited one of the outer suburbs of the city and then suddenly set forth. He travelled with many actors (entertainers), gladiators, racehorses, women, and all other forms of luxury (palace entertainments rather than military equipment).

When the emperor reached his destination, he did no harm to any of the enemy (Germans beyond the Rhine). In fact, when he had advanced only a short distance beyond the Rhine, he quickly returned. Then he set out again as though he might conduct a campaign against Britain. But he turned back from the edge of the ocean, frustrating his generals who were only able to gain slight success from these operations (only minor military awards).

The Military Build-up (AD 39–40)

A vast military build-up occurred on the Rhine frontier (AD 40). In total, the Romans had 20 legions in Europe (100,000 legionaries and a similar number of auxiliaries). Many of these forces might have been ordered to provide detachments for the expected Germanic War.

297 Cassius Dio, *Roman History*, 59.22
Caligula did not secure any financial surplus for the Roman state (excess funds stored in the treasury), but he did maintain its customary expenditures (...) he also marshalled 200,000 troops, or as some report, 250,000.

Preparations for War

In AD 40, Galba, the newly appointed governor of Upper Germany (South Rhine), readied the frontier armies for war.

298 Suetonius, *Galba*, 6
Galba was strict, not allowing any Petitions for Leave or other absence from the camps. He hardened the soldiers, both old and young, by constant exercise. He excluded any barbarians who had been filtering into Gaul (frontier security). Caligula therefore gave the highest praise to Galba when he reached Germany. No one else received higher commendation, or greater rewards, even though numerous troops were gathering from all the imperial provinces to converge on the region.

Frontier Activities (AD 40)

Suetonius describes a hunt staged by the emperor with the bodyguard sent ahead to secure the area.

299 Suetonius, *Caligula*, 45
The emperor could find no one to fight with (on the frontier). So, he had a few of his German bodyguard transported across the river (Rhine) and concealed on the far banks. He arranged to be interrupted during his dining with a panicked report that some great disturbance was occurring across the river and the enemy was approaching. He immediately rushed out with his friends and led part of the praetorian cavalry to the nearby woods. They thrashed about cutting branches and adorned themselves with these pieces like victory trophies.

The emperor returned by torchlight and taunted those who had not followed him, calling them timid and cowardly men. He presented his companions with victory crowns (military awards) ornamented with figures of the sun, moon, and stars. He called these objects *exploratoriae* (awards connected with military forces scouting ahead of a main army).

Sometime later, he seized some slaves from a common source (perhaps a dealer in barbarian captives). He secretly released these captives and sent them on ahead. Then suddenly during a banquet he got up with his companions and pursued these slaves as if they were fugitives. They were brought back in chains and the emperor reappeared displaying immoderate glee at his actions. When he returned to his table, someone announced that the army was fully assembled (the Rhine legions). He instructed the soldiers who delivered these messages to take a seat at the banquet while they were still in their armour (a breach of decorum).

Caligula in Combat (AD 40)

A passage in Frontinus suggests that the emperor fought some combats on the far side of the Rhine, but there is no mention of major battles.

300 Frontinus, *Stratagems*, 2.6.3 'Letting a Desperate Enemy Escape'
Gaius Caesar (Caligula) had surrounded and 'penned in' some Germans who began to fight more fiercely due to their desperation. In response he ordered that the Germans be allowed to escape. Then attacked them as they fled.

Exaggerated Fears of Caligula

301 Suetonius, *Caligula*, 51
Caligula issued many threats against the barbarians. But when he was riding in a chariot through a narrow gully on the far side of the Rhine, someone suggested that the sudden appearance of the enemy might cause panic (an ambush). Caligula immediately mounted a horse and hastily returned to the bridges (on the Rhine). He found the bridges crowded with oncoming military support staff and baggage supplies (personnel employed to transport provisions to the campaign forces). Caligula was too impatient to suffer delay, so he was passed along from hand to hand over the men's heads.

Confused Accounts

Imperial propaganda may have exaggerated the German threat, but the perceived danger was not resolved by a major battlefield victory. The transport of northern warships to Rome, as part of an undeserved triumph, encouraged fear and rumours of imperial weakness.

302 Suetonius, *Caligula*, 51

Soon after these events, there were reports of an uprising in Germany. Caligula prepared to flee from the city (of Rome) and equipped fleets for this purpose. He thought that the enemy might be victorious, seizing routes through the Alps as the Cimbri had done (in 102 BC) or they might capture Rome itself as the Senones had (the Gallic tribe that sacked Rome in 390 BC). If this occurred, Caligula planned his escape across the sea to more distant provinces (Greece, Egypt or North Africa).

Victory Games in Rome

Suetonius mentions a plot in Rome involving the Senators Lentulus Gaetulicus and Marcus Aemilius Lepidus. By relocating his government to the Rhine and surrounding himself with frontier soldiers, Caligula had protected himself and isolated conspirators. This might have been the true purpose of his 'German Campaign', but the public still demanded a triumph.

303 Suetonius, *Vespasian*, 23

During his praetorship, Vespasian seized every opportunity to win the favour of Caligula, who was in political disagreement with the Senate. Vespasian requested that the emperor's victory in Germany should be celebrated in unique games (gladiator shows and beast hunts). He also suggested that the conspirators (Lepidus and Gaetulicus) should be denied burial rites as an additional punishment.

National Celebrations Expected

304 Persius, *Satire*, 6.43

Have you heard, my friend? Caligula has requested a triumph (from the Senate) for destroying the armies of Germany. Dead ashes are being swept away from all the altars (in preparations for new sacrificial offerings). Caesonia (Caligula's wife) is already announcing contracts for weapons to decorate the doorposts (a custom replicating the traditional capture of enemy spoils including weapons). Royal cloaks will be needed and yellow fabric for the captives. There will be vast paintings of the Rhine (commissioned artworks). I will be staging a show for the gods, and our Leader's Guardian Spirit. What about a hundred pairs of gladiators to confirm his great deeds?

Fake German Triumph (AD 41)

In AD 41, Caligula is said to have staged a fake German triumph in Rome.

305 Suetonius, *Caligula*, 47

The Emperor (Caligula) gathered prisoners and deserters from barbarian armies in preparation for his triumph (in Rome). He selected men from all parts of Gaul who had the largest stature and seemed most suitable for the event. He arranged this with some of the Gallic chiefs and required the selected men to grow their hair long and dye it blond (to resemble the stereotypical German). These men were also required to learn German phrases and respond to names that were commonly used in that country.

The emperor also ordered that certain galleys which had entered the ocean (North Sea) were to be conveyed to Rome. These vessels were brought a great part of the way by land (perhaps overland between the Rhine and the Rhone river systems, which offered a route through Gaul). Meanwhile, Claudius wrote to his organisers in the city, instructing them:

> Make full preparations for a triumph which will occur at my arrival in Rome. Keep expenses minimal. But the event must be on a scale never seen before and consider all properties in the city subject to your priorities.

Chapter Thirteen

Germania during the Reigns of Claudius and Nero (AD 41–68)

The middle-aged Claudius became emperor in AD 41. He was the son of Nero Claudius Drusus and brother of Germanicus. However, Claudius selected Britain as the target for further imperial conquests and began the Roman invasion in AD 43. Between three and four Roman legions were engaged in the early conquest and subjugation of Britain (AD 43–83). The permanent garrison of Britannia included three legions relocated from the Rhine frontier. In AD 47, the Chauci attacked the North Rhine frontier and in AD 50, the Chatti plundered across the South Rhine. That year there was also unrest among the Suebic tribes occupying southern Germany.

Early Career of Vespasian (AD 41–43)

306 Suetonius, *Vespasian*, 4
In the reign of Claudius, Vespasian was sent to Germany as a legionary legate (commander of a legion). Vespasian achieved this posting through the influence of Narcissus (a leading freedman in the imperial court). From there he was transferred to Britain and fought the enemy in thirty engagements.

The Status of German Envoys in Rome

307 Suetonius, *Claudius*, 25
The Emperor Claudius allowed envoys from the Germans to sit in the front rows of the auditoriums. The Germans were led to upper seats occupied by the common people, but they saw the position of the other envoys. Representatives from the Armenian kingdom and the Parthian Empire were sitting with the senators in the front rows of the theatre. The Germans therefore acted with natural self-confidence and began making their way down to join them, loudly protesting that their merits and rank made them inferior to no one.

Operations by the Roman General Corbulo (North Germania, AD 47)

Gannascus was a member of the Canninefate tribe. He deserted from the Roman army to lead coastal pirate raids in the North Sea.

308 Tacitus, *Annals*, 11.18–20

Meanwhile, the Chauci, who were not warring against one another, were elated by the death of Sanquinius Maximus (the governor of Germania Inferior – North Rhine Province). Corbulo was sent as a replacement governor, but before his arrival, the Chauci raided the province under the leadership of Gannascus. Gannascus was of Canninefate ancestry (German allies in the Rhine delta) and he had served as an auxiliary in the Roman army. But he had deserted and as he was well acquainted with the peaceful and prosperous regions (west of the Rhine), he gathered a piratical fleet of light vessels to raid the coast of Gaul.

Corbulo showed caution when he reached the province (Germania Inferior), but soon achieved a great reputation from the campaign he enacted. He had triremes (from the *Classis Germanica* fleet) brought through the Rhine Channel (the Fossa Drusiana Canal). Other vessels were sorted according to their drafts (hull depth), for conveyance through various suitable canals and estuaries. Reaching the sea, the Roman ships engaged and sank the enemy vessels, expelling Gannascus and his piratical forces from this coast.

After the conflict, Corbulo recalled the legions. They were eager to pillage, but reluctant to toil, or perform arduous duties. He therefore brought back the older codes of military discipline. Severe prohibitions were put in place to prevent any soldier from leaving the marching columns, or carrying out any action without orders. All outpost and sentry duties, and every other task completed day or night, had to be conducted under arms (soldiers equipped and ready for immediate combat). It is recorded that two soldiers were punished by death. One was caught digging soil for the rampart without his side-arm (short sword), while another was seen excavating soil, equipped only with his dagger (an ineffectual weapon). These stories may be a false exaggeration, but they suggest the severity of the new commander. Corbulo was certainly strict, rigorous, and severe, even regarding trivial offences.

The measures enacted by Corbulo affected the Roman soldiers, who found their courage revived (renewed discipline and purpose). This impacted on the enemy, who felt their confidence diminish and their resolve weaken.

The Frisian tribe had been hostile since their rebellion (two decades earlier) and disaffected after their defeat by Lucius Apronius (the Roman commander in AD 28). But now they offered political hostages to Rome and remained in the territorial limits defined by Corbulo. Corbulo also imposed a senate, a magistracy, and laws upon the tribe (he gave imperial recognition to a tribal council, acknowledged their leaders and made them liable to Roman laws). To prevent his orders being neglected, he built a fortified outpost in their district (Frisian territory was absorbed into the Empire).

Corbulo also sent agents to persuade the Greater Chauci to surrender (the larger part of the tribe). These agents were also tasked with killing Gannascus by some ruse. The trap was successful (possibly false pledges, deception, then assassination). It was not dishonourable to kill a military deserter and oath-violator in such an ignoble manner. But the killing of Gannascus disturbed the Chauci and moved them closer to an uprising against Rome. The news regarding Gannascus pleased many of the Romans, but others perceived the threat and asked:

> Why is Corbulo inciting an enemy? He is a distinguished soldier and can expect success, but the conflict will still incur losses for the Roman state. These losses will be intolerable for a nervous emperor (Claudius) who will view the conflict as a wider threat to peace.

Claudius proved so opposed to further aggression in Germany, that he ordered all Roman garrisons to be withdrawn to the west bank of the Rhine.

Corbulo was already establishing a Roman encampment on enemy territory when he received this imperial dispatch. He was surprised by the new orders and a multitude of consequences filled his mind. There was danger in defying the emperor, plus the contempt of the barbarians (towards a weakened Rome), and to dismiss the orders would invite ridicule from the provincials (they too would perceive weakness). But Corbulo simply said, 'The generals of earlier times were happier men' (the Republican era, when there was no emperor to restrict the provincial commanders). Then he gave the orders to withdraw.

To further occupy the troops, Corbulo ordered the construction of a 23-mile-long canal between the Meuse and the Rhine (for troop movements and supply lines). This made it possible to evade the hazards of the North Sea (the difficult coastal stretch between the two river outlets).

The emperor had refused war, but still awarded Corbulo the insignia of a triumph. This honour was also granted to Curtius Rufus (governor of Germania Superior, South Rhine, in office AD 79–84). Rufus had opened a mine in search of silver deposits near Mattium (Maden, near Gudensburg, 140 miles west of the Rhine). The profits were slender and short-lived, but the legions suffered heavy losses when digging out the watercourses and constructing underground mine works (the Romans redirected streams to erode soil and expose ores). These operations would have been difficult enough in the open (but they were being conducted in the hills and woodlands of hostile territory, far beyond the frontiers). The legionaries were exhausted by their efforts and knowing that soldiers in other provinces faced similar hardships, they drafted a letter to the emperor in the name of the entire army. They begged him to award every general triumphal honours on achieving office (so the commander would not conduct unnecessary military operations in pursuit of further glory).

Corbulo – Governor of Germania Inferior (AD 47)

309 Cassius Dio, *Roman History*, 61.30

When Gnaeus Domitius Corbulo held command in Germany, he concentrated his legions on harassing barbarian groups, including the Cauchi. But when he was within enemy territory he was recalled by Claudius. This is because the emperor, learning of his valour and the discipline of his army, did not want Corbulo to become too powerful (a potential rival). When Corbulo received his instructions, he turned back, exclaiming, 'How happy were those who led our armies in former times.'

By this he meant that generals from an earlier era had been allowed to exhibit their prowess without danger (the Republican era). But he himself was blocked and inhibited by a jealous emperor. Even so, Corbulo obtained triumphal honours (for his military operations). Receiving his new command, he drilled his troops with increased thoroughness. Since the native tribes were at peace, Corbulo ordered his men to dig a canal all the way from the Rhine to the Maas River. This distance was about 23 miles and further projects were undertaken to prevent the rivers flowing backwards and causing inundations due to severe ocean flood tides.

Rhine Frontier (AD 50)

In AD 49, the Emperor Claudius married Agrippina the Younger, daughter of Germanicus (his deceased brother). This political marriage was considered incestuous and immoral by traditional Roman society. In AD 50, Agrippina had her birthplace awarded the status of a Veteran Colony (Cologne).

310 Tacitus, *Annals*, 12.27

Agrippina also wanted to demonstrate her political power over the allied peoples. She therefore procured the despatch of a colony of veterans to the chief town of the Ubii (German allies granted lands on the west banks of the Rhine). Her grandfather Agrippa had granted the Ubii these lands when they had crossed the Rhine under imperial protection (in 39 BC). Agrippina was born in the main town of this territory (the Roman military outpost at Ubiorum), so the new veteran colony in the district was named after her ('Colonia Claudia Ara Agrippinensium' – modern Cologne).

Chatti Warbands raid Roman Territory (AD 50)

311 Tacitus, *Annals*, 12.27–28

Around this time there was a widespread panic in Germania Superior (South Rhine frontier) as bands of Chatti plundered across the region. The threat was dealt with by a Roman commander named Lucius Pomponius. Pomponius had anticipated Chatti incursions and prepared a response force of Vangiones and Nemetes (subject Germans) along with allied cavalry. While the Chatti were still dispersed, the Romans harassed them vigorously from every direction. The general then divided his forces into two columns and sent one of these divisions along the left flank (east of the Rhine) to intercept and ambush the returning raiders (in enemy territory). The enemy were in high spirits after seizing Roman spoils and they were heavily asleep when the imperial forces attacked and defeated them. This happy achievement was enhanced when the victors recovered Roman prisoners. These were survivors from the defeat of Varus, now rescued from slavery after almost forty years of captivity.

The Roman column on the right flank (west of the Rhine) took a more direct route to engage the raiders (Chatti still plundering Roman territories). The enemy formed up for battle, but they were successfully defeated. This division returned to Mount Taunus (the Roman command station) with a large amount of recaptured plunder and a great deal of glory. Pomponius was waiting with the legions at Taunus in case the Chatti escalated the war by seeking greater vengeance against the Romans with a larger engagement. But the enemy was afraid of being caught between two opponents. On one side were the Romans (on the Rhine) and the other the hostile Cherusci (a rival tribe in inner Germany). The Chatti had been perpetually feuding with the Cherusci, but now the

Cherusci were sending envoys and hostages to Rome (indications of possible alliance). Pomponius was decreed the honour of a triumph for this success. He achieved even greater honour with the next generation of Romans due to his poetry, for these poems now constitute his greatest and most lasting glory.

Unrest in Suebic Territories (South Germany, AD 50)

312 Tacitus, *Annals*, 12.29–30

Around this same time, Vannius, the ruler of the Suebi (a central Germanic tribe), was expelled from his kingdom (Marcomannic realm). Vannius had been installed in power by Drusus Caesar (as a Roman client king in AD 17). At the start of his rule Vannius had been well respected and popular amongst his countrymen. But he became a tyrant (dictatorial) and provoked neighbouring tribes who encouraged insurrection in his territory. This led to his downfall. The revolt was orchestrated by Vibillius, king of the Hermunduri (another inner German tribe). Vibillius allied with Vangio and Sido, sons of Vannius' sister (nephews of the king) and they led the insurrection in Suebic territory.

Vannius repeatedly asked the Emperor Claudius for Roman military assistance, but the emperor refused to intervene in conflicts between barbarians (occurring far beyond imperial territory). He simply promised Vannius a safe refuge in the event of his expulsion from power.

Meanwhile, Claudius sent written orders to Publius Atellius Hister, the governor of Pannonia (the Danube frontier). He instructed Hister to assemble his legions along with some specially selected auxiliaries from the province (in a force of up to four legions). This army encamped on the riverbank (the frontier) as a show of Roman support for Vannius and a warning to the victorious insurgents who were becoming elated by their success. This Roman military display discouraged any impulse these Germans might have had to disturb the peace that was maintained in the Empire.

Furthermore, the Romans learned that an immense host of Ligii (an east Germanic tribe located near the Vistula River) was advancing towards the territory of Vannius (the Suebic homelands). The Ligii were joined by many other German tribes who had heard about the great fame of this wealthy realm. They knew that Vannius had gathered a vast fortune in plunder and tribute during his thirty-year rule. Vannius' own native force was infantry (Suebic warriors) and his cavalry was gathered from the Iazyges of Sarmatia (allies from the nearby steppe). This army could not hope to match the size of the invading force. Consequently, Vannius decided to place his supporters in fortified positions and prolong the war (either to exhaust the enemy or await Roman intervention).

But the Iazyges could not tolerate a siege (as steppe cavalry) and they therefore dispersed throughout the surrounding country. This made an engagement inevitable, as the Ligii and Hermunduri rushed to attack available targets. In response, Vannius and his supporters left their strongholds and assembled for battle. They were defeated, but Vannius gained respect for bravely fighting in person and receiving wounds across his chest. He then fled to the Danube where the Roman river fleet was waiting to receive him. Many of his supporters and adherents soon followed and each were granted land and permission to settle in Pannonia (the Roman province south of the Danube).

Vangio and Sido divided the Suebic kingdom between them (the two original usurpers). But they remained admirably loyal to us (successfully performing the role of Roman client kings). They were popular among their Seubic people when they were seeking power, but when they became rulers, they were despised because their despotic character was revealed.

Reign of Nero (AD 54–68)

Nero became emperor of Rome in AD 54. His mother was Agrippina the Younger, and his grandfather was Germanicus. He was 17 when he came to power through the instigations of Agrippina.

Unrest on the Rhine Frontier (AD 56)

313 Tacitus, *Annals*, 13.53

Up to this time the situation had been quiet in Germany (the Rhine frontier provinces) and triumphal decorations (military awards) had become less prestigious. The Roman generals expected to obtain greater glory by the maintenance of peace (rather than conducting aggressive campaigns against the enemy).

Paulinus Pompeius and Lucius Vetus were in command of the army (the provincial governors of Germania Superior and Inferior in AD 56). To keep the soldiers active, they completed the construction of an embankment started sixty-three years earlier by Drusus (the Elder). This earthwork was designed to confine the Rhine River to its existing stream (preventing overflow and keeping the river to a consistently deep and powerful stream). Vetus also prepared the construction of a canal connecting the Moselle (a tributary of the Rhine) to the Arar (a tributary of the Rhone). This would allow troops arriving from the sea (the Roman Mediterranean) to be conveyed up the Rhone and Arar (to inner Gaul). They could then take the canal across to the Moselle and the Rhine and travel downstream to the ocean (the North Atlantic). All the difficulties involved in this route would be removed (facilitating troop movement, supply lines and trade). There would be a waterborne communication route between the seas to connect the western shores (of the Mediterranean) with the far north (the Atlantic).

However, Aelius Gracilis, the governor of Gallia Belgica, discouraged this project. He did not want Vetus to send his legions to Gaul because that would increase his influence in the region. Gracilis said the project would incite the fears of the Emperor Nero (the concern that a regional commander was expanding his power and reputation). This is an accusation that often hinders and prevents large developments and praiseworthy undertakings.

The Frisii prepare for War (North Rhine, AD 58)

314 Tacitus, *Annals*, 13.54

Meanwhile, as the (assembled) army remained inactive, a rumour spread that the commanders had been deprived of authority to act against the enemy. In response the Frisii (Germans on the north coast) moved their youths into the forests and the marshlands (territories that were difficult to access). They transferred the rest of their non-fighting population over the lakes to the far riverbank (perhaps the Ems River, which was distant from the Roman frontier). Then their fighting men established a presence in the unoccupied lands that had been reserved for the use of our soldiers (strips of pastureland on the east side of the Rhine that had been claimed by the Empire). These operations were conducted by two leaders of the Frisii named Verritus and Malorix. They were joint 'kings', to the extent that German rulers and leaders could be called 'kings'.

The Frisii built dwellings on the land they seized and began cultivating the earth as though it were an ancestral possession. By this stage Dubius Avitus had succeeded Paulinus as the governor of Germania Inferior (the North Rhine region). Avitus threatened to attack the Frisii if they did not abandon the lands they had recently seized, or accept other territories from the Empire (the option to move to other imperial lands selected by the Romans). He therefore compelled Verritus and Malorix to become suppliants of Rome (the first stage in becoming client rulers).

The two Frisian leaders travelled to Rome and waited for an audience with the Emperor Nero. But Nero was occupied with other engagements and the barbarians were therefore given a tour of the city to witness its astonishing sights. They were taken into Pompey's Theatre so that they might behold the vastness of the Roman people (the theatre had a capacity of more than 20,000 spectators and seating was allocated according to social class). The Germans found no amusement in the theatre entertainment, but they did take advantage of this leisure time to ask their guide questions about the crowds who sat on the benches. They asked about the distinctions between the senior social classes (the nobility). Who exactly were the *equites*? Where were the senators? Then they saw some people in foreign costumes sat on the seats among the senators and asked who they were. They were told that this honour was granted to envoys from foreign nations that were distinguished for their bravery and for their friendship to Rome. The Frisii cried out that no men on earth surpassed the Germans in their military valour or their loyalty. Then they scrambled down through the Roman crowd and took their seats among the senators.

The spectators recognised this undertaking was a good-natured act. They understood that it was due to the impulsiveness of a primitive people who upheld an honourable rivalry. Nero gave both rulers the Roman franchise (an endorsement to rule as subject representatives of Rome). Then he ordered the Frisii to withdraw from the contested territory. But the occupiers refused to comply and expressed distain for the Roman commands. So, an auxiliary force of cavalry was dispatched to make a sudden attack on the territory (a land clearance). They slaughtered or captured anyone who stubbornly resisted.

The Ampsivarii seek Settlement Rights (AD 58); Bructeri and Tencteri threaten Hostilities

315 Tacitus, *Annals*, 13.55–56

The Ampsivarii now took possession of the contested frontier territory (another Germanic tribe). They were more powerful than the Frisii and possessed a larger population. They also had greater support from neighbouring tribes since they had been expelled from their original homelands by the Chauci (leaving lands near the Ems River). The Ampsivarii were outcasts who were searching for some new secure territories to occupy. Their case was pleaded by a man named Boiocalus who was well known among German tribes and a loyal supporter of Rome. He reminded the Romans that during the Cheruscan revolt against the Empire (in AD 9) he had been imprisoned on the orders of Arminius. Afterwards he had served under the leadership of Tiberius and of Germanicus (in subsequent Roman campaigns).

Boiocalus said he was adding further merit to fifty years of loyalty by bringing his tribe, the Ampsivarii, under Roman domination. He stated:

> A great plain lies ready to receive the flocks and herds of Roman soldiers who may one day settle there. But this land is currently an occasional grazing ground for cattle at a time when our men are starving. Surely the Romans do not prefer a wasteland to the support it could give to a friendly nation.
>
> Once these fields belonged to the Chamavi; then to the Tubantes and then to the Usipetes (earlier German tribes). As heaven is for the gods, so earth is for mankind. All empty lands can be taken by anyone.

Then Boiocalus looked up at the sun and invoked the other aspects of the sky (the moon, the planets and the stars). He addressed these heavenly bodies as though he stood in front of the gods themselves. He demanded:

> Do you want to behold a vacant land empty of people? It is better to submerge such a place beneath the sea than see it taken by those who plunder.

Avitus (the Roman governor) was impressed by this language, but he insisted that Ampsivarii must submit to the rule of a superior people. He said that those same gods whom the Ampsivarii asked for assistance, had willed that the Romans should decide their fate. Only the Romans could be the judge of what might be given, or taken, from the Ampsivarii.

This was his public declaration to the Ampsivarii. But to Boiocalus he gave a private reassurance that he would receive personal lands as recognition for his former allegiance to Rome (a personal refuge in Roman territory if his people were denied settlement and subsequently destroyed). Boiocalus was offended by this suggestion of disloyalty (that he could be bribed by Roman property and abandon his people). He challenged Avitus with the comment: 'We may currently lack a territory to live in, but at least we have found a land to die for.'

Boiocalus then left Avitus, with both men feeling vexed at the exchange (the mood had turned hostile and conflict was expected).

The Ampsivarii now called on the Bructeri and the Tencteri for military assistance (other Germanic tribes east of the Rhine). They also asked more distant tribes to be their allies in the upcoming conflict. Meanwhile, Avitus wrote to Curtilius Mancia who was commander of the upper army (governor of Germania Superior on the southern Rhine frontier). He asked Mancia to cross the Rhine with his troops and make a show of strength south of the enemy (the Germanic tribes hostile to Rome). As this occurred, Avitus led his own legions into the territory of the Tencteri and threatened them with extermination unless they dissociated themselves from the Ampsivarii. The Tencteri conceded and the terror-struck Bructeri followed their example. Other tribes took notice of the threat and decided to avoid the perils of a war that did not concern them.

The Ampsivarii were isolated by these military actions and their population retreated into the territories of the Usipetes and the Tubantes (German tribes on the northern Rhine frontier). But they were expelled from this region and sought refuge first with the Chatti and then with the Cherusci (inner Germanic tribes occupying lands around the Weser). Then the Ampsivarii became destitute outcasts driven between tribes who were either friends or foes. Their warrior youths were slain in strange lands and those who could not fight were seized and divided up as plunder.

Territory of the Ubii (Rhine allies) Destroyed by Fire (AD 58)

316 Tacitus, *Annals*, 13.57

Meanwhile, the Ubii, a German people in alliance with Rome, suffered greatly from an unexpected calamity. Fires suddenly erupted from the earth to destroy their country dwellings, crops, and villages (wildfires in Roman territories – on the west bank of the Rhine). The fires rushed across the landscape and reached the outskirts of the newly founded colony (the veteran settlement of Colonia Claudia Ara Augusta Agrippinensium – Cologne). The flames were not extinguished by rainfall, or water drawn up from the river. No moisture seemed to reduce their effect until some despairing countrymen began to hurl stones at the flames in their fury and frustration. The flames withdrew and when the men approached closer, the fire shrunk back (interpreted as a sign of its supernatural nature). So, they assaulted the fire with the blows of their clubs and other weapons. They drove back the fire as though the flames were a withdrawing mob of wild beasts. At last, the men stripped off their clothes and struck the fire with these garments. This clothing, soiled by common use, proved to be more effective in beating back and extinguishing the final flames (they used their clothing as fire beaters to extinguish the blaze).

War Between the Hermunduri and Chatti (AD 58)

317 Tacitus, *Annals*, 13.57

The same summer (in AD 58) a great battle was fought between the Hermunduri and the Chatti (major tribes in north Germany). Both tribes lay claim to a river between their territories which produced large amounts of salt (an essential component in food flavouring and preservation). It was their tradition to settle these disputes by warfare, but the site was also subject to profound superstitions. The Germans believe that such sites have a greater proximity to heaven and any mortal prayers made at these sacred locations will be more attentively heard by the gods. They believe that salt is produced in the rivers by a divine power that occupies the forests. In other countries salt is made by drying an overflow of water from the sea (natural evaporation in shallow pools), but in Germany salt is extracted using two opposite elements, fire and water. The salt is extracted when water is heated over a burning pile of wood (using metal pans to hold the water and capture the salt residue).

The war (over the salt resources) was a success for the Hermunduri and a disaster for the Chatti. This was because the Chatti had promised the victory to their gods Mars and Mercury (the Roman equivalent to the Germanic gods of war and craft – perhaps forerunners of Tyr and Woden). They promised these gods that when the Chatti obtained victory, the slain enemy army would be presented as a sacrificial offering. They vowed that everything on the vanquished side would be offered up for destruction, even the Hermunduri horses. But this violent fate recoiled back upon themselves (they became a sacrificial battlefield offering for the Hermunduri).

Epilogue

But what of the Caesars who had fought against the people of Germania? What did subsequent generations think of their achievements in these wars? There follows an assessment of the early Caesars by the Emperor Julian (AD 361).

Assessment of the Early Caesars

318 Emperor Julian, *The Caesars*

It is the season of the *Cronia* (the midwinter Saturnalia festival). It is the time which the god allows us to make merry. But, my dear friends, as I have no great talent for amusing or entertaining, I must take care not to talk mere nonsense.

> 'But Emperor – can there be anyone so dull and stupid as to take issue over jests? I always thought that such amusements were a relaxation of the mind and a relief from cautions and cares.'

Yes, your view is correct, but that is not how I see the matter. For by nature, I have no talent for banter, or parody, or joking. But I must obey the dictates of the god of this festival. So, would you like me to tell you an entertaining myth that might be worth hearing?

> 'I shall listen with great pleasure for, like you, I am not one to despise myths. I don't dismiss people who have the right attitude. I share the opinion of Plato who is admired by you and all other men. Since Plato often conveyed a serious lesson in his casual stories.'

By Zeus, that is indeed true!

> 'But what is your myth and of what type of story will you tell, O Emperor?'

It is not one of those traditional narratives such as Aesop (the ancient Greek writer of fables) composed. Perhaps you should call my story an invention of Hermes (the messenger god who practised deceptive arts). For it was from Hermes I learnt what I am going to tell you now. My narrative might be really true, or it might be a mixture of truth and fiction. As the saying goes, 'the outcome will decide'.

> 'You have composed a fine preface to this story. Exactly right for a myth and maybe even an ovation! But now, tell me the tale, whatever form it takes.'

Attend and listen. During the Saturnalia, at the festival of Cronia, Romulus (the founder of Rome) gave a banquet. He invited all the gods and all the Roman emperors. The couches for the gods were set and prepared in the sky as (Homer says) 'the gods will have their seat at Olympus forever uncontested'. Hercules took his place among them along with Quirinus (the deified Romulus) for it was the divine will that Romulus take this name. A banquet had been prepared in the sky for the gods (and the primordial Titans), and in the strata just below them, Quirinus had prepared an entertainment. This space below was illuminated by the moon and the radiance of the gods themselves.

Four couches were made ready for the superior gods. Cronus had a couch of gleaming ebony, with a lustre and blackness so intense and divine, that no one could look upon it for long. I think its radiance would have harmed the eyes as much as staring directly at the sun.

The couch of Zeus was more radiant than silver, but paler than gold. Perhaps it should be called 'electron', or maybe some other name? Hermes could not inform me precisely. On either side of these two deities sat the mother and daughter on golden thrones. Hera sat beside Zeus and Rhea was positioned next to Cronus.

As for the beauty of the gods, not even Hermes could describe it in the account he gave me. He said that their appearance transcended any spoken description. It could only be comprehended in the mind's eye. It was impossible to convey to mortal hearing or understanding. There will never be an orator gifted enough to describe the surpassing beauty that shines forth from the expressions of the gods.

A throne or couch had been prepared for each of the other gods according to their seniority. There was no dispute between deities, as Homer himself reveals. For the Muses (the patrons of literature, reason and art) had ordained which gods should take which place. Every god therefore sat at their appointed seat, which was firmly and immovably fixed in a permanent order. They rose when the Patriarch entered, but they never confounded or changed the order of things, or infringed on the claims of another god. Everyone knew their appointed place.

Now when the gods were seated in a circle, Silenus (the part-satyr mentor of Dionysus) moved position. I think he was still enamoured with Dionysus (the god of wine and drama) since this deity was forever young and attractive. Dionysus was sitting close to his father Zeus, but Silenus took a position next to him since he had raised Dionysus and been his tutor. Dionysus enjoys jesting and laughter and is a benefactor of the divine Graces (the goddesses who embody joy, creativity and beauty). So, Silenus amused Dionysus with a continual outpouring of sarcasms, jokes, jests, and other distractions.

But this Banquet of the Gods had been arranged for the Roman emperors. Julius Caesar entered first, and such was his passion for glory that he seemed ready to contend with Zeus himself for dominion. When Silenus saw him, he said:

> 'Take care, Zeus, lest this man in his lust for power decides to rob you of your empire. You can see that he is tall and handsome, but the top of his head is very like mine!' (the aged satyr pointed to his own bald head).

But the gods were paying little attention to Silenus and his jests, when suddenly Octavian (Augustus) entered. But this emperor had no ordinary appearance, he continually changed colour like a chameleon. He turned from pale to red. One moment his expression was gloomy, sombre, and overcast, the next instant he was exuberant and expressed all the charms of Aphrodite (goddess of Love and Beauty) and the three Graces.

Moreover, in the way he glanced around, he willingly took an aspect of the mighty Helios (the chariot-riding sun god). For when Augustus looked upon people, he preferred that they could not meet his gaze (as if staring at the sun).

> 'Good Heavens!' cried Silenus. 'What a mutable monster that is! What mischief might he do to us?

> 'Stop this frivolity,' commanded Apollo (the god of Sun and Light). 'After Zeus has considered this man, I shall transform him into solid gold. Zeus – take notice of my imitator.'

Zeus complied and recited a few sacred doctrines over Augustus. These verses resembled the incantations muttered by followers of Zamolxis (the chief god of the Dacians). These words immediately made Augustus wise and temperate.

The third emperor to approach the gods was Tiberius. His bearing and expression were solemn and grim. He was sober and martial in appearance. But as he turned to take his seat (at the dining couches) his naked back was exposed to view. The flesh was covered with countless scars, burns, and sores, painful welts, and bruises. Ulcers and abscesses covered his flesh as if they were brands burnt into the skin. These were the marks of a cruel and self-indulgent life.

Silenus (quoting Homer) cried out, 'Friend, you are now very different in appearance, than you were before.' And the deity suddenly seemed more serious than usual.

Dionysus therefore asked, 'Why so solemn, little father?'

Silenus replied, 'This man is an old satyr and he shocked me with his new appearance. I lost myself when I quoted Homer.'

> 'Take care,' said Dionysus, 'this man will tease you and tug on your ears. He will distress you like he tormented the grammarian Seleucus.'

> 'Let the plague take him in his little island,' cried Silenus. He was referring to the isle of Capri (where the emperor had retired). (A trespassing fisherman was once tortured by Tiberius by having his face scrubbed and lacerated with his catch.) So Silenus said, 'Let him loose to scratch the face of some wretched fishermen.'

While they were still joking together, a fierce monster entered the banquet. (It was the Emperor Caligula). All the gods turned away their eyes from the sight of this person. In that moment the goddess of justice (and moral order) commanded the avenging deities to hurl him into Tartarus (the deep abyss of Torment inhabited by wicked souls). This happened so fast that Silenus had no chance to say anything about him.

Then the Emperor Claudius entered. At once Silenus began to sing some (comic) verses from *The Knights* (an ancient Greek play written by Aristophanes). Except he changed the words so that the chorus flattered Claudius instead of Demos. He sang:

> 'Claudius, you are our all-powerful sovereign lord. All tremble before you, yet you are led around by the nose. You love to be flattered and fooled. You listen to the orators with gaping mouth and your mind is led astray.'

Then he looked at Quirinius (Romulus) and said:

> 'Quirinus, it is not kind of you to invite your descendant to a banquet without his freedmen Narcissus and Pallas. So send for them and fetch his wife Messalina. For without them this man is nothing but a dummy prop in a Tragedy play. He is almost lifeless (without these decision-makers).'

While Silinus was speaking, Nero entered, lyre in hand and wearing a laurel victory wreath. Silenus immediately turned to Apollo and said, 'This man models himself on you!'

> 'I will soon take that wreath from him,' replied Apollo. 'For he does not imitate me in all things, and even the aspects he copies are poorly performed.'

The victory wreath was seized from Nero and the Cocytus (the wailing river of lamentation) instantly swept him away (to Hades – the gloom-ridden underworld).

After Nero, several emperors of various sorts came crowding into the banqueting space. There was Vindex, Galba, Otho and Vitellius. They clustered together so that Silenus exclaimed:

> 'Ye gods, where have they found such a swarm of sovereigns? We are being suffocated by their smoke. For these brutes do not even spare the temples (when they squabble).'

Then Zeus turned to his brother Serapis (the chief Greco-Egyptian deity). He pointed at the Emperor Vespasian and said – 'Send this miser from Egypt to extinguish the flames. Have his eldest son (Titus) engage with Aphrodite Pandemos (the goddess who unifies communities). But shackle up his younger son (Domitian). Deal with him like that Sicilian monster (the cruel tyrant Phalaris who was roasted to death in his own torture device the Bronze Bull).'

* * *

Hermes conferred with his father Zeus. Then Zeus bade Hermes make the following proclamation:

> 'All you mortals who have entered this contest, know that according to our laws and decrees the victor is permitted to exult, but the vanquished

> must not complain. Depart then wherever you please. But in future every one of you should live under the guidance of the gods. Let every man now choose his own divine guardian and guide.' (...)

Julius Caesar wandered about for a long time, walking back and forth indecisively between the various deities. But finally mighty Ares (the god of war and courage) and Aphrodite (the goddess of passion) took pity on him. They summoned him over to join them. (...)

> 'As for you,' Hermes said to me, 'I have granted you the knowledge of your father Mithras (the Iranian solar god and master of secret cults). Keep his commandments. With this anchor and cable, obtain a secure position throughout your life. When you must depart from this world, you can with good hope, call upon Mithras as your guardian god.'

(This was the fate of the Roman emperors in the Afterlife as told by Hermes to the Emperor Julian.)

319 Seneca the Younger, *Moral Letters*, 47.10

You should remember that the man you call 'slave' sprang from the same human stock as yourself. He was raised beneath the same skies (the Northern Hemisphere) and just like you, he breathes, lives, and dies. It is possible that you could have been the slave and him the free-born man. Consider the consequences of the Varus massacres (Romans expelled from a subject territory and citizen survivors enslaved). Many men of distinguished birth, who were taking the first steps towards senatorial rank by service in the army, were caught in this disaster. They were humbled by fortune and set to work as some shepherd, or the caretaker of a rural hut. So, do you dare despise men that one day you might match in circumstance?

Index of Ancient Authors

Appian (second century AD)
Appian was a Greek historian who wrote a history of Roman conquests. He held public office in Alexandria and after receiving Roman citizenship went to Rome to practise Law. He became a procurator (government financial agent) under the Emperor Antoninus Pius (reigned AD 138 to AD 161). His *Roman History* is written in Greek.

Ammianus Marcellinus (born about AD 330 – died AD 395)
Ammianus was a Latin historian who wrote an account of the Later Roman Empire. He served as a soldier in Gaul and fought against the Persians on the Eastern frontiers. In AD 359, he served in the army commanded by the Emperor Julian during a failed invasion of Babylonia. Ammianus later resigned from the army and settled in Rome, where he composed his multivolume *History* in Latin. His account began in AD 96 with the reign of the Emperor Nerva, which was the year that Tacitus ended his account. Ammianus finished his study in AD 378 with the Gothic invasion of the Roman Empire (Goths – East Germans from the Far North).

Cassius Dio (born about AD 150 – died AD 235)
Cassius Dio was a Roman administrator and historian who wrote a multi-volume *Roman History* in Greek. Dio was a member of the Roman Senate. He served as the administrator of Pergamum and Smyrna, leading Greek cities in Anatolia. Returning to Rome he was made consul (senior magistrate in the Capitol). Afterwards he obtained the proconsulship (office of governor) in the Roman province of 'Africa' (Tunisia). Later he served as a legate in Dalmatia, then Pannonia (Danube frontier) before being granted a second consulship in the reign of the Emperor Severus Alexander (AD 229). His *Roman History* contains the insights of a soldier and senior statesman. Large extracts of his work survive as summaries by later authors.

Claudius Ptolemy (writing AD 150)
Claudius Ptolemy was a Greek mathematician, astronomer and geographer who lived in the Egyptian capital Alexandria during the Roman imperial era.

His *Geography* proposed new methods for constructing maps of the ancient world using data assembled by an earlier Greek geographer named Marinus of Tyre (active in about AD 100). Ptolemy's data includes a sequence of territories stretching from Ireland across Europe and Asia to China. Germany appears in book ten and is represented in Map 4 of Europe (preserved in medieval manuscripts). The map can either be plotted from the original co-ordinates listed by Ptolemy, or redrawn from the medieval renderings.

Jordanes (writing in AD 551)
Jordanes was a historian of Gothic ancestry who wrote an account of his people in Latin called the *Getica*. Jordanes probably lived in the Danube region after the fall of the Western Roman Empire (AD 476). The *Getica* was completed in AD 551.

Flavius Josephus (AD 37–100)
Josephus was a Jewish priest, scholar and historian from an aristocratic family. He was a commander in the Jewish Revolt against Rome (AD 66) and became a captive of the Roman general Vespasian. Josephus was freed when Vespasian became emperor and served as an advisor to his son Titus. After the conflict, Josephus was granted Roman citizenship and moved to Rome with the imperial family as his patron. Josephus wrote an account in Greek of the Jewish Revolt (AD 66–70) and a multivolume history of the Jews known as the *Antiquities*. These works provide interesting insights into the activities of the Roman Empire, along with ancient perceptions of Germanic peoples.

Julius Caesar (assassinated 44 BC)
Julius Caesar was a Roman general, politician and dictator. Caesar wrote an account of his military campaigns in Gaul leading to the conquest of the territory (58–52 BC). *The Gallic Wars* describes Roman conflict against the Germans who were intruding across the Rhine, written in the third person. Julius Caesar was about to launch a campaign of further conquests, which included new plans for Germania, when he was killed by a group of senators. They believed he wanted to end the republican system of government by personally retaining supreme power.

Juvenal (born about AD 60 – died about AD 127)
Juvenal was a Roman satirist and friend of the Latin poet Martial. Juvenal served as a military officer in preparation for a career in the administrative service of the Emperor Domitian. But he failed to obtain promotion and was banished for criticising the court favourites who influenced the allocation and award of

state offices. After the assassination of Domitian in AD 96, Juvenal returned to Rome where he published his *Satires*, offering a pessimistic and scathing view of contemporary Roman society.

Martial (born about AD 38 – died about AD 103)
Martial was a Roman poet and friend of the Latin satirist Juvenal. Early in his career, Martial wrote verses in praise of the dictatorial Emperor Domitian (reigned AD 81–96). But most of his epigrams concern the life and social conduct of people in Rome. Martial also wrote witty verses to accompany gifts exchanged between friends, clients and patrons during popular Roman festivals. These offer an important insight into the consumer culture of Rome and its attitudes towards Germanic society.

Orosius (writing in AD 414–417)
Orosius was a prominent Christian author and theologian from Roman Spain. He wrote a world history from the Christian perspective, which provides important information for events after AD 378.

Pliny the Elder (AD 23–79)
Pliny was the author of the *Natural History*, a vast encyclopaedic work considering mankind and the natural environment. Aged 23, Pliny began a military career in Germany, reaching the rank of cavalry commander. He returned to Rome to study and practise Law. He served as procurator (governor) of Spain and other provinces. Pliny devoted much of his time to writing, including a *History of Rome* and a multi-volume work describing Roman campaigns in Germany. In Rome, Pliny served in the advisory council of the Emperor Vespasian (AD 69–79). He was commander of the Roman fleet in the Bay of Naples when Mount Vesuvius erupted (AD 79). Pliny succumbed to volcanic fumes while leading a rescue attempt.

Plutarch (first to second century AD)
Plutarch was a Greek author and biographer who wrote the *Parallel Lives*. The work describes the character and careers of leading Roman generals and statesmen, paired with accounts of comparable Greek figures. Plutarch obtained the Chief Magistracy of Chaeronea, a leading Greek city in Boeotia, central Greece. He directed a philosophical school in the city and visited Rome as part of his official duties. He also held a lifelong priesthood position at Delphi, the most prominent religious centre in Greece.

Pomponius Mela (writing in about AD 43)
Mela was a Latin writer who composed a *Geography* in about AD 43. Little is known of his life, but he was cited as a source by Pliny the Elder in his *Natural History*. Mela's *Geography* contains a Roman perspective on Germania, the campaigns fought to control this territory, and imperial knowledge of the northern ocean.

Strabo (died after AD 21)
Strabo was a Greek historian and geographer writing during the reign of the first Emperor Augustus (27 BC to AD 14). Strabo lived in Alexandria, the Greek capital of Egypt, before moving to Rome. His *History* has not survived into the modern era, but his multi-volume *Geography* has been preserved. The *Geography* describes all the countries and populations known to the Greeks and Romans of his era, incorporating many historical details. Strabo wrote in Greek, the second language of the Roman Empire.

Suetonius (died after AD 122)
Suetonius was a Roman author who wrote a collection of short biographies concerning Julius Caesar and the first eleven Roman emperors (*The Twelve Caesars*). Suetonius was from the *equites*, the lesser nobility that held a rank below the ruling senatorial class. He began a legal career in Rome with the friendship and support of Pliny the Younger, the nephew of Pliny the Elder. Suetonius entered imperial service during the reign of the Emperor Hadrian (AD 117). He served as controller of the libraries, keeper of the archives, and adviser to the emperor on cultural matters. In about AD 121, he was briefly promoted to Secretary of the Imperial Correspondence. His work *The Twelve Caesars* describes the activities, behaviours and characteristics of the early Roman rulers up to the death of Emperor Domitian in AD 96. It contains many anecdotes that reveal their morals, capacity and intent. It offers an important insight into the inner politics of Rome.

Tacitus (died about AD 120)
Tacitus was a Roman orator, legal advocate, public official and Latin historian. Tacitus' father was the governor of Gallia Belgica, when Pliny held a military command on the Rhine frontier (AD 50s). Tacitus held the following career roles: military tribune attached to a legion, quaestorship with a possible provincial posting, praetorship with legal jurisdiction, and member of a Priestly College in Rome. He may also have served as a legionary commander for four years. Tacitus wrote the *Annals*, dealing with the Empire from AD 14 to AD 68, and the *Histories*, describing the era between AD 69 and AD 96. He also wrote a short

biography of his father-in-law, Gnaeus Julius Agricola, who was governor of Britain from AD 77 to AD 84, during the Roman conquest of Caledonia. In AD 98, Tacitus wrote an ethnography of the Germans, known as the *Germania*, which was possibly based on a multi-volume history by Pliny the Elder that has not survived.

Vellius Patercullus (born about 19 BC – died after AD 30)
Vellius Patercullus was a Roman soldier, political figure and Latin historian. Vellius served as a military tribune in Thrace, Macedonia, Greece and the eastern Mediterranean. He was a cavalry prefect and legate in Germany and Pannonia under the future Emperor Tiberius (AD 4). He held office as quaestor in AD 7 and praetor in AD 15. Velleius wrote a compendium of Roman history up to AD 29. He witnessed and participated in many of the events he describes about Roman conflicts in Germany.

Chronology

Germanic Migrations into Gaul and Italy (115–100 BC)

- 115–113 BC Cimbri and Teutones migrate into Gaul. They are joined by a Celtic tribe called the Ambrones.
- 113 BC Cimbri and Teutones defeat a Roman army at Noreia.
- 105 BC Germanic tribes invade Gallia Narbonensis, defeating the Romans at Arausio.
- 102 BC Rome defeats the Teutones at the Battle of Aquae Sextiae.
- 101 BC Rome defeats the Cimbri at the Battle of Vercellae (Raudian Plain).

Rhine Crossings (62–31 BC)

- 62 BC War between the Celtic Sequani and Aedui tribes in central Gaul. Sequani recruit Suebii (Germanic) warriors and allow them to cross the Rhine.
- 60 BC Sequani defeat the Aedui. The Suebii settle in Gaul.
- 59 BC Germanic King Ariovistus acknowledged as an ally of Rome.
- 58 BC Julius Caesar begins the Roman conquest of Greater Gaul.
- 58 BC Battle of Vosges, Caesar defeats the Germans settled west of the Rhine.
- 56 BC Caesar crosses the Rhine and conducts inconclusive campaign in Germania.
- 50 BC Caesar completes the conquest and subjugation of Greater Gaul.
- 44 BC Julius Caesar assassinated.
- 30s BC Germanic Ubii allowed to relocate across the Rhine to Oppidum 'Ubiorum' (modern Cologne).

Augustan Conquests (31 BC–AD 9)

- 31 BC Octavian wins the final civil war of the Roman Republic. Under the name 'Augustus' he becomes the first Roman emperor (27 BC).
- 17 BC Three Germanic tribes declare war on Rome. Marcus Lollius defeated by an alliance of Tencteri, Sugambri and Usipetes. Led by a warlord named Maelo, the Germans invade Belgica and seize the eagle standard of Legio V Alaudae.

- 14 BC Imperial prince, Drusus, legate (commander) of Tres Galliae, prepares the Roman invasion of Germania. Batavi brought into alliance and Roman military camps established along the Rhine.
- 12–9 BC Drusus campaigns in Germania Magna (Greater Germany).
- 9 BC–AD 9 West Germania as far as the Elbe is under Roman control.

Germanic Revolt and Resistance (AD 9–17)

- AD 9 Revolt: Battle in the Teutoburg Forest. Arminius and the Germans destroy three entire Roman legions. Rome withdraws from Germania Magna (Greater Germany) to the Rhine frontier.
- AD 10–13 The imperial princes Tiberius and Germanicus campaign in Germania.
- AD 14 Death of Emperor Augustus, succession of Tiberius.
- AD 14–16 Germanicus, son of Drusus, leads further retaliatory campaigns against the Germans.
- AD 17 Tiberius abandons plans to fix the Roman frontier on the Elbe. Rhine–Danube frontier now the northern limits of the Roman Empire.

Stalemate with Free Germany (AD 17–100)

- AD 37–41 Reign of Caligula (son of Germanicus).
- AD 40 Caligula prepares to invade Germany. Campaign halted.
- AD 41–54 Reign of Claudius (son of Drusus, brother of Germanicus).
- AD 43 Claudius conquers southern part of Britain.
- AD 47 Gnaeus Domitius Corbulo suppresses the Frisii.
- AD 54–68 Reign of Nero (grandson of Germanicus).
- AD 68–69 Roman Civil War: 'Year of the Four Emperors'.
- AD 69–70 Batavian Revolt.
- AD 81–96 Reign of Domitian.
- AD 83 Domitian invades Germania to engage the Chatti.
- AD 88 Romans defeated by Quadi and Marcomanni on the Danube frontier.
- AD 98 Tacitus writes the *Germania*.

Second and Third Century

- AD 161–180 Reign of Marcus Aurelius.
- AD 165–180 Antonine Pandemic, an ancestral form of smallpox, devastates the Roman population and its essential military forces. Casualties in affected

communities are as high as one-third (deaths and debilitating medical conditions that prevent further military service).

- AD 166–180 Marcomannic Wars. Marcomanni and Quadi threaten the Danube frontier. Sarmatians (steppe horsemen) attack the Lower Danube. Prolonged series of savage military campaigns conducted by the stoic Emperor Marcus Aurelius.
- AD 235–284 Third Century Crisis: upheaval and repeated civil wars in the Roman Empire.
- AD 284–305 Reign of Diocletian. Order restored in the Roman Empire. Diocletian reorganises Roman administration. The Empire is divided into East and West.

Age of Migrations (AD 370–476)

- AD 370–374 Huns defeat the Alani and Goths (east Germans) on the Pontic Steppe. The defeated populations flee westwards.
- AD 375 Visigoths ask Emperor Valens for sanctuary within imperial territories. The Tervingi are settled south of the Danube frontiers, but are abused by Roman officials.
- AD 376 Gothic Revolt. Battle of Marcianople: Goths defeat a Roman army in Thrace and seize imperial armouries.
- AD 378 Battle of Adrianople: Eastern Field Army destroyed by the Goths. Roman Emperor Valens killed in Battle.
- AD 406 Mass of Germanic tribes and steppe forces cross the Rhine frontier invading Gaul (Asding Vandals, Suebi, Marcomanni, Quadi and Alani).
- AD 410 Visigoth King Alaric sacks Rome.
- AD 428 The Asding Vandals cross from southern Spain into North Africa.
- AD 446 Final appeal of Roman provincials in Britain for imperial assistance against Pictish, Scots-Irish and Saxon invaders.
- AD 451 Battle of Catalaunian Fields: Attila invades Gaul with a vast army of Huns and vassal Germans. Invaders defeated by a coalition force of Romans, Visigoths, Burgundians and Salian Franks. Attila withdraws his army from the Western Empire.
- AD 450s The Anglo-Saxons begin the conquest of Britain.
- AD 453 The Vandals sack Rome.
- AD 476 Romulus Augustulus is deposed, the last emperor of Rome. Germanic soldier named Odoacer is declared king of Italy with the support of barbarian troops.
- AD 476 Fall of the Western Roman Empire.

Appendix A

German Statistics and Prospects for Conquest

Area

- Greater Germania (Rhine to Vistula, Danube to Baltic Sea): 190,000 square miles.
- *Germania Libera* ('Free Germany') between the Rhine and the Elbe: 90,000 square miles.
- Greater Gaul (Roman Gaul): 180,000 square miles.
- Roman campaign into Free Germany (military march to the Elbe): 400 miles (Velleius Paterculus, *History of Rome*, 2.106).
- Straight line distance from Bonna (Bonn) to the Elbe: 350 miles.
- Marcomanni Realm (Territory in southern Germania): 40,000 square miles.
- Size of Batavian territory: 8,500 square miles (100-mile frontier along the Rhine).

Routes and districts

- Amber Route: 'The distance from Carnuntum in Pannonia to the amber-producing coasts of Germany is about 600 miles' (Pliny, *Natural History*, 37.11).
- Sixty days to cross the Hercynian Forest (Pomponius Mela, *Geography*, 3.29).
- On one flank of the Suebic territories the lands are said to be desolate for about 600 miles (Julius Caesar, *Gallic War*, 4.2).
- The Lippe is about 600 stadia (60 miles) east of the Rhine (Strabo, *Geography*, 7.1.3).

Roman frontiers (early imperial period)

- Rhine frontier: 8 legions (80,000 soldiers).
- Danube: 6 legions (60,000 soldiers).

Information on Roman fleet sizes

- The Black Sea fleet, the *Classis Pontica*, included forty warships (Josephus, *Jewish War*, 2.16.3). The *Classis Britannica* would have been of equivalent or larger size.

- Trajan created a fleet of fifty military vessels for his conquest of Babylonia – a Euphrates River Fleet (Arrian, *Parthica*, 67).
- The *Classis Pannonica* patrolled and protected the Upper Danube between Raetia and Singidunum. The *Classis Moesica* guarded the Lower Danube from the Iron Gates, through the outflow of the river into the Black Sea, as far as the Crimean coast (total length of navigable river 1,500 miles).
- The Rhine Fleet, the *Classis Germanica*, possibly included fifty military vessels (total length of navigable river 750 miles). At least twenty-four ships were destroyed during the Batavian Revolt of AD 69 (Tacitus, *Histories*, 4.17). This was perhaps half the fleet, the part assigned to Germania Inferior (North Rhine).

Populations and military dynamics

- Population of ancient Sweden, southern tip of the landmass: 100,000 adults and adolescents. Hilleviones inhabit 500 villages (Pliny, *Natural History*, 4.13). The village of Hodde in Iron Age Denmark was encircled by a fenced perimeter and had an estimated population of over 200 people (first century BC).
- Scale of inter-tribal warfare: 60,000 Germans were killed when the Chamavi, Angrivarii and neighbouring tribes destroyed the rival Bructeri (Tacitus, *Germania*, 33).
- In a Germanic tribe, half of the active men could be assembled to fight in an offensive war. Half of the Suebic men could be mobilised (Julius Caesar, *Gallic War*, 4.1). The Lentienses mobilised 40,000 warriors, but Roman reports claimed they might have had 70,000 fighting men (Ammianus Marcellinus, *Roman History*, 31.10).
- A Germanic chief could lead 7,000 warriors, perhaps the entire fighting force of a tribe. Seven chiefs led an army of 35,000 warriors from the Alemannic coalition (AD 357) (Ammianus Marcellinus, *Roman History*, 16.12).
- Chiefs in command of 7,000 fighters. The Marcomannic coalition could field 70,000 infantry (Velleius Paterculus, *History of Rome*, 2.108) and they had ten chiefs, 'one from each of the tribes in their alliance' (Cassius Dio, *Roman History*, 71.10).
- Ratio of infantry warriors to cavalry 17:1. Derived from Marcomannic figures of 70,000 warriors and 4,000 cavalry (Velleius Paterculus, *History of Rome*, 2.108). This suggests that an army of 35,000 Germans could field more than 2,000 cavalry.
- Possible 10:1 cavalry ratio among Suebi (?). Tacitus describes swift infantry units attached to cavalry (Tacitus, *Germania*, 6). These were limited to 100 warriors per district. Perhaps one infantry runner per horseman? (Julius

Caesar, *Gallic War*, 1.48). The 100 could be part of the Suebic 1,000 warriors per district (Julius Caesar, *Gallic War*, 4.1).

Size of Germanic military coalitions

- 58 BC: King Ariovistus leading 66,000 warriors (?). Coalition of seven Germanic tribes: Harudes, Marcomanni, Triboci, Vangiones, Nemetes, Sedusii and Suebi (Julius Caesar, *Gallic War*, 1.51). Harudes had 24,000 men (Julius Caesar, *Gallic War*, 1.31). If each tribal component had 7,000 fighting men, then the total force might have numbered 66,000 warriors (42,000 from 6 tribes and 24,000 Harudes). This force could have been supported by over 3,000 cavalry (based on the 1:17 ratio).
- AD 9–17: War leader Armenius supported by 70,000 warriors (?). Revolt of the Cherusci, Chatti and Sugambri (three main tribes). Other tribal groups engaged: Caulci, Campsani, Bructeri, Usipetes, Chattuarii, Landi and Tubantes (seven tribes) (Strabo, *Geography*, 7.1.4). If each tribe contributed 7,000 warriors, then Rome might have engaged over 70,000 fighters during these campaigns.
- Suebic tribal coalition: 100,000 warriors capable of offensive warfare (Julius Caesar, *Gallic War*, 4.1).
- Marcomannic tribal coalition: 70,000 infantry and 4,000 cavalry (Velleius Paterculus, *History of Rome*, 2.108).
- Alemannic coalition: 35,000 warriors from 7 allied tribes (AD 357) (Ammianus Marcellinus, *Roman History*, 16.12).

Prospects for Roman conquest

- Roman conquest of Germania west of the Elbe (12–9 BC). Nero Claudius Drusus in command of seven Rhine frontier legions: four years.
- Romans retake Germania west of the Elbe (AD 15–16). Germanicus in command of eight Rhine frontier legions: two years.
- Roman army operating in Germany with a force of four legions (Tacitus, *Annals*, 2.16). Army composed of 30,000 infantry and 3,000 cavalry (Tacitus, *Annals*, 2.25).
- Roman conquest of Caledonia – Scotland north of Forth–Clyde frontier (AD 83–84). Agricola in command of four legions (the garrison of Britain): two years.
- A force of 20,000 soldiers conquer and occupy the territory of the Quadi and the Marcomanni in southern Germania (AD 177–180): four years?

- Forty days for a Roman army to march from Italy to the Rhine frontier (AD 357). 'The battle was fought near Argentorate (Strasburg), forty days' march from where Gratian was (in the Western military capital of Mediolanum – Milan) (see Ammianus Marcellinus, *Roman History*, 26.67).
- Three legions, perhaps 20,000 Roman troops, massacred at the Teutoburg Forest (AD 9). (Marcus Manilius, *Astronomicon*, 1.898).
- Marcomannic War. Roman military expedition north of the Danube (AD 170). Perhaps 20,000 soldiers killed (Lucian, *Alexander the False Prophet*, 48).

Other North European opponents and conquests (for comparison)

- Conquest of Roman Britain (southern region) achieved with 4 legions (40,000 soldiers). Area of southern Britain (the Wash to Anglesey in North Wales): 50,000 square miles.
- One legion and its auxiliary support required to conquer and retain Ireland (10,000 Roman soldiers) (see Tacitus, *Agricola*, 24). Area of Ireland: 32,000 square miles.
- Battle of Mons Graupius (AD 84). The Romans conquer Highland Scotland (Caledonia) with 11,000 auxiliaries and a reserve force of legionaries (perhaps 15,000 soldiers from 3 legions). Roman army: 8,000 auxiliary infantry with 3,000 cavalry facing more than 30,000 Caledonians. About 10,000 enemy are slain and 360 Romans killed. Over 20,000 enemy flee into the surrounding hills and forests (see Tacitus, *Agricola*, 29, 35, 37).
- Battle near Augustodunum (AD 21). Gallic revolt involving the Aedui (a Celtic tribe). A Roman force of 2 legions with auxiliaries (20,000 soldiers) defeated 40,000 Gauls. 'There were 40,000 enemy fighters, including one-fifth armed like our legionaries (8,000). The rest were equipped with spears, knives, and hunting weapons. They were also joined by slaves being trained as gladiators. These specialised fighters were called *crupellarii*. They were armed with native weapons that could not easily wound an enemy. But their armour was a complete covering of steel that made the gladiator almost impervious to wounds (…) Silius advanced against the enemy with two legions.' (Tacitus, *Annals*, 3.45–46).

Appendix B

Roman Revenues: The Economic Context*

Early Roman Empire (imperial era): forty provinces and six client kingdoms (landmass: 2 million square miles).

- The 'tribute-money from three provinces': 10 million sesterces (Seneca, *De Consolatione ad Helviam Matrem*, 10.4).
- Tribute imposed on Macedonia (167 BC): 2.5 million sesterces from a possible 5 million sesterces (Plutarch, *Aemilius Paulus*, 28.3).
- Annual revenues from the kingdom of Commagene in Anatolia (AD 18–38): 5 million sesterces (Suetonius, *Caligula*, 16).
- Annual tribute from the Chersonesos kingdom in Crimea (first century BC): 4.8 million sesterces (Strabo, *Geography*, 7.4.6).
- Funds offered by central and southern Iberia during Roman Civil War (49 BC): 18 million sesterces (Julius Caesar, *Civil War*, 3.4).
- Tribute from Greater Gaul (newly conquered in 50 BC): 40 million sesterces (Suetonius, *Julius Caesar*, 25).
- Roman revenues before Pompey's Eastern conquests (65 BC): 200 million sesterces (Plutarch, *Pompey*, 45).
- Revenues from Greater Anatolia plus Syria (61 BC): 140 million sesterces (Plutarch, *Pompey*, 45).
- Possible revenues from Anatolia (Asia Minor): 60+ million sesterces (suggested by Philostratus, *Lives of the Sophists,* 548).
- Revenues from the main territories of Herod's kingdom in Palestine (4BC): 22 million sesterces (Josephus, *Antiquities*, 17.11.4).
- Annual tribute from the province of Asia (500 cities in western Anatolia) (AD 125): 28 million sesterces (Philostratus, *Lives of the Sophists,* 548).
- Ancient evidence for Egyptian revenues: 576 million sesterces (Josephus, *Jewish War*, 2.16.4; *Antiquities*, 19.8.2).

* Figures extracted from McLaughlin, *The Roman Empire and the Indian Ocean* (2014) and *The Roman Empire and the Silk Routes* (2016).

Roman bullion revenues: 120+ million sesterces (during periods of high-level production)

- Spanish silver mines: less than 39 tons of silver, worth 36 million sesterces (Strabo, *Geography*, 3.2.10).
- Iberian gold mines (AD 73): more than 7 tons of gold, worth 80 million sesterces (*Pliny, Natural History*, 33.21).
- Gold mine in Dalmatia (Croatia) (discovered in AD 55): 70 million sesterces worth of gold (*Pliny, Natural History*, 33.21).